CURRENT ECONOMIC ISSUES: PROGRESSIVE PERSPECTIVES FROM *DOLLARS & SENSE*

Eleventh Edition

EDITED BY CHRIS STURR, RAMAA VASUDEVAN,

AND THE *DOLLARS & SENSE* COLLECTIVE

CURRENT ECONOMIC ISSUES
Eleventh Edition

ISBN: 978-1-878585-68-4
Published by:
Economic Affairs Bureau, Inc.
Dollars & Sense
29 Winter Street
Boston, MA 02108
617-447-2177
dollars@dollarsandsense.org
www.dollarsandsense.org

Current Economic Issues is edited by the Dollars & Sense Collective, which also publishes *Dollars & Sense* magazine and the classroom books *Real World Macro, Real World Micro, Real World Globalization, Real World Banking, The Wealth Inequality Reader, The Environment in Crisis, Introduction to Political Economy, Unlevel Playing Fields: Understanding Wage Inequality and Discrimination, Striking a Balance: Work, Family, Life*, and *Grassroots Journalism*.

The 2007 Collective:
Faisal Chaudhry, Amee Chew, Daniel Fireside, Ellen Frank, Amy Gluckman, Tyler Hauck, Mary Jirmanus, Toussaint Losier, James McBride, John Miller, Laura Orlando, Larry Peterson, Smriti Rao, Alejandro Reuss, Bryan Snyder, Chris Sturr, Ramaa Vasudevan, Jeanne Winner, and James Woolman.

Cover Design: Nick Thorkelson
Cover Art: Mauricio Alberto Cordero
Production: Noel Cunningham and Chris Sturr

Manufactured by Vision Lithographics
Printed in U.S.A.

CONTENTS

Chapter 1

BUSINESS CYCLES, EMPLOYMENT, AND WAGES

UNEQUAL RECOVERY

Unemployment rates show African Americans losing ground while whites regain their footing.

DENA LIBNER
May/June 2005

The current economic recovery has been called many things, especially "jobless" and "wageless." But the recovery has also been exceedingly unequal. Although the recession ended in late 2001, and despite overall job growth and improvements in the white unemployment rate, the black unemployment rate is worsening. The trend has caught economists by surprise.

African-American employment is generally more "elastic," or responsive to changes in the business cycle, than white employment; it falls sooner than white unemployment during recessions, but rises more quickly during recoveries. Not so this time.

Whites enjoyed a 0.4 percentage point decrease in unemployment over the first 13 quarters of the current recovery (the fourth quarter of 2001 through the first quarter of 2005) while African Americans faced a 0.8 percentage point *increase* in unemployment. During the equivalent period of the 1990s recovery, the African-American unemployment rate improved by 0.6 percentage points (falling 50% more than white unemployment), according to analysis by Economic Policy Institute senior economist Jared Bernstein (see Figure 1).

In many other respects, the recent recession and current recovery are comparable to the early 1990s. Both decades' recessions were at least partly the result of falling investor and consumer confidence brought on by wars in the Middle East. Both recoveries were "jobless"; GDP growth was not matched by strong growth in employment.

Given the parallels, what explains today's post-recession rise in African-American unemployment? No consensus explanation has emerged, but several factors likely contribute.

First, racial discrimination, a persistent feature of labor markets, may actually intensify in slack labor markets. Research conducted by economist William M. Rodgers suggests that discrimination may decline during boom periods, and, he speculates, the reverse may also hold. When there are many unemployed workers vying for a job, employers can indulge their personal preferences or prejudices. Conversely, when job markets are tight, employers cannot afford to keep their biases in play. "It makes sense that, in a period of slow job growth, workers are hired not just for their skill but also because of their race," Rodgers says.

Another culprit is the extremely weak demand for labor. Although the early 1990s and current recoveries are both described as "jobless," the current one is *extra* "jobless." In 1994, the economy generated 321,080 jobs per month on average, according to the Bureau of Labor Statistics. In comparison, the 2004 average of 182,830 jobs per month was positively tepid. The recession that began in 2001 resulted in the loss of 2.7 million jobs. Only 3.1 million jobs have

FIGURE 1
QUARTERLY CHANGE IN UNEMPLOYMENT
Current Recovery and Last Recovery by Race

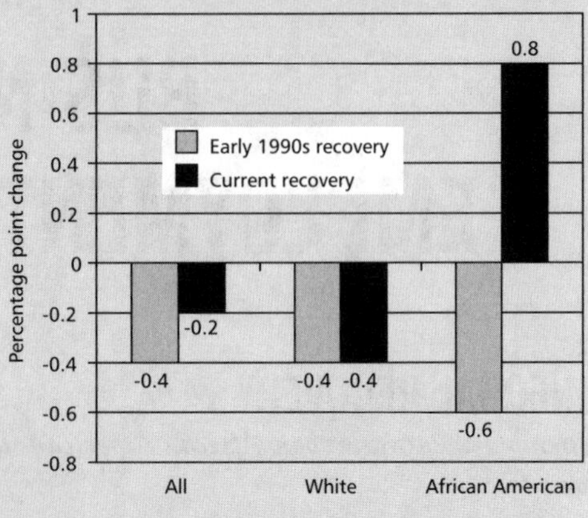

(bars — Early 1990s recovery; Current recovery)

All: −0.4, −0.2
White: −0.4, −0.4
African American: −0.6, 0.8

Source: Analysis of Bureau of Labor Statistics data by Economic Policy Institute senior economist Jared Bernstein.

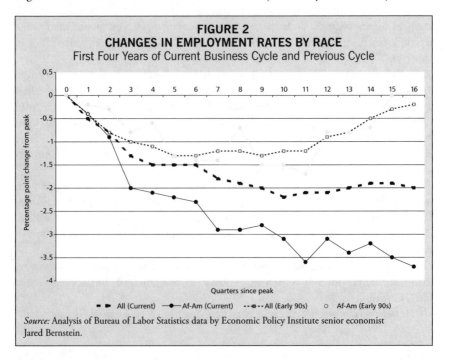

FIGURE 2
CHANGES IN EMPLOYMENT RATES BY RACE
First Four Years of Current Business Cycle and Previous Cycle

Quarters since peak

■ ■ All (Current) ● Af-Am (Current) - -�– - All (Early 90s) ○ Af-Am (Early 90s)

Source: Analysis of Bureau of Labor Statistics data by Economic Policy Institute senior economist Jared Bernstein.

been added since, so the net job creation since 2001 is 400,000 jobs—less than the number of new workers entering the labor force. "There is a job deficit in the millions relative to what you would expect at this stage, and that wasn't the case three years into the last recovery," notes Bernstein.

Rodgers adds, "At least 150,000 new jobs must be created per month just to absorb the labor market's natural population growth. Average monthly job growth well in excess of 150,000 new jobs is needed before displaced workers, particularly African Americans, are re-employed." For instance, the 110,000 jobs created in March of this year was not enough to absorb even the natural growth of the work force, let alone make a dent in national unemployment (or African-American unemployment.)

In the early 1990s, the African-American employment rate tracked the overall employment rate (see the top lines of Figure 2). In the current recovery, the African-American employment rate is significantly outperformed by the (weak) overall employment rate. (The employment rate—also called the employment-to-population ratio—is the percentage of working-age people who have jobs.)

The influx of immigrants may also play a role. During the 1990s, the immigrant population grew by 11.3 million—faster than at any other time in history. In the context of weak overall job growth and the contraction of the manufacturing sector, competition from immigrants for scarce jobs in the service, office, and clerical occupations may have compounded African Americans' already fragile employment situation. Steven A. Camarota, director of research at the Center for Immigration Studies, points out that "between March of 2000 and March of 2004, the number of adults working actually increased, but all of the net change went to immigrant workers." During that period, Camarota continues, the number of *unemployed* adult natives increased by 2.3 million, while the number of *employed* adult immigrants increased by 2.3 million.

One thing is certain. The black unemployment rate hit a staggering 10.6% in the first quarter of 2005, up from 9.8% in 2001, widening the already dramatic gap with the white unemployment rate (which hovers at 4.4%). With more than one in 10 African Americans unemployed today, many who experienced some degree of economic opportunity and mobility in the 1990s are finding themselves losing ground—well into what is supposed to be a recovery.

Resources: Jared Bernstein, "African Americans in the current recovery," Economic Snapshots. The Economic Policy Institute, April 6, 2005 <www.epinet.org>; Steven A. Camarota, "A Jobless Recovery? Immigrant Gains and Native Losses," Center for Immigration Studies, October 2004 <www.cis.org>.

MISSING JOBS STILL LOST

JOHN MILLER
November/December 2004

> "MISSING JOBS FOUND"
>
> ... It turns out that this economic expansion is different from those in the past, but not in the way that many thought. New jobs are being created as usual, but they are different kinds of jobs. The U.S. economy is undergoing a structural change as more people become self-employed or form partnerships, rather than working for large corporations.
>
> This transformation confounds the government's employment surveyors because they rely on the payroll data of about 400,000 existing companies ...
>
> These [new] jobs show up in the "household survey." The government collects this data from workers rather than companies, and while it is more volatile month-to-month due to the smaller sample size (60,000 households), over the past three years it consistently told us that something unusual is happening. If you believe the payroll figures, the U.S. still has to create 700,000 more new jobs before it will return to the peak pre-recession level of 2001. But according to what individual Americans are saying, we've already surpassed that level by two million jobs.
>
> In short, these are good times for most American workers ...
>
> —*Wall Street Journal*, October 11, 2004

The Bush administration may have struck out trying to find weapons of mass destruction in Iraq, but the *Wall Street Journal* editors say they have found the jobs that have gone missing during this jobless economic recovery.

Using the household survey of employment as their Geiger counter, the *Journal*'s editors claim to have unearthed hundreds of thousands of new jobs overlooked by the traditional payroll survey of employment favored by the Bureau of Labor Statistics, the Congressional Budget Office, and most economists. With those extra jobs, the household survey has the Bush administration adding jobs to the economy, not losing them, and the recovery, as of September, creating 1,628,000 jobs on top of replacing the jobs lost since the last recession began, in March 2001. That picture is far more to the liking of the *Journal*'s editors than the one painted by the payroll survey, which depicts the Bush administration as losing jobs and the recovery still down 940,000 jobs since the onset of the recession some three and a half years ago. Replacing the jobs lost to the recession is something the average postwar recovery managed to accomplish within two years.

But the truth is that, when used appropriately, the payroll and household employment surveys tell "the same (sad) story," in the words of Cleveland Federal Reserve Bank economists Mark Schweitzer and Guhan Venkatu. "Both surveys," they note, "show that employment has performed poorly in this recovery relative to the usual post-World War II experience." By historical standards, over four million jobs remain missing in today's economy.

Why the Payroll Survey Is More Accurate Than the Household Survey

Federal Reserve Board Chair Alan Greenspan feels the *Journal* editors' pain. Still, he can't bring himself to endorse using the household survey to measure monthly employment growth. Earlier this year, Greenspan told Congress, "Having looked at both sets of data … it's our judgment that as much as we would like the household data to be the more accurate, regrettably that turns out not to be the case."

Why do Alan Greenspan, the Bureau of Labor Statistics (BLS) that conducts both surveys, and the nonpartisan Congressional Budget Office regard the payroll survey to be "the more accurate," to provide "more reliable information," and to "better reflect the state of the labor market" than the household survey?

The first reason is statistical reliability. The payroll or establishment survey, which the BLS calls the Employment Statistics Survey, asks employers at about 400,000 worksites how many people they employ. The payroll sample includes every firm with 1,000 employees or more and covers about one-third of the total number of workers. The household survey—its formal name is the Current Population Survey—asks people in 60,000 households about their employment status. That is a small fraction of the total number of workers; the sample size of the payroll survey is 600 times larger. As a result, the household survey is subject to a large sampling error, about three times that of the payroll survey on a monthly basis.

Second, the payroll survey is better anchored in a comprehensive count of employment than the household survey. The household survey checks its result against a direct count of employment only once a decade when the decennial census is completed. On the other hand, every year the BLS adjusts the payroll survey's estimate of employment to correspond to the unemployment insurance tax records that nearly all employers are required to file. The preliminary revision based on the March 2004 benchmark added 236,000 workers, or a two-tenths of one percent increase in employment. The *Journal* suggests the revision shows the payroll numbers to be faulty; on the contrary, it should be taken as sign of their reliability, especially since the household survey is "benchmarked" but once a decade.

Beyond statistical reliability, the two surveys differ conceptually as well. Some of those differences narrow the gap between the job count of the two surveys, while others widen that gap. For instance, the two surveys treat multiple jobholders differently. The payroll survey counts each job reported by employers, even if the same worker holds two jobs. The household survey, on the other hand, counts multiple jobholders as employed only once. Also, while the household survey sample is quite limited, it does equally well counting jobs at new firms and long-established firms. The more thorough payroll survey only slowly integrates new firms into its sample, which can present problems in periods of rapid job growth. Finally, the household survey counts the self-employed, while the payroll survey of business establishments does not.

It is this third point that the *Journal* editors have seized on to explain why the payroll survey has undercounted the growth of jobs in the current recovery. They put it this way: "[W]hen a higher ratio of people make their livelihood as independent consultants to their old company, or as power sellers on eBay, they don't show up in the establishment survey."

Perhaps—if it were true that a higher ratio of people are self-employed. But even Harvard economist Robert Barro, a senior fellow at the conservative Hoover Institute, isn't buying it. In his March *Wall Street Journal* op-ed piece, Barro called "the large expansion of self-employment" explanation "a non-starter." Self-employment in the household survey just hasn't risen that much. As a ratio of household employment, self-employment rose somewhat after 2002, but even now that ratio is barely above its level at the onset of the recession in 2001, and it remains well below its level throughout most of the 1990s. What's more, an increase in self-employment is common in a weak labor market and typically disappears as labor market conditions improve and many of the self-employed find wage and salary employment. Finally, Barro estimates that "self-employment and other measurable differences between the two surveys explain only 200,000 to 400,000 of the extra three million jobs in the household survey."

The Same Sad Story

Even the household survey indicates this recovery has done far less to create jobs than other postwar recoveries. According to the household survey, the current recovery had added just 1.5% to total employment by January 2004, some 26 months after the recession officially ended in November 2001. Other postwar recoveries added an average of 5.5% to the number of jobs over the same period. The payroll survey paints an even more dismal picture: it shows the U.S. economy losing 0.5% off its job base during 26 months of recovery, while prior recoveries since 1949 added an average of 6.9% to employment in that amount of time.

Economists Schweitzer and Venkatu agree that it is more sensible to compare each employment survey to its own results during other postwar business cycles rather than to the other survey. They compare the ratio of employment (measured by the household survey) to total population in this recovery with the average pattern over postwar business cycles. In a recession, the employment-population ratio typically declines for about a year and a half and then returns to its previous level within about three years. But in this recovery, the employment-population ratio has declined nearly continuously. As a result, after three years of economic recovery, that ratio now stands at 62.3% (in September 2004), a full two percentage points below its 2001 pre-recession level of 64.3%.

By that standard, the U.S. economy is still missing 4,252,000 jobs—the number required to simply return to the employment-population ratio in 2001, and to equal the performance of the average postwar recovery. Schweitzer and Venkatu conclude that "both measures [the payroll survey and the household survey] show a surprisingly similar picture of the weak labor market performance that has prevailed during this recovery relative to previous business cycle periods."

The continuous decline in the ratio of employment to population makes clear why the unemployment rate is not higher, given the weak labor market. It is not because new jobs have gone uncounted; after all, unemployment rates are derived from the household survey. Rather, it is because many people have stopped looking for jobs and thus have dropped out of the unemployment statistics. The labor force participation rate—the fraction of the population either working or looking for work—has fallen sharply since George Bush took office; if it had stayed at its January 2001 level, the official unemployment rate would be 7.4%.

Still Missing

By any measure—the payroll survey, the household survey, or even the unemployment rate—the *Wall Street Journal* has not managed to locate the missing jobs in the U.S. economy. An honest inspection of the data reveals what most working people already know: when it comes to creating jobs, this recovery is the weakest since the Great Depression. That truth will continue to go missing on the editorial pages of the *Wall Street Journal*.

Sources: "Missing Jobs Found," *Wall Street Journal* 10/11/04; Mark Schweitzer and Guhan Venkatu, "Employment Surveys Are Telling the Same (Sad) Story," Economic Commentary (Federal Reserve Bank of Cleveland, 5/15/04); Robert Barro, "Go Figure," *Wall Street Journal*, 3/9/04; Bureau of Labor Statistics, "Employment from the BLS household and payroll surveys: summary of recent trends," 10/8/04; Elise Gould, "Measuring Employment Since the Recovery: A comparison of the household and payroll surveys," (Economic Policy Institute, December 2003); Steven Hipple, "Self-employment in the United States: an update," *Monthly Labor Review*, July 2004.

BERNANKE'S DILEMMA

WILLIAM GREIDER
November/December 2005

If Ben Bernanke is unlucky, he may inherit the whirlwind when he succeeds Alan Greenspan as Federal Reserve chairman early next year. The Greenspan Fed is once again pursuing a high-risk strategy while concealing its real intentions from the public: raising short-term interest rates in the name of fighting inflation, but actually aiming to defuse the price bubble in housing. The last time the Fed tried this maneuver, it was hoping to subdue the stock market bubble. That gambit ended badly: shareholders lost $6 trillion, and instead of subsiding gently, the bubble collapsed and the economy went into recession.

This time, as sophisticated financial-market analysts understand, the Fed's true objective is asset deflation—though neither Greenspan nor Bernanke will acknowledge even that a housing bubble exists. Raising short-term rates, the Fed assumes, will induce financial markets to raise rates on long-term loans like mortgages, and higher interest on mortgages would definitely dampen housing prices.

Trouble is, the Fed strategy has so far failed utterly. Long-term rates are not rising. If Bernanke persists with Greenspan's strategy, short-term rates may rise higher than long-term rates. That unnatural condition means the imminent threat of recession, which is what has occurred repeatedly when the Fed has induced this state of inverted short-term and long-term rates.

A recession, as always, imposes the worst pain and loss on the weakest parties—the newly unemployed, families already struggling with debt, and small businesses already squeezed by energy costs and other negatives. Thorstein Veblen called it "the slaughter of the innocents." It's simply wrong for the Fed to put the real, Main Street economy at risk in order to solve a financial problem, the housing bubble, that Greenspan, Bernanke and their colleagues at the Fed won't even acknowledge exists, let alone admit their culpability in creating.

If Bernanke, like Greenspan, is convinced that long-term rates need to rise, there's a better way to do it—an ingenious strategy proposed by Paul McCulley, Fed watcher at PIMCO, the giant bond investment house. Contrary to conventional thinking, McCulley suggests the Fed can effectively force long-term rates to rise if it now starts to *reduce* short-term rates. Inflation vigilantes in the bond market would be alarmed, McCulley explains, believing that the central bank has given in to the return of price inflation that depresses the value of long-term financial assets. In that event, bond-market players would bid up bond rates to protect themselves. Pushing long-term rates up would address the housing bubble; doing so without raising short-term rates would be easier on the Main Street economy.

The logic is persuasive, but don't count on Bernanke to grasp it. Like Greenspan, he belongs to the orthodox school: Markets are logical and efficient, so there should be no need for central bankers to game or surprise market players to induce them to react one way or another. Holding firm to their economic principles—in this case, protecting the interests of the wealth holders and financial markets—is often more important to central bankers than protecting the economic well-being of the overall society.

But perhaps Bernanke will turn out to be a more supple thinker than the excessively admired Greenspan. We will soon find out.

MEASURING THE FULL IMPACT OF MINIMUM WAGE LAWS

Workers who were earning less than the new wage floor are not the only ones who benefit from a higher minimum wage.

JEANNETTE WICKS-LIM
May/June 2006

Raising the minimum wage is quickly becoming a key political issue for this fall's midterm elections. In the past, Democratic politicians have shied away from the issue while Republicans have openly opposed a higher minimum wage. But this year is different. Community activists are forcing the issue by campaigning to put state minimum-wage proposals before the voters this fall in Arizona, Colorado, Ohio, and Missouri. No doubt inspired by the 100-plus successful local living-wage campaigns of the past ten years, these activists are also motivated by a federal minimum wage that has stagnated for the past nine years. The $5.15 federal minimum is at its lowest value in purchasing-power terms in more than 50 years; a single parent with two children, working full-time at the current minimum wage, would fall $2,000 below the poverty line.

Given all the political activity on the ground, the Democrats have decided to make the minimum wage a central plank in their party platform. Former presidential candidate John Edwards has teamed up with Sen. Edward Kennedy (D-Mass.) and ACORN, a leading advocacy group for living wage laws, to push for a $7.25 federal minimum. Even some Republicans are supporting minimum wage increases. In fact, a bipartisan legislative coalition unexpectedly passed a state minimum wage hike in Michigan this March.

Minimum-wage and living-wage laws have always caused an uproar in the business community. Employers sound the alarm about the dire consequences of a higher minimum wage both for themselves and for the low-wage workers these laws are intended to benefit: Minimum wage mandates, they claim, will cause small-business owners to close shop and lay off their low-wage workers. A spokesperson for the National Federation of Independent Business (NFIB), commenting on a proposal to raise Pennsylvania's minimum wage in an interview with the Philadelphia Inquirer, put it this way: "That employer may as well be handing out pink slips along with the pay raise."

What lies behind these bleak predictions? Mark Shaffer, owner of Shaffer's Park Supper Club in Crivitz, Wisc., provided one explanation to the Wisconsin State Journal: "… increasing the minimum wage would create a chain reaction. Every worker would want a raise to keep pace, forcing up prices and driving away customers." In other words, employers will not only be forced to raise the wages of those workers earning below the new minimum wage, but also the wages of their co-workers who earn somewhat more. The legally required wage raises are difficult enough for employers to absorb, they claim; these other raises—referred to as ripple effect raises—aggravate the situation. The result? "That ripple effect is going to lay off people."

Ripple effects represent a double-edged sword for minimum-wage and living-wage proponents. Their extent determines how much low-wage workers will benefit from such laws. If the ripple effects are small, then a higher minimum (or living) wage would benefit only a small class of workers, and boosting the minimum wage might be dismissed as an ineffective antipoverty strategy. If the ripple effects are large, then setting higher wage minimums may be seen as a potent policy tool to improve the lives of the working poor. But at the same time, evidence of large ripple effects provides ammunition to employers who claim they cannot afford the costs of a higher wage floor.

So what is the evidence on ripple effects? Do they bloat wage bills and overwhelm employers? Do they expand the number of workers who get raises a little or a lot? It's difficult to say because the research on ripple effects has been thin. But getting a clear picture of the full impact of minimum and living wage laws on workers' wages is critical to evaluating the impact of these laws. New research provides estimates of the scope and magnitude of the ripple effects of both minimum-wage and living-wage laws. This evidence is crucial for analyzing both the full impact of this increasingly visible policy tool and the political struggles surrounding it.

Why Do Employers Give Ripple-Effect Raises?

Marge Thomas, CEO of Goodwill Industries in Maryland, explains in an interview with The Gazette (Md.): "There will be a ripple effect [in response to Maryland's recent minimum wage increase to $6.15], since it wouldn't be fair to pay people now making above the minimum wage at the same level as those making the new minimum wage." That is, without ripple effects, an increase in the wage floor will worsen the relative wage position of workers just above it. If there are no ripple effects, workers earning $6.15 before Maryland's increase would not only see their wages fall to the bottom of the wage scale, but also to the same level as workers who had previously earned inferior wages (i.e., workers who earned between $5.15 and $6.15).

Employers worry that these workers would view such a relative decline in their wages as unfair, damaging their morale—and their productivity. Without ripple effect raises, employers fear, their disgruntled staff will cut back on hard-to-measure aspects of their work such as responding to others cheerfully and taking initiative in assisting customers.

So employers feel compelled to preserve some consistency in their wage scales. Workers earning $6.15 before the minimum increase, for example, may receive a quarter raise, to $6.40, to keep their wages just above the new $6.15 minimum. That employers feel compelled to give non-mandated raises to some of their lowest-paid workers because it is the "fair" thing to do may appear to be a dubious claim. Perhaps so, but employers commonly express anxiety about the costs of minimum-wage and living-wage laws for this very reason.

The Politics of Ripple Effects

Inevitably, then, ripple effects come into play in the political battles around minimum-wage and living-wage laws—but in contradictory ways for both opponents and supporters. Opponents raise the specter of large ripple effects bankrupting small businesses. At the same time, though, they argue that minimum-wage laws are not effective in fighting poverty because they do not cover many workers—and worse, because those who are covered are largely teens or young-adult students just working for spending money. If ripple effects are small, this shores up opponents' assertions that minimum-wage laws have a limited impact on poverty. Evidence of larger ripple effects, on the other hand, would mean that the benefits of minimum-wage laws are larger than previously understood, and that these laws have an even greater potential to reduce poverty among the working poor.

The political implications are complicated further in the context of living-wage laws, which typically call for much higher wage floors than state and federal minimum-wage laws do. The living-wage movement calls for wage floors to be set at rates that provide a "livable income," such as the federal poverty level for a family of four, rather than at the arbitrary—and very low—level current minimum-wage laws set. The difference is dramatic: the living-wage ordinances that have been passed in a number of municipalities typically set a wage floor twice the level of federal and state minimum wages.

So the mandated raises under living-wage laws are already much higher than under even the highest state minimum-wage laws. If living-wage laws have signifi-cant ripple effects, opponents have all the more ammunition for their argument that the costs of these laws are unsustainable for employers.

How Big are Ripple Effects?

My answer is a typical economists' response: it depends. In a nutshell, it depends on how high the wage minimum is set. The reason for this is simple. Evidence from the past 20 years of changes to state and federal minimum wages suggests that while there is a ripple effect, it doesn't extend very far beyond the new minimum. So, if the wage minimum is set high, then a large number of workers are legally due raises and, relatively speaking, the number of workers who get ripple-effect raises is small. Conversely, if the wage minimum is set low, then a small number of workers are le-gally due raises and, relatively speaking, the number of workers who get ripple-effect raises is large.

In the case of minimum-wage laws, the evidence suggests that ripple effects do dramatically expand their impact. Minimum wages are generally set low relative to the wage distribution. Because so many more workers earn wages just above the minimum wage compared to those earning the minimum, even a small ripple effect increases considerably the number of workers who benefit from a rise in the mini-mum wage. And even though the size of these raises quickly shrinks the higher the worker's wage rate, the much greater number of affected workers translates into a significantly larger increase in the wage bills of employers.

For example, my research shows that the impact of the most recent federal minimum-wage increase, from $4.75 to $5.15 in 1997, extended to workers earning wages around $5.75. Workers earning between the old and new minimums generally received raises to bring their wages in line with the new minimum—an 8% raise for those who started at the old minimum. Workers earning around $5.20 (right above the new minimum of $5.15) received raises of around 2%, bringing their wages up to about $5.30. Finally, those workers earning wages around $5.75 received raises on the order of 1%, bringing their wages up to about $5.80.

This narrow range of small raises translates into a big overall impact. Roughly 4 million workers (those earning between $4.75 and $5.15) received mandated raises in response to the 1997 federal minimum wage increase. Taking into account the typical work schedules of these workers, these raises translated into a $741 million increase to employers' annual wage bills. Now add in ripple effects: Approximately 11 million workers received ripple-effect raises, adding another $1.3 billion to em-ployers' wage bills. In other words, ripple-effect raises almost quadrupled the num-ber of workers who benefited from the minimum-wage increase and almost tripled the overall costs associated with it.

Dramatic as these ripple effects are, the real impact on employers can only be gauged in relation to their capacity to absorb the higher wage costs. Here, there is evi-dence that businesses are not overwhelmed by the costs of a higher minimum wage, even including ripple effects. For example, in a study I co-authored with University of Massachusetts economists Robert Pollin and Mark Brenner on the Florida ballot measure to establish a $6.15 state minimum wage (which passed overwhelmingly in 2004), we accounted for ripple-effect costs of roughly this same magnitude. Despite almost tripling the number of affected workers (from almost 300,000 to over 850,000) and more than doubling the costs associated with the new minimum wage (from $155 million to $410 million), the ripple effects, combined with the mandated wage increases, imposed an average cost increase on employers amounting to less than one-half of 1% of their sales revenue. Even for employers in the hotel and restaurant industry, where low-wage workers tend to be concentrated, the average cost increase was less than 1% of their sales revenue. In other words, a 1% increase in prices for hotel rooms or restaurant meals could cover the increased costs associated with both legally mandated raises and ripple-effect raises.

The small fraction of revenue that these raises represent goes a long way toward explaining why economists generally agree that minimum-wage laws are not "job killers," as opponents claim. According to a 1998 survey of economists, a consensus seems to have been reached that there is minimal job loss, if any, associated with minimum-wage increases in the ranges that we've seen.

Just as important, this new research revises our understanding of who benefits from minimum wage laws. Including ripple-effect raises expands the circle of minimum-wage beneficiaries to include more adult workers and fewer teenage or student workers. In fact, accounting for ripple effects decreases the prevalence of teenagers and traditional-age students (age 16 to 24) among workers likely to be affected by a federal minimum-wage increase from four out of ten to three out of ten. In other words, adult workers make up an even larger majority of likely minimum-wage beneficiaries when ripple effects are added to the picture.

The Case of Living-Wage Laws

With living-wage laws, the ripple effect story appears to be quite different, however—primarily because living wage laws set much higher wage minimums.

To understand why living-wage laws might generate far less of a ripple effect than minimum-wage hikes, it is instructive to look at the impact of raising the minimum wage on the retail trade industry. About 15% of retail trade workers earn wages at or very close to the minimum wage, compared to 5% of all workers. As a result, a large fraction of the retail trade industry workforce receives legally mandated raises when the minimum wage is raised, which is just what occurs across a broader group of industries and occupations when a living-wage ordinance is passed.

My research shows that the relative impact of the ripple effect that accompanies a minimum-wage hike is much smaller within retail trade than across all industries. Because a much larger share of workers in retail receive legally required raises when the minimum wage is raised, this reduces the relative number of workers receiving ripple effect raises, and, in turn, the relative size of the costs associated with ripple effects. This analysis suggests that the ripple effects of living wage laws will likewise be smaller than those found with minimum-wage laws.

To be sure, the ripple effect in the retail trade sector may underestimate the ripple effect of living-wage laws for a couple of reasons. First, unlike minimum-wage hikes, living-wage laws may have ripple effects that extend across firms as well as up the wage structure within firms. Employers who do not fall under a living-wage law's mandate but who are competing for workers within the same local labor market as those that do may be compelled to raise their own wages in order to retain their workers. Second, workers just above living-wage levels are typically higher on the job ladder and may have more bargaining power than workers with wages just above minimum-wage levels and, as a result, may be able to demand more significant raises when living-wage laws are enacted.

However, case studies of living-wage ordinances in Los Angeles and San Francisco do suggest that the ripple effect plays a smaller role in the case of living-wage laws than in the case of minimum-wage laws. These studies find that ripple effects add less than half again to the costs of mandated raises—dramatically less than the almost tripling of costs by ripple effects associated with the 1997 federal minimum-wage increase. In other words, the much higher wage floors set by living-wage laws appear to reverse the importance of legally required raises versus ripple-effect raises.

Do the costs associated with living-wage laws—with their higher wage floors—overwhelm employers, even if their ripple effects are small? To date, estimates suggest that within the range of existing living-wage laws, businesses are generally able to absorb the cost increases they face. For example, Pollin and Brenner studied a 2000 proposal to raise the wage floor from $5.75 to $10.75 in Santa Monica, Calif. They estimated that the cost increase faced by a typical business would be small, on the order of 2% of sales revenue, even accounting for both mandated and ripple-effect raises. Their estimates also showed that some hotel and restaurant businesses might face cost increases amounting to up to 10% of their sales revenue—not a negligible sum. However, after examining the local economy, Pollin and Brenner concluded that even these cost increases would not be likely to force these businesses to close their doors. Moreover, higher productivity and lower turnover rates among workers paid a living wage would also reduce the impact of these costs.

Ultimately, the impact of ripple-effect raises appears to depend crucially on the level of the new wage floor. The lower the wage floor, as in the case of minimum-wage laws, the more important the role of ripple-effect raises. The higher the wage floor, as in the case of living-wage laws, the less important the role of ripple-effect raises.

Making the Case

The results of this new research are generally good news for proponents of living- and minimum-wage laws. Ripple effects do not portend dire consequences for employers from minimum and living wage laws; at the same time, ripple-effect raises heighten the effectiveness of these laws as antipoverty strategies.

In the case of minimum-wage laws, because the cost of legally mandated raises relative to employer revenues is small, even ripple effects large enough to triple the cost of a minimum-wage increase do not represent a large burden for employers. Moreover, ripple effects enhance the somewhat anemic minimum-wage laws to make them more effective as policy tools for improving the lot of the working poor. Accounting for ripple effects nearly quadruples the number of beneficiaries of a minimum-wage hike and expands the majority of those beneficiaries who are adults—in many instances, family breadwinners.

However, ripple effects do not appear to overwhelm employers in the case of the more ambitious living-wage laws. The strongest impact from living-wage laws appears to come from legally required raises rather than from ripple-effect raises. This reinforces advocates' claims that paying a living wage is a reasonable, as well as potent, way to fight poverty.

Sources: Fairris, D. et al. Examining the evidence: The impact of the Los Angeles living wage ordinance on workers businesses. (Los Angeles Alliance for a New Economy, 2005); Fuchs, V. et al. "Economists' Views About Parameters, Values and Policies: Survey Results in Labor and Public Economics," Journal of Economic Literature (Sept. 1998); Pollin, R., Brenner, M. and Wicks-Lim, J. "Economic Analysis of the Florida Minimum Wage Proposal" (Center for American Progress, 2004); Pollin, R. and Brenner, M. "Economic Analysis of the Santa Monica Living Wage Proposal," (Political Economy Research Institute, 2000); Reich, M. et al. Living wages and economic performance. (Institute of Industrial Relations, 2003); Wicks-Lim, J. "Mandated wage floors and the wage structure: Analyzing the ripple effects of minimum and prevailing wage laws." (Ph.D. dissertation, University of Massachusetts-Amherst, 2005).

BUMPY LANDING
Rough Ride Continues as Economy Slows

JOHN MILLER
July/August 2007

Landing a plane is tricky business. A pilot must contend with a host of variables—weather, visibility, runway conditions, and air traffic—to make a safe landing.

The same holds for landing an economy, according to the conventional analysis. The pilot of the U.S. macroeconomy, the chair of the Federal Reserve Board, must check inflationary expectations, corral labor costs, and shrink debt burdens to slow the economy while not pushing it off the runway of moderate economic growth into a recession or a full-blown crash.

If all goes according to plan, the economy will coast in at a 2% to 3% growth rate, land softly, and refuel with lower costs and higher profit margins for the next economic takeoff.

Much of the economics profession seems to think that Fed chair Ben Bernanke will be able to pull off just such a soft landing. The consensus forecast of business economists sees the economy growing "just enough to keep investors happy and inflation at bay" in 2007. The *Wall Street Journal's* survey of 60 business economists predicts 2.5% GDP growth for the year, the slowest growth rate in five years but fast enough to avoid a recession. Even Lakshman Achuthan, managing director at the Economic Cycle Research Institute, who—unlike 95% of U.S. economists—accurately predicted the 2001 recession, expects an uptick in the vast U.S. service sector in 2007, keeping the economy out of recession.

But others, including former Fed chair Alan Greenspan, won't rule out a hard landing that drives the economy into recession. Speaking via satellite to investors in Singapore, Hong Kong, and Australia, Greenspan labeled the current expansion, now in its sixth year, "long in the tooth" and put the probability of the U.S. economy slipping into a recession by the end of 2007 at one-third.

Some see recession as the most likely scenario for 2007. Nouriel Roubini, director of the RGE Monitor and economist at the Stern School of Business at NYU, says, "The [U.S.] economy will experience a hard landing, at best in the form of a growth recession (growth in 0%-1% range) for most of 2007, or more likely, an actual recession." For Dean Baker and Mark Weisbrot, chief economists at the Center for Economic and Policy Research, the enormity of the housing bubble makes a "housing crash recession" a near certainty in 2007.

Recession or no, this much is clear. The economy will slow in 2007, and the landing, no matter how soft it may feel to the passengers in first class, will be a bumpy one for those in the economy seats. After all, the last five years of economic expansion have been a rough ride for most everyone one in the back of the economic plane. Working people never saw their real wages take off, and the usual ration of new jobs never materialized. This February, Fed chair Bernanke took the unusual step of calling upon policymakers to put in place "some limits on the downside risks to individuals" to protect the dynamism essential for economic progress, although his monetary policy will likely do just the opposite.

Not a Pretty Picture

The current economic expansion began in November 2001, following an eight-month economic slowdown brought on by the bursting of the stock market bubble and the collapse of the Internet-driven investment boom of the late 1990s.

The 2001 recession had been neither long nor deep. Nonetheless, the economic recovery that followed was far from robust. The economic plane seemed to do little more than taxi down the runway despite the efforts of the Fed to get the economy airborne through record low interest rates and the Bush administration's repeated pro-rich tax cuts. During the first two and half years of the expansion, economic growth was sluggish, never reaching 3.0%; real personal income (income of households adjusted for inflation) grew much more slowly than in past recoveries; and the economy continued to lose jobs.

The economy finally took off in the third quarter of 2003 when GDP growth rates spiked to 7.5% following the invasion of Iraq in March of that year, which produced the biggest quarterly increase in military spending since the Korean War. After that, consumer spending fueled by the housing bubble and investment spending bolstered by ever-rising corporate profits kept the economy airborne. The expansion logged growth rates between 3% and 4% until slowing to just over a 2% growth rate in the second half of 2006, and to 1.3% in the first quarter of 2007.

All told, annual GDP growth in this expansion has averaged just 2.9%, well below the 4.2% average in earlier postwar business cycles of similar length. Employment growth continues to be the weakest of any postwar economic recovery, just 0.9% a year as opposed to an average of 2.4%—and just one-half the rate posted by the "jobless recovery" of the 1990s. In addition, wages and salaries improved just 1%

a year on average in the current expansion, far below the 2.6% average of postwar expansions, with most of those gains coming only in the past year.

But in two areas this expansion has been exceptional. First, at 64 months, it already has steamed past the usual 51-month length of postwar expansions. Second, it has racked up a record level of corporate profits.

The two are closely related. What typically brings a capitalist expansion to a close is increasing business costs, usually rising wages, which cut into profit margins and bring investment to a halt. Long-running economic expansions tighten labor markets. With jobs plentiful, the balance of class power tilts toward workers, allowing them to push for higher wages which, in turn, eat into corporate profits.

While this expansion might be getting old, the usual signs of aging have not been apparent. Corporate cost cutting, including the outsourcing of manufacturing and white-collar jobs, has kept workers' bargaining power in check, performing a kind of liposuction on any unsightly bulges in wages and salaries. And because labor is the largest expense for business overall, preventing wage gains is the equivalent of a botox injection for corporate profits.

This pro-corporate cosmetic surgery has not been pretty. The current economic recovery has done more to improve profits and far less to raise wages than any other expansion since World War II. A recent study conducted by the Washington, D.C.-based Center on Budget and Policy Priorities, reports the alarming details. From 2001 to 2006, corporate profits rose 12.8% a year after adjusting for inflation, compared to the 8.3% average growth rate in other postwar recoveries of equal duration. By contrast, over the same period inflation-adjusted wages and salaries grew just 1.9% a year, well below the 3.8% average annual rate posted by earlier postwar expansions. For three years of the expansion, real wages actually declined. And even total labor compensation (the sum of all paychecks plus employee benefits, including rapidly rising health insurance premiums) grew at just a 2.5% annual rate in this expansion, well below the 4.1% average rate for earlier postwar expansions. (See Table 1.)

For the first time on record, a larger share of the income growth from an economic expansion went into corporate profits, some 46% of it, than to wages and salaries. As a result, by the end of 2006 wages and salaries had fallen to just a 51.6% share of national income, the lowest level on record, with data going back to 1929. At the same time, corporate profits as a share of national income reached 13.8%, the highest level on record.

And what there was for income gains was unevenly distributed. From the be-

TABLE 1
AVERAGE ANNUAL GROWTH RATES IN THE FIVE YEARS
FOLLOWING THE END OF A RECESSION

Recession Ending In	1949	1954	1958	1961	1970	1975	1980	1982	1991	2001	Average for Post-World War II Recoveries (not including current recovery)
Wages and Salaries	5.8%	3.5%	4.4%	5.4%	1.9%	3.8%	2.3%	4.4%	2.4%	1.9%	3.8%
Corporate Profits	7.2%	7.4%	10.0%	12.1%	6.6%	6.6%	6.6%	10.1%	8.4%	12.8%	8.3%

Source: CBPP calculations based on Commerce Department data.

ginning of the expansion in 2001 until 2005, the average income of the richest 5% of households rose 3.1% after adjusting for inflation, while the average income of the middle fifth of the population rose just 0.9%, and the poorest fifth just 0.7%. This expansion was the first in 40 years to fail to reduce the poverty rate, which rose from 11.7% in 2001 to 12.6% in 2005. And 5.4 million more people were without health insurance in 2005 than when the expansion began in 2001.

Good Jobs at Good Wages: Don't Hold Your Breath

Joshua Feinman, chief economist at Deutsche Asset Management, attempts to put the best face on the situation in a 2006 article with the surprisingly honest title "Is Capital Eating Labor's Lunch?" That proposition, admits Feinman, has "the ring of plausibility." After all, real wages for the median American worker have stagnated, while a cumulative 14% increase in labor productivity added to corporate profits from third quarter 2001 through the end of 2005.

Still Feinman is not convinced for two reasons. First, he finds that the share of national income going to corporate profits has reached record levels in large part because interest costs have fallen, with record low interest rates as emerging Asian nations have parked money in "safe investments" in the United States. Second, returns to labor usually lag in periods with slack labor markets and strong productivity gains. He likens the current period to the first five years of the long 1990s expansion, which saw compensation begin to catch up only at the end of the expansion.

In other words, the current tilt of the benefits of growth away from labor is perhaps not unprecedented, and corporate profits have benefited from an abundance of capital flowing into the United States from the developing world. Both of these assessments might strike most workers as cold comfort.

But for the editors of the *Wall Street Journal*, it is enough to convince them that better wages are on their way. The editors point out that as the economy moves from recovery to sustained expansion, productivity grows first, which boosts profits, then employment picks up, and finally wages rise as labor markets tighten. Like Feinman, they cite the first five years of the 1990s expansion, when unemployment remained high and wages stagnated.

No one should hold her breath waiting for this expansion to produce higher wages and better jobs. The editors' catch-up argument is predicated on sustained job creation tightening labor markets and tilting the balance of class power in labor's favor.

But the great American jobs machine seems to be out of order. The current expansion has created fewer jobs and added fewer work hours than any other expansion since World War II. Economist Jared Bernstein of the labor-funded Economic Policy Institute documents just how dismal job creation has been over five years of this economic expansion. From November 2001 through November 2006, the payrolls of private employers and the government grew just 4.5%—much more slowly than the other three postwar expansions five years in length for which we have data. (See "Payroll Growth at Five.")

The current expansion has a long way to go even to match the performance of the jobless recovery of the early 1990s. At this point, the 1990s expansion had seen payrolls grow 9.5% and had replaced the jobs lost in the previous recession in 31 months, as opposed to the 45 months this expansion took to accomplish that feat. Had the current business cycle added jobs at the same rate as the 1990s cycle, it would have created 12 million jobs by now, not 5 million. That shortfall should be enough to dash any optimism about improving labor market conditions.

During this expansion the U.S. economy has *lost* 2.9 million manufacturing jobs. Job growth has been concentrated in the service sector. Even information technology, the great promise of the 1990s, lost more than 1.1 million jobs in the last five years.

Given those numbers, it seems reasonable to ask "What's Really Propping Up the Economy?" as did a September 2006 cover story in *Business Week*. Their answer was a health care industry that added 1.7 million jobs over the last five years. The rest of the private sector added none: the jobs created by the housing boom were more than outweighed by the losses from the info tech bust. The remaining job growth this decade came from the public sector.

Paul Craig Roberts, supply-side economist and fierce critic of the Bush administration, goes yet further. The U.S. economy is experiencing "a job-depression," in his view. For Roberts, the Bureau of Labor Statistics list of ten fastest growing occupations from 2004 to 2014 only confirms the sorry state of the U.S. labor market. Seven of those jobs are in health care, and the other three are in information services. (See Table 2.) Home health aide, a job paying up to $20,184 a year, tops the list. So much for good wages. And in a fit of xenophobia, Roberts rails that most of the

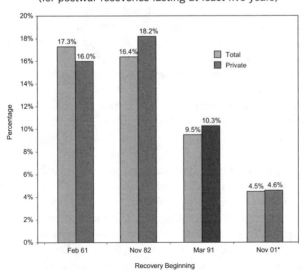

PAYROLL GROWTH AT FIVE
Total (private + government) and Private Payroll Growth Five Years into Recovery
(for postwar recoveries lasting at least five years)

Source: Jared Bernstein, "Jobs recovery at five reveals uniquely weak expansion," Economic Policy Institute, 12/13/06 <www.epi.org/content.cfm/webfeatures_snapshots_20061213>; from BLS Establishment data.

better computer jobs on the list are likely to go to foreigners holding work visas.

Offshore outsourcing and offshore production, which have battered service-sector as well as manufacturing workers, have surely contributed to U.S. labor market woes. Even dyed-in-the-wool free-trader Alan Blinder, former Clinton administration economic advisor and vice-chair of the Fed, now argues that outsourcing is sapping the U.S economy's ability to create good jobs at good wages. Blinder estimates that as many as 40 million American jobs are now at risk of being shipped out of the country in the next decade or two, including computer programmers, actuaries, bookkeepers, film and video editors, and even economists. That is more than double the total number of workers employed in manufacturing today. With that wide swath of the U.S workforce in tradable jobs exposed to competition from abroad, it could be long time before any economic expansion enhances workers' bargaining power enough to push up wages.

That is true even though the official unemployment rate remains historically low at about 4.5%. The continuous decline in the ratio of employment to population explains why the unemployment rates are no higher despite the weak labor market. Many people have stopped actively looking for jobs and dropped out of the unemployment statistics. The labor force participation rate—the fraction of the population either working or actively looking for work—has fallen sharply since George Bush took office; if it had stayed at its January 2001 level, the official unemployment rate would be above 7%.

TABLE 2
FASTEST-GROWING OCCUPATIONS, 2004 TO 2014

Rank	Occupation	Projected Employment Growth 2004-2013	Income	Education Required
1	Home health aide	56%	up to $20,184	Short-term on-the-job training
2	Network systems and data communications analyst	54.6%	$43,605 and up	Bachelor's degree
3	Medical assistant	52.1%	$20,185 to $28,589	Moderate on-the-job training
4	Physician assistant	49.6%	$43,605 and up	Bachelor's degree
5	Computer software engineer, applications	48.4%	$43,605 and up	Bachelor's degree
6	Physical therapy assistant	44.2%	$20,185 to $28,589	Associate's degree
7	Dental hygienist	43.3%	$43,605 and up	Associate's degree
8	Computer software engineer, systems software	43%	$43,605 and up	Bachelor's degree
9	Dental assistant	42.7%	$20,185 to $28,589	Moderate on-the-job training
10	Personal and home care aide	41%	up to $20,184	Short-term on-the-job training

Source: Bureau of Labor Statistics, "Occupational employment projections to 2014," Monthly Labor Review Nov. 2005, Table 2 <www.bls.gov/emp/emptab21.htm>; found at Forbes.com <www.forbes.com/2007/03/09 jobs-boomers-labor-lead-careers_cx_hc_0309jobs_slide_8.html?thisSpeed=15000>

Bumpy Landing

And those were the good times. Today the economy is beset with a constellation of seemingly intractable problems: a slumping housing market, an ever widening trade deficit, slowing business spending, and consumers up to their eyeballs in debt with few prospects for better jobs or higher wages.

But it is the bursting of the housing bubble that has spooked even the most optimistic. Everyone acknowledges that the turmoil in the subprime mortgage market has created serious financial problems for the least well-off homeowners. Subprime loans—loans to borrowers with poor credit records—made up a record 13% of a $10.2 trillion mortgage market in 2006 and financed about one-half of the jump in homeownership rates from 65% to 69% over the last decade.

But these loans came with inordinate risks that left these new homeowners vulnerable to foreclosure. Some 80% had adjustable rate mortgages, or ARMs, with interest payments that increase as interest rates rise in the economy. And 47% of mortgages issued last year to subprime customers contained "creative features"— such as interest-only payments or low initial "teaser" interest rates—that make the burden of these loans rise precipitously over time. On top of that, borrowers have taken on ever more debt relative to their assets: the value of their loans reached 86.5% of the value of their property in 2006, up from 78% in 2000.

When interest rates were low and home prices rising, these loans remained viable. But since the Fed hiked short-term interest rates by four percentage points beginning in 2004 and the rise in housing prices slowed in 2005, subprime borrowers could no longer keep up with their payments. Foreclosures on subprime mortgage markets soared, more than doubling last year from 2005. At least 20 subprime mortgage lenders have gone out of business.

The biggest worry is that the subprime meltdown will spread to the broader housing market and the economy. But even if the subprime mortgage crisis is contained, that is hardly good news for working people and the poor. Business Week reporter Peter Coy argues that the Fed rate hikes have turned into "a regressive tax on weak borrowers." Families with ARMs will see their monthly payments skyrocket as short-term interest rates rise. In contrast, better mortgage holders may benefit as lenders flee the subprime market and rush into the safer traditional mortgage market, lowering those mortgage rates.

But that assumes the crumbling housing market will not spread across the economy, driving it into recession. There is real reason to think otherwise.

First, the housing recession seems to be getting worse, not better. After a run-up in housing prices led to a near doubling of sales of new and existing homes since the mid-1990s, inflation-adjusted home prices are now dropping—down between 4% and 5% in real terms nationwide from their levels at the same point in 2005, and down much more sharply in overvalued areas such as parts of Florida and California. Homes for sale averaged 6.9 months of supply in the six months ending in October 2006, the largest average supply since 1991.

Second, the subprime mortgage crisis does seem to be spreading. The same risky loans—teaser rates, interest-only, and ARMs—are now found in near-prime and some prime mortgages, making up as much as one-half of new loans in those markets. And default and foreclosure rates rose sharply for those mortgage loans as well last year.

Third, the sheer size of the housing bubble puts the economy at risk. The Federal Reserve Bank of Dallas estimates that after the run-up in housing prices from 2001 to 2005 and the bursting of the stock market bubble, real estate and stock wealth represent about equal shares of total household net wealth. Historically, a $100 rise in housing wealth has produced about a $6 rise in long-run consumption, while the same increase in stock wealth has generated only a $4 gain. And this expansion has been especially dependent on consumption, which rose as a share of GDP from about 67% in the late nineties to 70% over the last five years. In other words, a hit to home prices has a greater effect on the macroeconomy than a drop-off in stock prices—cause for concern since the deflation of the housing bubble is still underway.

All this leads economists Baker and Weisbrot from the Center for Economic and Policy Research to predict that the bursting of the housing bubble will do just as much to depress the economy as the bursting of the stock market bubble that brought on the 2001 recession, especially since recession-like conditions have already taken hold in the automobile industry and manufacturing generally.

Many economists still believe that Ben Bernanke will be able to engineer a soft landing of the economy even under these precarious conditions. As they see it, if the economy is heading toward a hard landing, the Fed will aggressively cut interest rates to perk up spending and prevent a recession. The Fed tried just such a strategy in 2001, rapidly cutting interest rates, but it did not prevent a recession then. And with today's glut of tech goods, housing, and autos and other consumer durables, it seems unlikely the Fed would be able to rescue the economy this time either.

On top of that, an ever-widening trade deficit will further hamstring Fed interest rate policy. Last year, the U.S. current account deficit, the broadest measure of the balance of trade in goods and services, expanded to a record $763.6 billion, a full percentage point over the 5%-of-GDP level financial analysts have traditionally used as a marker of financial distress in developing countries.

That large a deficit makes cutting interest rates risky business. Lower interest rates make U.S. bonds less attractive to investors. To finance last year's record trade deficit, the United States needed to borrow on average more than $70 billion a month in foreign funds. If the Fed lowered interest rates, it would have a hard time keeping foreigners buying the bonds that pay for the trade deficit. And should some large foreign creditors dump their dollar holdings, the value of the dollar would plummet, causing interest rates to spike and the U.S. stock and bond markets to tumble. That would be a hard landing indeed.

Better Economic Policy

Despite the constrained flight pattern of a capitalist economy, better public policy could surely reduce the turbulence in today's economy.

First off, if Ben Bernanke were sincerely interested in placing "limits on the downside risks in today's economy," he would not burst the housing bubble by hammering those already saddled with deceptive and predatory mortgages. Teaser rates,

ARMs with no limits or controls, and other risky and predatory mortgage practices should never have been allowed in the first place. The Fed chair was in a position to institute the proper regulatory oversight that might have pricked the housing market bubble without the worst-off having to endure a painful credit crunch.

Similarly, if the editors of the *Wall Street Journal* were truly interested in heralding in an era of higher wages, they would surely endorse increasing the minimum wage, one of the key ingredients that allowed working people to make some nice wage gains in the second half of the 1990s.

Finally public investment, which has fallen to about *one-half* its levels during the 1960s and 1970s relative to the size of the economy, must be restored to maintain the nation's economic competitiveness and reduce the trade deficit. That means increased public investments in education, job training, and child care as well as in basic infrastructure, the environment, energy, and research and development.

The Campaign for America's Future, the pro-labor policy group, has outlined just such an industrial policy, dubbed the Apollo Project for Good Jobs and Energy Independence. Their program would develop energy efficiency technologies while it creates good jobs by making our economy more competitive. It would dramatically reduce imports of foreign oil and help U.S companies take the lead in emerging markets for efficient appliances and alternative fuels.

Policies that would provide immediate relief from the harmful effects of outsourcing and offshore production are also needed. The list should include wage insurance, education opportunities, job placement help for displaced workers, and national health care, financed by rolling back President Bush's upper-income tax cuts which have stood in the way of an economic growth that spreads its benefits widely.

Those policies would make for a smoother economic ride for most of us.

Sources: Aviva Aron-Dine and Isaac Shapiro, "Share of National Income Going to Wages and Salaries at record low in 2006," Center on Budget and Policy Priorities, 3/29/07; Jared Bernstein, "Jobs recovery at five reveals uniquely weak expansion," Economic Policy Institute, 12/13/06; Eduardo Porter and Jeremy Peter, "This Expansion Looks Familiar," *New York Times*, 4/6/07; Nouriel Roubini, "Who is to Blame for the Mortgage Carnage and Coming Financial Disaster?" RGE Monitor 3/19/07; Nouriel Roubini, "The Housing and Global Bust," *RGE Monitor* 3/18/07; Christian Weller, "The U.S Economy in Review: 2006" Center for American Progress, 12/21/06; Christian Weller, "The End of the Great American Housing Boom," Center for American Progress, 12/06; Mark Weisbrot, "Economy Looks Bad for 2007," Center for Economic and Policy Research, 1/07; Dean Baker, "Recession Looms for the U.S. Economy in 2007," Center for Economic and Policy Research, 11/06; Nick Timiraos, "The Subprime Market's Rough Road," *Wall Street Journal*, 2/17/07; Peter Coy, "Under the Fed's Hammer," *Business Week*, 3/19/07; "What's Really Propping Up the Economy," *Business Week* 9/25/06; David Wessel and Bob Davis, "Pain From Free Trade Spurs Second Thoughts," *Wall Street Journal* 3/28/07; Paul Craig Roberts, "Nuking the Economy," *Counterpunch* 2/11/06; Paul Craig Roberts, "Data Shows America's Job Growth Benefits Immigrants, Outsourcers," *Counterpunch*, 3/3/06; "The Coming of Wage," Wall Street Journal, 10/2/06; "Good Jobs at Good Wages," *Wall Street Journal* 7/11/06; "The Current Depression" *Wall Street Journal*, 2/3/07; Joshua Feinman, "Is Capital Eating Labor's Lunch?" Deutsche Asset Management, 10/06; John V. Duca, "Making Sense of the U.S. Housing Slowdown," *Economic Letter*, Federal Reserve Bank of Dallas, 11/06.

Chapter 2

LABOR LAW, BARGAINING POWER, AND WORK CONDITIONS

UNREGULATED WORK

Is enforcement the next battle in the fight for workers' rights?

SIOBHÁN McGRATH AND NINA MARTIN
September/October 2005

Guillermo* regularly puts in 70-hour weeks as a prep cook in a New York City restaurant. He came to the United States from Ecuador six years ago because he heard that "you can earn something for your family." But these aspirations soured after he wasn't paid for three weeks. Small sums of money and continued promises from the boss keep Guillermo returning to work each day for his 12-hour shifts.

Non-payment of wages plagues Guillermo and his co-workers, but their employer uses other tactics to reduce labor costs as well. Guillermo explains, "Workers have to punch out as if they had worked eight hours. So after eight hours, they punch out and then work four more hours. It is almost like a threat that if you don't punch the card, you're fired." With an average wage of about $300 per week, these long hours translate into just over $4 per hour. Some of Guillermo's co-workers have left the restaurant for other jobs, usually at food establishments, but often the working conditions they face are frustratingly similar.

Brenda, an African-American grandmother, is a child care worker in Brooklyn. Formerly a home health care worker, Brenda's own health no longer permits her to make the long commute to her patients' homes. Caring for children in her home seemed like a good way to replace this lost income. The parents of the children she cares for receive subsidized child care as they move from welfare to work. Brenda has no sick days or vacation days, and she only has health insurance through her husband's job.

Worse, her pay often dips below minimum wage. But the city's Human

---
* The names of the workers have been changed.

Resources Administration, which cuts her check, maintains that this does not break the law. Even though the city effectively sets her pay, it classifies her as an "independent contractor," rather than an employee. So Brenda doesn't have the same rights as a regular employee, such as the minimum wage, overtime, or paid leave.

Unfortunately, the experiences of Guillermo and Brenda are far from unique. Violations of employment and labor laws are a growing problem in U.S. workplaces. Employers in many sectors of the economy are breaking the law in order to cut costs, gain a competitive edge, and boost profits, and workers are suffering the consequences. In some industries, the abuses have become so common that they are now routine practice. And enforcement by the government has steadily declined, so that more and more workers are facing abusive and unsafe conditions at work. Anyone who pays attention knows that U.S. workers in certain industries and occupations have long been vulnerable to employer abuses. But today, illegal and abusive practices are becoming common in a far larger swath of the economy, and the will and resources to enforce worker-protection laws are shrinking.

We are part of a large research team working out of three universities that is studying this phenomenon—what we call "unregulated work"—in New York City and Chicago. Over the past two years we have conducted in-depth interviews with over 400 workers, employers, government officials, community groups, union staff, and policy advocates. The next phase of our project will be a survey of workers in unregulated jobs, in order to estimate the size of this hidden zone of the economy. To date, we have found unregulated work in 14 industries. While many people are familiar with the conditions faced by garment workers and construction day laborers, the tentacles of unregulated work stretch into many other sectors of the economy, including workplaces as diverse as restaurants, grocery stores, security companies, nail salons, laundries, warehouses, manufacturers, building services firms, and home health care agencies.

We have documented considerable variety in how employers violate laws. They pay their workers less than minimum wage, fail to pay them overtime, refuse to pay them for all hours worked, or simply don't pay them at all. They disregard health and safety regulations by imposing unsafe conditions, forcing employees to work without providing necessary safety equipment, and failing to give training and information. The list of ways employers break the law goes on: they refuse to pay Unemployment Insurance or Workers' Compensation; they discriminate against workers on the basis of race, gender and immigration status; they retaliate against attempts to organize; they refuse medical leaves.

Such stories of substandard working conditions may sound familiar—they carry strong echoes of the experiences of workers at the beginning of the last century. At that time, the solution was to pass laws to create wage minimum standards, protect workers who speak up for their rights, and eventually, guarantee workplace safety and outlaw discrimination. That these very laws are now being so widely violated poses new challenges. While efforts to pass new laws raising workplace standards are still critical, a new battle has emerged to ensure that existing laws are enforced.

What Explains Unregulated Work?

The rise of unregulated work is closely tied to many of the same factors that are thought to be responsible for declining wages and job security in key sectors of the economy. Over the last 30 years, for example, global economic competition has been extinguishing the prospects of workers in manufacturing. Local manufacturers struggle to drive down their costs in order to compete against firms located in Asian or Latin American countries where wages and safety standards are lower.

Yet unregulated work cannot be explained simply as a byproduct of globalization. It's true that the competitive pressure felt in manufacturing may ripple through other parts of the economy, as wage floors are lowered and the power of labor against capital is diminished. But we found businesses that serve distinctly local markets—such as home cleaning companies, grocery stores, and nail salons—engaging in a range of illegal work practices, even though they are insulated from global competition.

Declining unionization rates since the 1970's also contribute to the spread of unregulated labor. One effect has been a general rise in inequality accompanied by lower wages and workplace standards: a weaker labor movement has less influence on the labor market as a whole, and offers less protection for both unionized and non-union workers. More directly, union members are more likely to report workplace violations to the relevant government authority than non-union workers, as a number of studies have shown. So it makes sense that employers are increasingly committing such violations in the wake of a long-term decline in the percentage of workers in unions.

But even the powerful one-two punch of globalization and de-unionization provides only a partial explanation. Government policy is also instrumental in shaping unregulated work—not only employment policies per se, but also immigration, criminal justice, and welfare "reform" policies that create pools of vulnerable workers. In this environment employers can use a variety of illegal and abusive cost-cutting strategies. Perhaps most significantly, they are deciding whether or not to break the law in an era of declining enforcement, when they are likely to face mild penalties or no penalties at all.

Immigration Policy

The deeply flawed immigration policy in the United States creates a labor supply that is vulnerable at work. For example, employers often convince undocumented workers that they have no rights at the workplace. If undocumented workers demand to be paid the minimum wage, their employers threaten not just to fire them, but also to "call immigration." Armed with such threats, employers break the law with little fear of being held accountable. Yet this strategy is only possible because US immigration policy currently denies an estimated 10 million undocumented immigrants legal recognition, thereby ensuring a steady stream of vulnerable workers. In spite of the protections they have on paper, undocumented workers consistently report feeling that government assistance is off-limits because of their immigration status.

The victims of unregulated work are not, however, limited to undocumented immigrants. Immigrants who are authorized to work are also a significant part of this workforce. Employers sometimes simply assume that people from certain countries are undocumented. Some workers are hampered by a lack of proficiency in English. Many new arrivals also lack knowledge of U.S. labor and employment laws and employers can, and do, exploit this ignorance.

For example, the newly arrived Polish women we interviewed who work at A-1 Cleaning in Chicago are usually very pleased to have quickly found work that does not require a full command of English. A Polish immigrant founded the home cleaning company, using his ties in the community to find new workers. But this is not a story of ethnic solidarity. This employer often fails in his duty to inform these workers that their rights under U.S. law include such novel concepts as a minimum wage and overtime pay, and routinely violates these rights. If employees don't fully understand workplace regulations and their rights under the law, an unscrupulous employer can get them to work for less than minimum wage.

Prison, Welfare, and Discrimination

Immigrants are not the only workers made more vulnerable to workplace exploitation by government policies. Many workers, like Brenda, were born and raised in the United States but face barriers to employment in the more regulated part of the labor market. Predictably, race, ethnicity, and gender play a role in determining who ends up in the unregulated workforce. In addition, people leaving the welfare rolls or coming out of prison are especially vulnerable: they are pushed to find work as soon as possible, yet the stigma attached to having been on welfare or in prison limits the options available to them. For "ex-offenders," this is compounded by the fact that they are legally barred from certain jobs. Similarly, some features of welfare reform policies, such as abrupt or arbitrary benefit cutoffs, or "work first" policies that force people to take the first job offered, only make it more difficult to find a satisfactory job. Ironically, the only stable employment history some workers are able to build is in unregulated work, but because they are "off the books" this does not translate into better prospects in formal jobs, so they stay mired in exploitative jobs.

Employers also keep workers trapped in unregulated jobs through illegal discrimination. In New York City's restaurant industry, for example, a white college student applying for a job will be given a front-of-the-house job such as waiting tables, seating people, or operating the cash register. A Mexican worker, regardless of language skills or immigration status, will instead be funneled into a back-of-the-house job such as dishwashing, cooking, or janitorial work. These behind-the-scenes workers are then more vulnerable to violations and extremely unlikely to be promoted to better positions.

Externalization and Exclusion from Legal Protection

New business strategies in recent decades have produced a clear shift towards the "externalization" of work. Various forms of subcontracting and outsourcing are now widespread, and allow employers to evade responsibility for mistreating workers. When workers complain about abusive or illegal practices, the firm and its subcontractor can always point fingers at each other. Overall, the growth of outsourcing has driven many jobs into spaces where the reach of regulation is weak or nonexistent.

Employers also insulate themselves from workers' demands for improved working conditions by hiring temporary workers or using subcontractors. Some use placement agencies to do their dirty work, routinely asking them to screen workers on the basis of gender, race, age and other characteristics. In one of the most egregious examples we discovered, some employment agencies in New York demand sensitive health information from job seekers. A group of workers explained to us that these agencies also post signs refusing job applications from western Africans or South Africans. In this way, they seem to believe that they are screening out potentially HIV-positive candidates for their clients. One of the main services these agencies provide, then, is to discriminate simultaneously on the basis of national origin and disability.

Tapping into a contingent workforce of day laborers allows many employers to keep their costs to an absolute minimum. The emergence of day labor corners in many cities is one of the most visible examples of unregulated work. Day laborers are hired for a variety of jobs, including construction, cleaning, and moving. Besides the often dangerous and difficult working conditions they face, day laborers may work for employers who scrimp on promised wages or fail to pay them at all.

Chicago's largest day labor corner is on the city's northwest side, in the parking lot of a gas station. Known colloquially as the "slave station", the corner is the morning destination for large numbers of men who hope to find a day's work. Many of the men are Polish; others are Mexican, Ecuadorian, Guatemalan, and Ukrainian. They have often just arrived in the city and have large debts incurred while traveling to the United States. Contractors actively try to bid down wages of workers by playing them off against one another. While the going wage in the area for these jobs is between $8 and $10 per hour, day laborers are sometimes forced to accept as little as $4 per hour rather than go without work.

Some workers are especially vulnerable to employers' abuses because they are located outside the reach of some, or even all, legal protections. For example, although domestic workers are covered by minimum wage laws and other protections, they are not covered by the National Labor Relations Act, and so they don't have the right to organize. This means that their employers are effectively given free reign to fire them for complaining about their jobs or demanding better treatment. Farm workers are similarly vulnerable, since they are exempt from protection of many labor laws.

Employers are increasingly misclassifying their workers as "independent contractors" in order to evade workplace regulations. The problem, as Cathy Ruckelshaus of the National Employment Law Project points out, is that this classification is only supposed to be applied to independent businesspersons. "You have to ask yourself, especially in the case of some of the low-wage workers," she says, "whether these people are actually running their own businesses or not." Child care workers, construction day laborers, janitors, street vendors, delivery people and bathroom attendants have been placed into this category, when in fact they were dependent upon their employer for scheduling, job assignments, equipment and training— signaling their status as traditional employees.

The Enforcement Problem

Our fieldwork indicates that unregulated work is a growing feature of business strategies at the bottom of the labor market. Very few attempts have been made to estimate the prevalence of workplace violations, but our preliminary findings are in line with evidence gathered by other researchers. For example, in the late 1990s the U.S. Department of Labor (DOL) carried out several surveys to assess compliance with the Fair Labor Standards Act (FLSA)—the law that regulates the minimum wage, overtime, and the use of child labor. Among their results: in 1999, only 42% of restaurants in Chicago and only 35% of garment shops in New York City were in compliance with FLSA.

Unfortunately, just as employer violations appear to be increasing, the resources allocated to enforcement are waning. Data we recently received from the Department of Labor shows that while the number of workplaces in the United States more than doubled between 1975 and 2004, the number of compliance actions by the DOL's Wage and Hour Division (WHD) declined by more than a third. As Howard Wial, a senior researcher at the Brookings Institution, writes, "The general picture that emerges ... is that there has been a long-term decline in the adequacy of enforcement resources, which has probably resulted in a long-term decline in the amount of attention that the WHD pays to low-wage workers."

So employers are unlikely to be the target of WHD inspections, and if they are, penalties are unlikely to be high enough to provide a deterrent. An unprincipled employer may find that it is cheaper to break the law—and run the slight risk of getting caught—than it is to comply. David Weil, an economist at Boston University, conducted a cost-benefit analysis of compliance in the garment industry, including data on the annual likelihood of inspection, the average underpayment per worker, and the median civil penalty. He found that for an apparel contractor with 35 workers, "the potential cost of not complying [with minimum wage requirements] is $121 versus a benefit of $12,205, implying that an apparel employer should clearly choose not to comply."

The problem of unregulated work is not just a "race to the bottom." It is a race that is taking place below the bottom. The legal floors on wages and working conditions are increasingly irrelevant to American employers. For the workers who populate this segment of the labor market, there is no guarantee that workplace laws will protect them.

Workers Push Back

The good news is that on the ground, community groups and other advocates are taking action. Workers are protesting for the wages owed them even as they are filing complaints with the Department of Labor or filing suits in court. In New York, workers have also collaborated with the state Attorney General's office, which has undertaken a number of initiatives to bring law-breaking employers into compliance. Immigrant workers in particular are organizing, either with unions or through Worker Centers, on the basis of industry and occupation. Day-labor groups across the country are creating "job centers," where wage rates and rules for hiring are collectively set and enforced by workers.

Advocates are also using legislation to pressure the relevant government agencies to enforce the law to protect workers. Campaigns are also underway to pass state legislation that would tie businesses' operating licenses to their compliance with labor and employment laws. In 2003, a new law in California increased employers' responsibility for violations carried out by their subcontractors. And a local law passed the same year in New York City increased the responsibility of employment agencies for the actions of their clients who hire domestic workers.

Clearly, a greater commitment to workplace enforcement, backed up by sufficient resources, will be necessary to combat the increasing number of violations of workers' rights. Yet more enforcement alone will not be enough. A deeply flawed immigration policy also needs to be fundamentally changed, so that all workers enjoy the minimum standards under the law, regardless of their citizenship status. In practice, our current immigration system accepts people into the country but then effectively denies them rights in the workplace. This creates a steady stream of vulnerable workers. Comprehensive immigration reform, with a sound path to legalization, is an essential component of efforts to guarantee workers' rights. Similarly, comprehensive changes to welfare and penal policies would make people returning to the workforce less vulnerable to exploitation in the unregulated workforce.

The growth of unregulated jobs has created a new terrain in the battle for workers' rights. While continuing efforts to raise the minimum wage and improve workplace standards are critical, in practice employers are routinely violating the standards that already exist. A greater commitment to enforcement, comprehensive reform in a range of areas of government policy (including immigration, penal, and welfare policy), and efforts to close the loopholes employers are currently taking advantage of, will all be necessary to fulfill the promise of protective labor legislation.

WHAT'S GOOD FOR WAL-MART ...

JOHN MILLER
January/February 2006

"Is Wal-Mart Good for America?"
It is a testament to the public relations of the anti-Wal-Mart campaign that the question above is even being asked.

By any normal measure, Wal-Mart's business ought to be noncontroversial. It sells at low costs, albeit in mind-boggling quantities....

The company's success and size ... do not rest on monopoly profits or price-gouging behavior. It simply sells things people will buy at small markups and, as in the old saw, makes it up on volume.... You may believe, as do service-workers unions and a clutch of coastal elites—many of whom, we'd wager, have never set foot in Wal-Mart—that Wal-Mart "exploits" workers who can't say no to low wages and poor benefits. You might accept the canard that it drives good local businesses into the ground, although both of these allegations are more myth than reality.

But even if you buy into the myths, there's no getting around the fact that somewhere out there, millions of people are spending billions of dollars on what Wal-Mart puts on its shelves. No one is making them do it…. Wal-Mart can't make mom and pop shut down the shop anymore than it can make customers walk through the doors or pull out their wallets.

What about the workers? … Wal-Mart's average starting wage is already nearly double the national minimum of $5.15 an hour. The company has also recently increased its health-care for employees on the bottom rungs of the corporate ladder.

—*Wall Street Journal* editorial, December 3, 2005

"Who's Number One? The Customer! Always!" The last line of Wal-Mart's company cheer just about sums up the *Wall Street Journal* editors' benign view of the behemoth corporation. But a more honest answer would be Wal-Mart itself: not the customer, and surely not the worker.

The first retail corporation to top the Fortune 500, Wal-Mart trailed only Exxon-Mobil in total revenues last year. With 1.6 million workers, 1.3 million in the United States and 300,000 offshore, Wal-Mart is the largest private employer in the nation and the world's largest retailer.

Being number one has paid off handsomely for the family of Wal-Mart founder Sam Walton. The family's combined fortune is now an estimated $90 billion, equal to the net worth of Bill Gates and Warren Buffett combined.

But is what's good for the Walton family good for America? Should we believe the editors that Wal-Mart's unprecedented size and market power have redounded not only to the Walton family's benefit but to ours as well?

Low Wages and Meager Benefits

Working for the world's largest employer sure hasn't paid off for Wal-Mart's employees. True, they have a job, and others without jobs line up to apply for theirs. But that says more about the sad state of today's labor market than the quality of Wal-Mart jobs. After all, less than half of Wal-Mart workers last a year, and turnover at the company is twice that at comparable retailers.

Why? Wal-Mart's oppressive working conditions surely have something to do with it. Wal-Mart has admitted to using minors to operate hazardous machinery, has been sued in six states for forcing employees to work off the books (i.e., unpaid) and without breaks, and is currently facing a suit brought by 1.6 million current and former female employees accusing Wal-Mart of gender discrimination. At the same time, Wal-Mart workers are paid less and receive fewer benefits than other retail workers.

Wal-Mart, according to its own reports, pays an average of $9.68 an hour. That is 12.4% below the average wage for retail workers even after adjusting for geography, according to a recent study by Arindrajit Dube and Steve Wertheim, economists at the University of California's Institute of Industrial Relations and long-time Wal-Mart researchers. Wal-Mart's wages are nearly 15% below the average wage of workers at large retailers and about 30% below the average wage of unionized grocery workers. The average U.S. wage is $17.80 an hour; Costco, a direct competitor of Wal-Mart's Sam's Club warehouse stores, pays an average wage of $16 an hour (see box on p. 32).

Wal-Mart may be improving its benefits, as the *Journal's* editors report, but it needs to. Other retailers provide health care coverage to over 53% of their workers, while Wal-Mart covers just 48% of its workers. Costco, once again, does far better, covering 82% of its employees. Moreover, Wal-Mart's coverage is far less comprehensive than the plans offered by other large retailers. Dube reports that according to 2003 IRS data, Wal-Mart paid 59% of the health care costs of its workers and dependents, compared to the 77% of health care costs for individuals and 68% for families the average retailer picks up.

A recent internal Wal-Mart memo leaked to the *New York Times* confirmed the large gaps in Wal-Mart's health care coverage and exposed the high costs those gaps impose on government programs. According to the memo, "Five percent of our Associates are on Medicaid compared to an average for national employees of 4 percent. Twenty-seven percent of Associates' children are on such programs, compared to a national average of 22 percent. In total, 46 percent of Associates' children are either on Medicaid or are uninsured."

A considerably lower 29% of children of all large-retail workers are on Medicaid or are uninsured. Some 7% of the children of employees of large retailers go uninsured, compared to the 19% reported by Wal-Mart.

Wal-Mart's low wages drag down the wages of other retail workers and shutter downtown retail businesses. A 2005 study by David Neumark, Junfu Zhang, and Stephen Ciccarella, economists at the University of California at Irvine, found that Wal-Mart adversely affects employment and wages. Retail workers in a community with a Wal-Mart earned 3.5% less because Wal-Mart's low prices force other businesses to lower prices, and hence their wages, according to the Neumark study. The same study also found that Wal-Mart's presence reduces retail employment by 2% to 4%. While other studies have not found this negative employment effect, Dube's research also reports fewer retail jobs and lower wages for retail workers in metropolitan counties with a Wal-Mart. (Fully 85% of Wal-Mart stores are in metropolitan counties.) Dube figures that Wal-Mart's presence costs retail workers, at Wal-Mart and elsewhere, $4.7 billion a year in lost earnings.

In short, Wal-Mart's "everyday low prices" come at the expense of the compensation of Wal-Mart's own employees and lower wages and fewer jobs for retail workers in the surrounding area. That much remains true no matter what weight we assign to each of the measures that Wal-Mart uses to keep its costs down: a just-in-time inventory strategy, its ability to use its size to pressure suppliers for large discounts, a routinized work environment that requires minimal training, and meager wages and benefits.

How Low are Wal-Mart's Everyday Low Prices?

Even if one doesn't subscribe to the editors' position that it is consumers, not Wal-Mart, who cause job losses at downtown retailers, it is possible to argue that the benefit of Wal-Mart's low prices to consumers, especially low-income consumers, outweighs the cost endured by workers at Wal-Mart and other retailers. Jason Furman, New York University economist and director of economic policy for the 2004 Kerry-Edwards campaign, makes just such an argument. Wal-Mart's "staggering" low prices are 8% to 40% lower than people would pay elsewhere, according to Furman. He calculates that those low prices on average boost low-income families' buying power by 3% and more than offset the loss of earnings to retail workers. For Furman, that makes Wal-Mart "a progressive success story."

But exactly how much savings Wal-Mart affords consumers is far from clear. Estimates vary widely. At one extreme is a study Wal-Mart itself commissioned by Global Insight, an economic forecasting firm. Global Insight estimates Wal-Mart created a stunning savings of $263 billion, or $2,329 per household, in 2004 alone.

At the other extreme, statisticians at the U.S. Bureau of Labor Statistics found no price savings at Wal-Mart. Relying on Consumer Price Index data, the BLS found that Wal-Mart's prices largely matched those of its rivals, and that instances of lower prices at Wal-Mart could be attributed to lower quality products.

Both studies, which rely on the Consumer Price Index and aggregate data, have their critics. Furman himself allows that the Global Insight study is "overly simplistic" and says he "doesn't place as much weight on that one." Jerry Hausman, the M.I.T. economist who has looked closely at Wal-Mart's grocery stores, maintains that the CPI data that the Bureau of Labor Statistics relies on systematically miss the savings offered by "supercenters" such as Wal-Mart. To show the difference between prices at Wal-Mart and at other grocers, Hausman, along with Ephraim Leibtag, USDA Economic Research Service economist, used supermarket scanner data to examine the purchasing patterns of a national sample of 61,500 consumers from 1988 to 2001. Hausman and Leibtag found that Wal-Mart offers many identical food items at an average price about 15%-25% lower than traditional supermarkets.

While Hausman and Leibtag report substantial savings from shopping at Wal-Mart, they fall far short of the savings alleged in the Global Insight study. The Hausman and Leibtag study suggests a savings of around $550 per household per year, or about $56 billion in 2004, not $263 billion. Still, that is considerably more than the $4.7 billion a year in lost earnings to retail workers that Dube attributes to Wal-Mart.

But if "Wal-Mart hurts wages, not so much in retail, but across the whole country," as economist Neumark told *Business Week*, then the savings to consumers from Wal-Mart's everyday low prices might not outweigh the lost wages to all workers. (Retail workers make up just 11.6% of U.S. employment.)

Nor do these findings say anything about the sweatshop conditions and wages in Wal-Mart's overseas subcontractors. One example: A recent Canadian Broadcasting Corporation investigative report found that workers in Bangladesh were being paid less than $50 a month (below even the United Nation's $2 a day measure of poverty) to make clothes for the Wal-Mart private label, Simply Basic. Those workers included 10- to 13-year-old children forced to work long hours in dimly lit and dirty conditions sewing "I Love My Wal-Mart" t-shirts.

The Costco Alternative?
Wall Street Prefers Wal-Mart

In an April 2004 online commentary, *Business Week* praised Costco's business model but pointed out that Costco's wages cause Wall Street to worry that the company's "operating expenses could get out of hand." How does Costco compare to low-wage Wal-Mart on overhead expenses? At Costco, overhead is 9.8% of revenue; at Wal-Mart, it is 17%. Part of Costco's secret is that its better paid workers are also more efficient: Costco's operating profit per hourly employee is $13,647; each Wal-Mart employee only nets the company $11,039. Wal-Mart also spends more than Costco on hiring and training new employees: each one, according to Rutgers economist Eileen Appelbaum, costs the company $2,500 to $3,500. Appelbaum estimates that Wal-Mart's relatively high turnover costs the company $1.5 to $2 million per year.

Despite Costco's higher efficiency, Wall Street analysts like Deutsche Bank's Bill Dreher complain that "Costco's corporate philosophy is to put its customers first, then its employees, then its vendors, and finally its shareholders. Shareholders get the short end of the stick." Wall Street prefers Wal-Mart's philosophy: executives first, then shareholders, then customers, then vendors, and finally employees.

Average Hourly Wage		Percentage of U.S. Workforce in Unions		Employees Covered by Company Health Insurance		Employees Who Leave After One Year	
Wal-Mart	Costco	Wal-Mart	Costco	Wal-Mart	Costco	Sam's Club*	Costco
$9.68	$16.00	0.0%	17.9%	48%	82%	21%	6%

* Sam's Club is the Wal-Mart unit that competes directly with Costco.

In 2004, Wal-Mart paid CEO Lee Scott $5.3 million, while a full-time employee making the average wage would have received $20,134. Costco's CEO Jim Senegal received $350,000, while a full-time average employee got $33,280. And *Business Week* intimates that the top job at Costco may be tougher than at Wal-Mart. "Management has to hustle to make the high-wage strategy work. It's constantly looking for ways to repackage goods into bulk items, which reduces labor, speeds up Costco's just-in-time inventory, and boosts sales per square foot. Costco is also savvier ... about catering to small shop owners and more affluent customers, who are more likely to buy in bulk and purchase higher-margin goods."

Costco's allegedly more affluent clientele may be another reason that its profit per employee is higher than Wal-Mart's and its overhead costs a lower percentage of revenue. However, Costco pays its employees enough that they could afford to shop there. As the *Business Week* commentary noted, "the low-wage approach cuts into consumer spending and, potentially, economic growth."

—Esther Cervantes

Making Wal-Mart Do Better

Nonetheless, as Arindrajit Dube points out, the relevant question is not whether Wal-Mart creates more savings for consumers than losses for workers, but whether the corporation can afford to pay better wages and benefits.

Dube reasons that if the true price gap between Wal-Mart and its retail competitors is small, then Wal-Mart might not be in a position to do better—to make up its wage and benefit gap and still maintain its price advantage. But if Wal-Mart offers consumers only minor price savings, then its lower wages and benefits hardly constitute a progressive success story that's good for the nation.

If Wal-Mart's true price gap is large (say, the 25% price advantage estimated by Hausman), then Wal-Mart surely is in a position to do better. For instance, Dube calculates that closing Wal-Mart's 16% overall compensation gap with other large retailers would cost the company less than 2% of sales. Raising prices by two cents on the dollar to cover those increased compensation costs would be "eminently absorbable," according to Dube, without eating away much of the company's mind-boggling $10 billion profit (2004).

Measures that set standards to force Wal-Mart and all big-box retailers to pay decent wages and provide benefits are beginning to catch on. Chicago, New York City, and the state of Maryland have considered or passed laws that would require big-box retailers to pay a "living wage" or to spend a minimum amount per worker-hour for health benefits. The Republican board of Nassau County on Long Island passed an ordinance requiring that all big-box retailers pay $3 per hour toward health care. Wal-Mart's stake in making sure that such proposals don't become law or spread nationwide goes a long way toward explaining why 80% of Wal-Mart's $2 million in political contributions in 2004 went to Republicans.

Henry Ford sought to pay his workers enough so they could buy the cars they produced. Sam Walton sought to pay his workers so little that they could afford to shop nowhere else. And while what was good for the big automakers was probably never good for the nation, what is good for Wal-Mart, today's largest employer, is undoubtedly bad for economic justice.

Sources: "Is Wal-Mart Good for America?" *Wall Street Journal*, 12/3/05; "Gauging the Wal-Mart Effect," *WSJ*, 12/03/05; Arindrajit Dube & Steve Wertheim, "Wal-Mart and Job Quality—What Do We Know, and Should We Care?" 10/05; Jason Furman, "Wal-Mart: A Progressive Success Story," 10/05; Leo Hindery Jr., "Wal-Mart's Giant Sucking Sound," 10/05; A. Bernstein, "Some Uncomfortable Findings for Wal-Mart," *Business Week Online*, 10/26/05, and "Wal-Mart: A Case for the Defense, Sort of," *Business Week Online*, 11/7/05; Dube, Jacobs, and Wertheim, "The Impact of Wal-Mart Growth on Earnings throughout the Retail Sector in Urban and Rural Counties," *Institute of Industrial Relations Working Paper*, U-C Berkeley, 10/05; Dube, Jacobs, and Wertheim, "Internal Wal-Mart Memo Validates Findings of UC Berkeley Study," 11/26/05; Jerry Hausman and Ephraim Leibtag, "Consumer Benefits from Increased Competition in Shopping Outlets: Measuring the Effect of Wal-Mart," 10/05; Hausman and Leibtag, "CPI Bias from Supercenters: Does the BLS Know that Wal-Mart Exists?" *NBER Working Paper No. 10712*, 8/04; David Neumark, Junfu Zhang, and Stephen Ciccarella, "The Effects of Wal-Mart on Local Labor Markets," *NBER Working Paper No. 11782*, 11/05; Erin Johansson, "Wal-Mart: Rolling Back Workers' Wages, Rights, and the American Dream," (American Rights at Work, 11/05); Wal-Mart Watch, "Spin Cycle"; CBC News, "Wal-Mart to cut ties with Bangladesh factories using child labour," 11/30/05; National Labor Committee, "10 to 13-year-olds Sewing 'I Love My Wal-Mart' Shirts," 12/05; Global Insight, "The Economic Impact of Wal-Mart," 2005.

THE RISE OF MIGRANT WORKER MILITANCY

IMMANUEL NESS

September/October 2006

Testifying before the Senate immigration hearings in early July, Mayor Michael Bloomberg affirmed that undocumented immigrants have become indispensable to the economy of New York City: "Although they broke the law by illegally crossing our borders or overstaying their visas, and our businesses broke the law by employing them, our city's economy would be a shell of itself had they not, and it would collapse if they were deported. The same holds true for the nation." Bloomberg's comment outraged right-wing pundits, but how much more outraged would they be if they knew that immigrant workers, beyond being economically indispensable, are beginning to transform the U.S. labor movement with a bold new militancy?

After years of working in obscurity in the unregulated economy, migrant workers in New York City catapulted themselves to the forefront of labor activism beginning in late 1999 through three separate organizing drives among low-wage workers. Immigrants initiated all three drives: Mexican immigrants organized and struck for improved wages and working conditions at greengroceries; Francophone African delivery workers struck for unpaid wages and respect from labor contractors for leading supermarket chains; and South Asians organized for improved conditions and a union in the for-hire car service industry. (In New York, "car services" are taxis that cannot be hailed on the street, only arranged by phone.) These organizing efforts have persisted, and are part of a growing militancy among migrant workers in New York City and across the United States.

Why would seemingly invisible workers rise up to contest power in their workplaces? Why are vulnerable migrant workers currently more likely to organize than are U.S.-born workers? To answer these questions, we have to look at immigrants' distinct position in the political economy of a globalized New York City and at their specific economic and social niches, ones in which exploitation and isolation nurture class consciousness and militancy.

Labor Migration and Industrial Restructuring

New immigrant workers in the United States, many here illegally, stand at the crossroads of two overwhelming trends. On one hand, industrial restructuring and capital mobility have eroded traditional industries and remade the U.S. political economy in the last 30 years in ways that have led many companies to create millions of low-wage jobs and to seek vulnerable workers to fill them. On the other hand, at the behest of international financial institutions like the International Monetary Fund, and to meet the requirements of free-trade agreements such as NAFTA, governments throughout the global South have adopted neoliberal policies that have restructured their economies, resulting in the displacement of urban workers and rural farmers alike. Many have no choice but to migrate north.

A century ago the United States likewise experienced a large influx of immigrants, many of whom worked in factories for their entire lives. There they formed social networks across ethnic lines and developed a class consciousness that spurred the organizing of unions; they made up the generation of workers whose efforts began with the fight for the eight-hour day around the turn of the last century and culminated in the great organizing victories of the 1930s and 1940s across the entire spectrum of mining and manufacturing industries.

Today's immigrants face an entirely different political-economic landscape. Unlike most of their European counterparts a century ago, immigration restrictions mean that many newcomers to the United States are now here illegally. Workers from Latin America frequently migrate illegally without proper documentation; those from Africa, Asia, and Europe commonly arrive with business, worker, student, or tourist visas, then overstay them.

The urban areas where many immigrants arrive have undergone a 30-year decline in manufacturing jobs. The growing pool of service jobs which have come in their stead tend to be dispersed in small firms throughout the city. The proliferation of geographically dispersed subcontractors who compete on the basis of low wages encourages a process of informalization—a term referring to a redistribution of work from regulated sectors of the economy to new unregulated sectors of the underground or informal economy. As a result, wages and working conditions have fallen, often below government-established norms.

Although informal work is typically associated with the developing world—or Global South—observers are increasingly recognizing the link between the regulated and unregulated sectors in advanced industrial regions. More and more the regulated sector depends on unregulated economic activity through subcontracting and outsourcing of work to firms employing low-wage immigrant labor. Major corporations employ or subcontract to businesses employing migrant workers in what were once established sectors of the economy with decent wages and working conditions.

Informalization requires government regulatory agencies to look the other way. For decades federal and state regulatory bodies have ignored violations of laws governing wages, hours, and workplace safety, leading to illegally low wages and declining workplace health and safety practices. The process of informalization is furthered by the reduction or elimination of protections such as disability insurance, Social Security, health care coverage, unemployment insurance, and workers compensation.

By the 1990s, substandard jobs employing almost exclusively migrant workers had become crucial to key sectors of the national economy. Today, immigrants have gained a major presence as bricklayers, demolition workers, and hazardous waste workers on construction and building rehab sites; as cooks, dishwashers, and busboys in restaurants; and as taxi drivers, domestic workers, and delivery people. Employers frequently treat these workers as self-employed. They typically have no union protection and little or no job security. With government enforcement shrinking, they lack the protection of minimum-wage laws and they have been excluded from Social Security and unemployment insurance.

These workers are increasingly victimized by employers who force them to accept 19th-century working conditions and sub-minimum wages. Today, New York

City, Los Angeles, Miami, Houston, and Boston form a nexus of international labor migration, with constantly churning labor markets. As long as there is a demand for cheap labor, immigrants will continue to enter the United States in large numbers. Like water, capital always flows to the lowest level, a state of symmetry where wages are cheapest.

In turn, the availability of a reserve army of immigrant labor provides an enormous incentive for larger corporations to create and use subcontracting firms. Without this workforce, employers in the regulated economy would have more incentive to invest in labor-saving technology, increase the capital-labor ratio, and seek accommodation with unions.

New unauthorized immigrants residing and working in the United States are ideal workers in the new informalized sectors: Their undocumented legal status makes them more tractable since they constantly fear deportation. Undocumented immigrants are less likely to know about, or demand adherence to, established labor standards, and even low U.S. wages represent an improvement over earnings in their home countries.

Forging Migrant Labor Solidarity

The perception that new immigrants undermine U.S.-born workers by undercutting prevailing wage and work standards cannot be entirely dismissed. The entry of a large number of immigrants into the underground economy unquestionably reduces the labor market leverage of U.S.-born workers. But the story is more complicated. In spite of their vulnerability, migrant workers have demonstrated a willingness and a capacity to organize for improvements in their wages and working conditions; they arguably are responding to tough conditions on the job with greater militancy than U.S.-born workers.

New York City has been the site of a number of instances of immigrant worker organizing. In 1998, Mexicans working in greengroceries embarked on a city-wide organizing campaign to improve their conditions of work. Most of the 20,000 greengrocery workers were paid below $3.00 an hour, working on average 72 hours a week. Some did not make enough to pay their living expenses, no less send remittances back home to Mexico. Following a relentless and coordinated four-year organizing campaign among the workers, employers agreed to raise wages above the minimum and improve working conditions. Moreover, the campaign led state Attorney General Eliot Spitzer to establish a Greengrocer Code of Conduct and to strengthen enforcement of labor regulations.

In another display of immigrant worker militancy, beginning in 1999 Francophone African supermarket delivery workers in New York City fought for and won equality with other workers in the same stores. The workers were responsible for bagging groceries and delivering them to affluent customers in Manhattan and throughout the city. As contractors, the delivery workers were paid no wage, instead relying on the goodwill of customers in affluent neighborhoods to pay tips for each delivery.

The workers were employed in supermarkets and drug stores where some others had a union. Without union support themselves, delivery workers staged a significant strike and insurrection that made consumers aware of their appalling conditions of work. In late October, workers went on strike and marched from supermarket to supermarket, demanding living wages and dignity on the job. At the start of their campaign, wages averaged less than $70 a week. In the months following the strike the workers all won recognition from the stores through the United Food and Commercial Workers that had earlier neglected to include them in negotiations with management. The National Employee Law Project, a national worker advocacy organization, filed landmark lawsuits against the supermarkets and delivery companies and won backwage settlements as the courts deemed them to be workers—not independent contractors in business for themselves.

Immigrant workers have organized countless other campaigns, in New York and across the country. How do new immigrants, with weak ties to organized labor and the state, manage to assert their interests? The explanation lies in the character of immigrant work and social life; the constraints immigrant workers face paradoxically encourage them to draw on shared experiences to create solidarity at work and in their communities.

The typical migrant worker can expect to work twelve-hour days, seven days a week. When arriving home, immigrant workers frequently share the same apartments, buildings, and neighborhoods. These employment ghettos typify immigrant communities across the nation. Workers cook for one another, share stories about their oppressively long and hard days, commiserate about their ill treatment at work, and then go to sleep only to start anew the next day.

Migrant women, surrounded by a world of exploitation, typically suffer even more abuse their male counterparts, suffering from low wages, long hours, and dangerous conditions. Patterns of gender stratification found in the general labor market are even more apparent among migrant women workers. Most jobs in the nonunion economy, such as construction and driving, are stereotypically considered "men's work." Women predominate in the garment industry, as domestic and child care workers, in laundries, hotels, restaurants, and ever more in sex work. A striking example of migrant women's perilous work environment is the massive recruitment of migrant women to clean up the hazardous materials in the rubble left by the collapse of the World Trade Center without proper safety training.

Isolated in their jobs and communities, immigrant workers have few social ties to unions, community groups, and public officials, and few resources to call upon to assist them in transforming their workplaces. Because new immigrants have few social networks outside the workplace, the ties they develop on the job are especially solid and meaningful—and are nurtured every day. The workers' very isolation and status as outsiders, and their concentration into industrial niches by employers who hire on the basis of ethnicity, tend to strengthen old social ties, build new ones, and deepen class solidarity.

Immigrant social networks contribute to workplace militancy. Conversely, activism at work can stimulate new social networks that can expand workers' power. It is through relationships developed on the job and in the community that shared social identities and mutual resentment of the boss evolves into class consciousness and class solidarity: migrant workers begin to form informal organizations, meet with coworkers to respond to poor working conditions, and take action on the shop floor in defiance of employer abuse.

Typically, few workplace hierarchies exist among immigrants, since few reach supervisory positions. As a result, immigrant workers suffer poor treatment equally at the hands of employers. A gathering sense of collective exploitation usually transforms individualistic activities into shared ones. In rare cases where there are immigrant foremen and crew leaders, they may recognize this solidarity and side with the workers rather than with management. One former manager employed for a fast-food sandwich chain in New York City said: "We are hired only to divide the workers but I was really trying to help the workers get better pay and shorter hours."

Migrant workers bring social identities from their home countries, and those identities are shaped through socialization and work in this country. In cities and towns across the United States, segmentation of migrant workers from specific countries reinforces ethnic, national, and religious identities and helps to form other identities that may stimulate solidarity. Before arriving in the United States, Mexican immigrant workers often see themselves as peasants but not initially as "people of color," while Francophone Africans see themselves as Malian or Senegalese ethnics but not necessarily "black." Life and work in New York can encourage them to adopt new identifications, including a new class consciousness that can spur organizing and militancy.

Once triggered, organizing can go from workplace to workplace like wildfire. When workers realize that they can fight and prevail, this creates a sense of invincibility that stimulates militant action that would otherwise be avoided at all costs. This demonstration effect is vitally important, as was the case in the strikes among garment workers and coal miners in the history of the U.S. labor movement.

"Solidarity Forever" vs. "Take This Job and Shove It"

The militancy of many migrant workers contrasts sharply with the passivity of many U.S.-born workers facing the same low wages and poor working conditions. Why do most workers at chain stores and restaurants like Wal-Mart and McDonalds—most of whom were born in the United States—appear so complacent, while new immigrants are often so militant?

Migrants are not inherently more militant or less passive. Instead, the real workplace conditions of migrant workers seem to produce greater militancy on the job. First, collective social isolation engenders strong ties among migrants in low-wage jobs where organizing is frequently the only way to improve conditions. Because migrants work in jobs that are more amenable to organizing, they are highly represented among newly unionized workers. Strong social ties in the workplace drive migrants to form their own embryonic organizations at work and in their communities that are ripe for union representation. Organizing among migrant workers gains the attention of labor unions, which then see a chance to recruit new members and may provide resources to help immigrant workers mobilize at work and join the union.

Employers also play a major role. Firms employing U.S workers tend to be larger and are often much harder to organize than the small businesses where immigrants work. In 2003, the Merriam-Webster dictionary added the new word

McJob, defined as "a low-paying job that requires little skill and provides little opportunity for advancement." The widely accepted coinage reflects the relentless 30-year economic restructuring creating low-end jobs in the retail sector.

Organizing against Home Depot, McDonalds, Taco Bell, or Wal-Mart is completely different from organizing against smaller employers. Wal-Mart uses many of the same tactics against workers that immigrants contend with: failure to pay overtime, stealing time (intentionally paying workers for fewer hours than actually worked), no health care, part-time work, high turnover, and gender division of labor. The difference is that Wal-Mart has far more resources to oppose unionization than do the smaller employers who are frequently subcontractors to larger firms. But Wal-Mart's opposition to labor unions is so forceful that workers choose to leave rather than stay and fight it out. Relentless labor turnover mitigates against the formation of working class consciousness and militancy.

The expanding non-immigrant low-end service sector tends to produce unskilled part-time jobs that do not train workers in skills that keep them in the same sector of the labor market. Because jobs at the low end of the economy require little training, workers frequently move from one industry to the next. One day a U.S.-born worker may work as a sales clerk for Target, the next day as a waiter at Olive Garden. Because they are not stuck in identity-defined niches, U.S. workers change their world by quitting and finding a job elsewhere, giving them less reason to organize and unionize.

The fact that U.S.-born workers have an exit strategy and migrant workers do not is a significant and important difference. Immigrant workers are more prone to take action to change their working conditions because they have far fewer options than U.S.-born workers. Workers employed by companies like Wal-Mart are unable to change their conditions, since they have little power and will be summarily fired for any form of dissent. If workers violate the terms of Wal-Mart's or McDonalds' employee manual by, say, arriving late, and then are summarily fired, no one is likely to fend for them, as is usually the case among many migrant workers. While migrant workers engage in direct action against their employers to obtain higher wages and respect on the job, U.S. workers do not develop the same dense connections in labor market niches that forge solidarity. Employers firing new immigrants may risk demonstrations, picket lines, or even strikes.

Immigrant workers are pushed into low-wage labor market niches as day laborers, food handlers, delivery workers, and nannies; these niches are difficult if not impossible to escape. Yet immigrant workers relegated to dead-end jobs in the lowest echelons of the labor market in food, delivery, and car service work show a greater eagerness to fight it out to improve their wages and conditions than do U.S. workers who can move on to another dead-end job.

The Role of Unions

Today's labor movement is in serious trouble; membership is spiraling downward as employers demand union-free workplaces. Unionized manufacturing and service workers are losing their jobs to low-wage operations abroad. Unions and, more importantly, the U.S. working class, are in dire straits and must find a means to triumph over the neoliberal dogma that dominates the capitalist system.

As organizing campaigns in New York City show, migrant workers are indispensable to the revitalization of the labor movement. As employers turn to migrant labor to fill low-wage jobs, unions must encourage and support organizing drives that emerge from the oppressive conditions of work. As the 1930s workers' movement demonstrates, if conditions improve for immigrants, all workers will prosper. To gain traction, unions must recognize that capital is pitting migrant workers against native-born laborers to lower wages and improve profitability. Although unions have had some success organizing immigrants, most are circling the wagons, disinterested in building a more inclusive mass labor movement. The first step is for unions to go beyond rhetoric and form a broad and inclusive coalition embracing migrant workers.

KENTUCKY RIVER THREATENS TO SWAMP LABOR

An NLRB ruling could eliminate millions of workers' right to unionize.

PAUL BIGMAN
September/October 2006

Kentucky River. If the name doesn't worry you, you need to know more about the latest effort to eliminate labor unions. There are currently three cases, collectively referred to as the "Kentucky River" cases, working their way through the National Labor Relations Board (NLRB) that could ultimately deprive millions of U.S. workers of the right to union representation.

The cases are efforts to fine-tune a 2001 Supreme Court decision in NLRB v. Kentucky River Community Care. The Court ruled 5-4 that registered nurses at a Kentucky nursing home were supervisors because they used independent judgment to direct other employees. In dissent, Justice John Paul Stevens warned that this decision could lead to the elimination of the right to organize for most professionals. The NLRB is expected to rule this fall on three more cases that could dramatically expand the definition of "supervisor"—and strip millions of other workers of their right to organize.

U.S. labor laws already exclude large numbers of workers. A 2002 Government Accountability Office report estimated that 32 million U.S. workers were excluded from coverage under federal labor laws. Of those, almost 11 million were private sector managers and supervisors, whose right to union representation was eliminated by the 1947 Taft-Hartley Act.

Generally, a supervisor is someone who can hire, fire, or discipline other workers, but corporations are fighting to dramatically expand the definition. This is the core issue in the Kentucky River cases, many of which deal with nurses in hospitals and nursing homes. Hospital managers throughout the country have decided that virtually all of their RNs should be viewed as supervisors, not because they hire or fire other workers, but because they provide training and direction to less highly skilled personnel.

The immediate impact of an NLRB ruling on the Kentucky River cases could be to deprive almost one million RNs and licensed practical nurses of the right to collective bargaining. But as many as eight million workers could lose their right to choose union representation based on the precedent from these cases, according to an Economic Policy Institute estimate, including hundreds of thousands of journeymen in the building trades, computer systems analysts, cooks, secretaries, cashiers, and electricians.

These cases are only one part of a broad assault on collective bargaining rights being waged by corporations and their government allies. Companies have curtailed their workers' right to organize through increased use of temp agencies and "leased workers," as well as efforts to redefine everyone from truckers to grocery delivery workers as "independent contractors."

Public sector workers are also under attack. The Bush administration eliminated collective bargaining rights for 165,000 workers when it transferred them into the Department of Homeland Security and is now moving to place 750,000 civilian workers in the Department of Defense under the National Security Personnel System (NSPS), which would gut collective bargaining and abrogate existing contracts. Still on tap is the Working for America Act, which would extend the NSPS to most federal workers.

And now, with the Kentucky River cases—along with over 50 other cases now before the NLRB that also address the definition of an "employee"—millions of additional workers could see their right to join a union disappear without a hearing. That's right: despite rallies organized on short notice in two dozen cities throughout the country and letters from scores of members of Congress, the NLRB refuses to hear oral argument on the cases. In fact, it's been over five years since this NLRB has accepted oral argument on anything—the first time in the board's 70-year history that it has gone five years without any live testimony.

Given the largely Bush-appointed board's track record—it has decided, for example, that neither graduate students in private universities nor temp agency employees have the right to organize—a ruling against the workers seems likely. But the fight won't end there. Labor, led by nurses' unions and joined by allies such as Jobs with Justice, is mobilizing workers to stand up to employers attempting to redefine workers as supervisors, sponsoring legislation to restore rights removed by the NLRB, and holding actions at regional NLRB offices. The battle to prevent corporate interests from eliminating the very right to union representation is not one that workers can afford to lose.

Resources: "Supervisor in Name Only," EPI Issue Brief #225 (Economic Policy Institute, 7/12/06); "The Fight to Protect Workplace Democracy," AFL-CIO Exec. Council statement (8/8/06).

Chapter 3

SOCIAL PROGRAMS
Health, Welfare, and Education

WELFARE REFORM TEN YEARS LATER
Welfare "as we knew it" ended in 1996; poverty didn't.

RANDY ALBELDA
January/February 2006

I n 1996, the U.S. government radically changed its cash assistance program for poor families with children—commonly called welfare. Now that nearly a decade has passed, including periods of both expansion and recession in the overall economy, what do we know about the impact of welfare "reform" on poor families?

Welfare reform was touted as a transformation in U.S. social policy that would move families, and particularly single mothers, off of the program and free them from dependence on the government. If that was the aim, then the change has succeeded. Once a primary source of support for single mother families, welfare now serves a smaller and smaller percentage of poor families and leaves more and more poor families "independent" of assistance. But if the aim was to reduce poverty and promote economic independence, then the plan has not worked. The evidence suggests that many low-income families are struggling as hard as they did under welfare's previous incarnation, but with a far weaker safety net.

Refresher on Welfare Policies

In August 1996, President Clinton signed the Personal Responsibility and Work Opportunity Reconciliation Act. Along with cuts to Food Stamps and Supplemental Security Income (SSI), the bill eliminated Aid to Families with Dependent Children (AFDC), the major welfare program, replacing it with Temporary Assistance for Needy Families (TANF).

TANF has four main components:

1. It ends the federal guarantee of cash assistance to poor families by giving states broad leeway in structuring their programs.

What this means: With the stroke of a pen, lawmakers erased the hard-earned struggles of the welfare rights movements of the 1960s and 1970s to assure that

43

low-income families knew their rights and received the assistance they were eligible for. With federal eligibility requirements eliminated, states can now define "needy" any way they want. States are not obliged to provide cash assistance at all and can completely privatize their welfare systems. The lack of uniform eligibility provisions opens the door to the systematic denial of benefits that was common until the 1960s.

2. It establishes a new fiscal relationship between the federal government and the states in the antipoverty arena: the federal government now provides only fixed block grants to states, while no longer providing them with a financial incentive to spend additional money to help low-income families.

What this means: Under TANF's block grant structure, states can spend as much as they please, but will not receive an extra penny from the feds. The formula that sets the size of each state's block grant contains no automatic adjustments for either inflation or need. This represents a dramatic change from AFDC, which was a matching grant: for every dollar a state spent on the program, it received at least one federal dollar. Now, once a state's federal TANF money is gone, there is no more. When a recession comes and the number of poor families rises, states do not necessarily have any more resources to help out than they do during good times.

3. It establishes a lifetime limit of 60 months, not necessarily consecutive, for receiving assistance from federal TANF funds.

What this means: For the first time since welfare began, there is now a time limit on receiving benefits. States are not allowed to allocate federal TANF dollars to any adult who has received TANF benefits for 60 months—regardless of how much assistance she received in any single month or how long it took to accrue 60 months of aid. In 1996, the average amount of time any AFDC recipient received aid over her lifetime was seven years (84 months). Sixty months is an arbitrary number and will not serve the needs of many poor families.

States can exempt families from or provide extensions to their time limits, and most do for a few families, especially those who have members with severe physical disabilities. However, states must often use their own funds to extend the time limit; the current political climate and state budgetary pressures make it unlikely they will do so for more than a handful of families.

4. It penalizes states that do not force a substantial percentage of their adult recipients into narrowly defined work programs.

What this means: The law now requires recipients whose youngest child is more than one year old to do some form of paid or unpaid work after 24 months of receiving benefits. Although previous federal provisions also had work requirements, they exempted women with disabled children or children under age six, and most job training counted toward the work requirement. Now, most job training no longer counts as "work." Further, unless states specifically opt out, adult recipients with children older than one must perform community service (also called workfare) after only two months of benefits.

In addition to the work requirements, states must meet overall work participation rates or risk losing some of their federal grant. As of 2005, states must show that 50% of single mothers on welfare are working—at least 30 hours a week if their youngest child is six or older, and at least 20 hours if they have children under six. The requirement is structured so as to discourage states from providing education and training that would allow at least some women to move into decently paying jobs. States can provide education and training if they want, but most of those programs do not count toward the work participation requirement. To hit their quotas, states are under pressure to place women into the labor market immediately.

The bottom line? The new law is designed to encourage states to reduce spending and cut welfare rolls by pushing women into the low-wage labor market without the vital supports that make employment possible.

Has Welfare Reform "Worked"?

Advocates of the new welfare model tout the rapid and steep decline in caseloads as their main indicator of how well welfare reform has worked. However, this measure only denotes success if receiving welfare is inherently bad. In and of itself, fewer people on welfare does not mean less poverty, more personal responsibility, or greater self-sufficiency.

Let's compare changes in welfare usage with changes in poverty rates. The poverty rate for single mothers fell from 42% in 1996 to 36% in 2004 (a 14% decline). But over that same period, the percentage of families using welfare fell by close to 60%. So while welfare usage has plummeted, the poverty rate for single mothers— the group most likely to use and need cash assistance—has decreased only slightly.

Even a modest decline in single-mother poverty may appear to be good news. But there are limitations to what the poverty rate tells us. The formula used to determine the poverty threshold is outdated; the threshold—$15,067 for a family of three in 2004, for example—is hardly enough to even minimally support a family. So it may be more appropriate to look at changes in the percentage of families with incomes below 150% or even 200% of the poverty line to really get a sense of how low-income families are faring. These figures show much less improvement. In 2004, 31.2% of U.S. residents had incomes below 200% of the poverty line, compared to 33.3% in 1996—only a 6% change. A second and more serious problem is that the poverty rate only measures income; it does not take into account the additional costs families incur when they move from welfare to work, such as child care and transportation. Without accounting for these costs, it is impossible to assess real changes in families' economic well-being.

Whether you view cash assistance as a positive or negative force in people's lives, it has historically been a crucial safety net for poor mothers. There is no doubt that welfare is much less of an alternative for low-income families than it was prior to 1996. In 2002, the most recent year for which the figure is available, only 5.3% of children received welfare, even though 16.7% of them were officially poor. (Since 2002 the child poverty rate has risen—to 17.6% in 2003 and 17.8% in 2004.) In other words, less than a third of poor children receive welfare. Compare this to 1996, when well over half of poor children received welfare; that year, 20.5% of children were poor and 12.5% received benefits.

Work ≠ Wellbeing

Not surprisingly, employment rates of those leaving welfare and of poor single mothers overall have increased. Three-quarters of those leaving welfare find employment within a year of leaving, versus about two-thirds prior to the 1996 law. In 1996, 54% of mothers with children under age six and with incomes 200% or less of the poverty line were in the labor force. By 2002, that figure had jumped to 67%. Restricting welfare has no doubt forced more low-income mothers of young children into the labor market.

However, employment has not guaranteed economic security for low-income families. Studies of people leaving welfare consistently find that welfare leavers' wages average between $7 and $8 per hour—above the minimum wage, but usually not enough to support a family. Moreover, many people leaving welfare are not employed full-time or year-round. For this reason, a summary of studies in 15 states found that in the late 1990s welfare leavers were earning on average about $2,700 per employment quarter—less than $11,000 a year! Nor do many of those leaving welfare land jobs with the employer-sponsored benefits that are vital for families with children. About half had employer-sponsored health insurance, and no more than half had sick leave with pay or pension coverage. Finally, research shows that 20% to 33% return to welfare within a year of leaving. Ironically, these results are only marginally better than before welfare reform.

The evidence on families who hit their time limits provides few surprises. Families hitting the limit tend to be larger, less often white, and headed by a parent who is less likely to have a high school diploma than families who leave welfare before hitting their time limits. In short, the families with the most needs, those most likely to face employment discrimination or receive the lowest wages, are the ones who are getting kicked off the rolls. Most families who hit their time limits describe extreme hardships and report that they are worse off than they were while receiving benefits. Moreover, evidence does not bear out the stereotyped view that recipients dodge work until they are forced off of welfare: employment rates for those who leave upon hitting their time limits do not differ from those who leave without reaching their limit.

If we look at all low-income single mothers rather than just those leaving welfare, we find that families at the bottom are no better off as a result of welfare reform. An Institute for Women's Policy Research study looked at low-income single parents with incomes below 200% of the poverty level in 1995 and in 2000. Over the study period—one of sustained economic growth—the researchers found that inflation-adjusted earnings increased by a meager $100 a month for this group, and that their families' access to health benefits declined.

A federal government study looked at the bottom 20% of single-mother families between 1996 and 2002 and found those families slightly worse off in the package of government benefits ("means-tested income") and earnings they received. For families in the next 20%, the study found only very slight improvement. (See figure.)

The way low-income single mothers are packaging their resources has changed significantly since welfare reform. Families are relying much more on earnings than

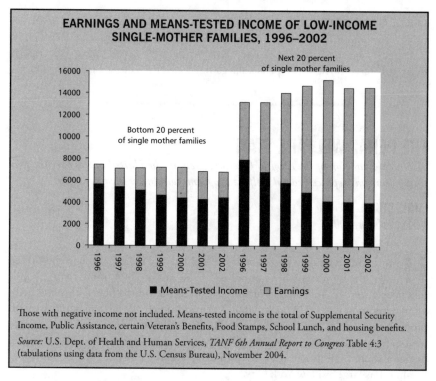

EARNINGS AND MEANS-TESTED INCOME OF LOW-INCOME
SINGLE-MOTHER FAMILIES, 1996–2002

Those with negative income not included. Means-tested income is the total of Supplemental Security Income, Public Assistance, certain Veteran's Benefits, Food Stamps, School Lunch, and housing benefits.

Source: U.S. Dept. of Health and Human Services, *TANF 6th Annual Report to Congress* Table 4:3 (tabulations using data from the U.S. Census Bureau), November 2004.

on public resources—but still are not much better off. Furthermore, these data do not acknowledge the value of the time with their children that these moms lose. If the time children spend with their mothers is worth anything, then substituting earnings for benefits represents a loss of resources to the family.

New welfare rules, same poverty problems. Most single mothers *cannot* work their way out of poverty—definitely not without supplemental support. Welfare reform has meant more paid work, but proponents can't claim that it has improved the lives of poor families. There are many possible policy steps that could be taken to help single mothers and other low-wage workers get the most out of an inhospitable labor market. But ultimately, old-fashioned cash assistance to poor families must remain part of the formula.

This article was adapted from "Farewell to Welfare, But Not Poverty" by Randy Albelda and Chris Tilly, in *Women: Images and Realities, A Multicultural Anthology* (3rd ed.).

Resources: M. Greenberg and S. Savner, *A Brief Summary of Key Provisions of the Temporary Assistance for Needy Families Block Grant of H.R. 3734* (Center for Law and Social Policy, 8/96); Randy Albelda and Chris Tilly, *Glass Ceilings and Bottomless Pits: Women's Work, Women's Poverty* (South End Press, 1997); A. DeWeever-Jones, J. Peterson, and X. Song, *Before and After Welfare Reform: The Work and Well-Being of Low-Income Single Parent Families* (Institute for Women's Policy Research, 2003); U.S. Census Bureau, *Historical Tables on Poverty* (http://www.census.gov/ hhes/www/poverty/poverty.html); U.S. Dept. of Health and Human Services, *TANF 6th Annual Report to Congress*, 11/04; D. Bloom et al., *Welfare Time Limits: State Policies, Implementation and*

Effects on Families (MDRC, 2002); K. Christopher, "Welfare as We [Don't] Know It: A Review and Feminist Critique of Welfare Reform Research in the United States," *Feminist Economics*, 7/04; G. Acs and P. Loprest, *Final Synthesis Report of Findings from ASPE "Leavers" Grants* (U.S. Dept. of Health and Human Services, at http://aspe.hhs.gov/hsp/leavers99/synthesis02/index.htm#EE).

THE PENAL WELFARE STATE
The huge expansion of the criminal justice system in the United States over the past thirty years has replaced social welfare programs with mass incarceration.

CHRIS STURR
January/February 2006

However much we may know about the high rates of incarceration in the United States, the numbers still astound. As of the end of 2004, more than 2.1 million people were incarcerated in prisons or jails in the United States; this makes for an incarceration rate of 724 per 100,000. An additional 4.9 million adults were on probation or parole, and about half a million juveniles were in detention or on probation, for a total of more than 7.5 million people under supervision by the criminal justice system. If all those people lived in one place, the resulting metropolis would be almost as large as New York City.

The number of people in prison or jail in the United States has not always been so high. Throughout the 20th century, until the 1970s, the number of people in federal or state prisons hovered around 200,000. However, beginning in the early 1970s, the numbers began to climb; the number of people in prison now tops 1.36 million. The United States imprisons people at a far higher rate than other countries. The rates of incarceration for comparable industrialized countries are many times lower than the U.S. rate of 724 per 100,000 (for prisons and jails combined): Canada's rate is 116 per 100,000; France's is 80; Finland's is 50. The U.S. rate is also considerably higher than the country with the next highest rate, Russia (529 per 100,000).

How are we to understand this crisis of mass incarceration? At first glance, three factors stand out.

The "War on Drugs"—laws, sentencing policies, and enforcement initiatives ostensibly aimed at reducing drug abuse—has clearly contributed to the huge increase in incarceration. Since the mid-1970s, with the passage of the Rockefeller Drug Law in New York state and similar provisions in California, states have adopted tough drug laws and longer sentences for drug-related crimes, while the federal government has made funding for state and local police contingent on targeted enforcement of drug laws. As a result, arrests, convictions, and incarceration for drug-related crimes have shot up. The share of state prisoners incarcerated for drug-related crimes rose from 21.3% to 57.9% between 1991 and 1997; 56.3% of federal prisoners are in for drug-related crimes.

"Tough on crime" policies in general have also contributed to the prison boom.

Throughout the 1980s and 1990s, states and the federal government adopted mandatory minimum sentences, including "Three Strikes" laws that mandate long sentences for a third felony conviction; many states also adopted "truth in sentencing" laws that have reduced the possibility of parole. The federal parole system was eliminated in 1987, and there has been a huge increase in the number of life sentences without parole. In general, indeterminate sentencing and judicial discretion—the hallmarks of the judicial system until the early seventies—have been steadily eroded. The result has been marked increases in the average sentences for all categories of crimes. Prisoners are being kept in prison for longer than ever before, and are paroled much less frequently than they used to be.

Race and racism are perhaps the most striking features of the prison boom. In the early 1970s, about one-third of state and federal prisoners were African-American or Latino; today about two-thirds are. The rates of incarceration, when broken down by race/ethnicity and gender, follow a striking racial pattern. The incarceration rate for all men in the United States is 1,346 per 100,000; but for non-Latino white men the rate is much lower—717 per 100,000. Latino and African-American men take up the slack, with rates of 1,717 and 4,919 respectively. Racism at every stage of the criminal justice system contributes to these disparities. For example, 13% of the U.S. population is African-American, and 13% of drug users are African-American. Yet African-Americans represent 35% of those arrested, 54% of those convicted, and 74% of those incarcerated, for drug-related crimes.

In fact, there is little correspondence between the huge increase in incarceration and the ostensible aims of tougher drug and sentencing policies. The prison boom has not had a corresponding impact on the crime rate or on rates of drug abuse, and crime rates in the United States continue to be comparable to those of other advanced industrialized societies. The United States has a rate of crime victimization (21%) comparable to those of Finland (19%), France (21%) and Canada (24%), even though the incarceration rate here is more than six times as high.

While the prison crisis is clearly a consequence of the drug war, harsher penalties, and racism, what has led to these policies, and why has racism begun to take the form of an incarceration boom?

Surely a core part of the answer is that the prison boom is clearly also an *economic* phenomenon. In 2001, spending on the criminal justice system at all levels of government topped $167 billion (vs. $36 billion in 1982); the number of people employed by the criminal justice system was 2.3 million people in 2001 (an increase of 81% over 1982). The sheer amount of money expended on policing, courts, and incarceration, and the number of people—prisoners, supervisees, or employees—caught up in the criminal justice system, show that the "prison-industrial complex" has become a huge sector of the economy.

How has the U.S. economy become so largely a *penal* economy?

One simple answer is private profit. Corporations have reaped huge profits from prison construction and from the provision of subcontracted services to prisoners (food, health care, pay phones); the market for calls made from prison pay phones alone is estimated at $1 billion a year. The operation of prisons themselves is another source of profit: as of 2001, 6.1% of state prisoners, 11.9% of federal prisoners, and 10.1% of Homeland Security detainees were housed in private facilities, chiefly those run by the two corporations holding a 75% market share in the industry, Wackenhut and Corrections Corporation of America. Yet another source of profit is prison labor; a wide variety of companies—including such familiar ones as Victoria's Secret, Dell, Motorola, and Microsoft—have taken advantage of the low cost, and armed supervision, of prison labor.

But private profits don't tell the whole economic story. Mass incarceration also has an impact on the labor market. The beginning of the prison boom coincided with de-industrialization and the increasing export of manufacturing jobs overseas. As jobs have been lost in the United States, low-skill workers have become less economically useful as wage-laborers. Prisons absorb some low-skill workers as prisoners, others as guards or service workers. One key factor contributing to the low unemployment rate in the United States, in comparison with European social welfare states, is its high rate of incarceration. If prisoners were counted among the unemployed, the difference would be much less.

Some economists have also argued that the U.S. criminal justice system functions as a kind of "penal Keynesianism." Just as in "military Keynesianism," —government use of military spending as economic stimulus to regulate the cycles of capitalism—spending on prisons is arguably now being used in a similar way. Building prisons has also become a key economic development strategy in many rural areas (as ineffective as that strategy has proven to be). Other interests—for example, prison guards (and their unions), local police departments, and social service agencies—have come to depend on the flow of government money through the prison economy.

When viewed in the context of recent changes in the global economy and the neoliberal policies of the U.S. government abroad and at home—including attacks on the welfare state and the privatization or elimination of many government services—the prison boom can be seen as a matter of exchanging *social* welfare policies for *penal* welfare policies. There has been a shift toward policies that favor private, corporate interests, with the complicity of professionals and civil servants; the burden of this shift has fallen squarely on the economically and politically disenfranchised communities—largely African-American and Latino—that have been most adversely affected by the prison crisis. Other issues—the high rates of incarceration among Native Americans; the increasing rate of incarceration among women, especially women of color; the increase in detention of immigrants by Homeland Security; the high incidence of rape in prison and the special burdens faced by lesbian, gay and trans prisoners—must also be part of our picture of the shift to a penal economy.

It has long been clear that mass incarceration does not solve the social problems it purports to—it neither reduces crime and drug abuse nor makes our communities safer. But pointing out the ineffectiveness of current policies in achieving their *stated* aims is not enough if those policies have now become crucial for maintaining our current economic and political status quo. Activist strategies against the prison crisis and efforts to build alternatives to mass incarceration must take into account the real—economic and political—causes and functions of the prison crisis.

Sources: Bureau of Justice Statistics (www.ojp.usdoj.gov/bjs/); Sentencing Project (www.

sentencingproject.org); Prison Policy Initiative (prisonpolicy.org, prisonsucks.com); Christian Parenti, *Lockdown America* (Verso, 1999); David Garland, *The Culture of Control* (University of Chicago Press, 2001); Jens Soering, *An Expensive Way to Make Bad People Worse* (Flashpoint, 2004); Loïc Wacquant, *Deadly Symbiosis: Race and the Rise of Neoliberal Penality* (Cambridge, 2006); Nils Christie, *Crime Control as Industry* (Routledge, 2000).

MEDICARE PART D GETS AN "F"

JAMES WOOLMAN AND JAMES McBRIDE
January/February 2006

Medicare Part D, the new drug benefit package that went into effect at the beginning of 2006, is projected to cost $724 billion over 10 years. Not only is it expensive, it's confusing, and it provides more benefits to insurance companies than to enrollees. Here are five key reasons Medicare Part D deserves an "F":

1. Meager Benefits

Despite the program's huge cost, the actual benefits are minimal. A standard plan requires members to pay a $32 monthly premium, a $250 deductible, and 25% of drug costs up to $2,250. After that, they must pay 100% of the costs until their total drug spending reaches $5,100, then 5% of costs exceeding $5,100. Subsidies are available for low-income enrollees (those whose incomes are under 150% of the federal poverty line), but most participants will still have to pay the majority of their drug costs out of pocket (see Figure 1).

In addition, analysts predict one in four enrollees will actually end up spending *more* under the new plan than they would have without it. This is because many seniors who already have prescription drug coverage—through an employer, a supplemental Medicare policy, or Medicaid —will lose this coverage and be forced to accept the less generous benefits provided by Part D.

To make matters worse, the new drug plan may undermine one important source of prescription drugs for hundreds of thousands of people without health insurance: the pharmaceutical companies' patient assistance programs for the indigent. Some companies have said that anyone who signs up for Medicare D will become ineligible for such programs; others have indicated they will drop anyone who is even eligible for the new benefit.

2. Less Negotiating Power

Because conservatives have decreed that markets will always provide the lowest prices and the greatest efficiency, the new Medicare drug law explicitly bans the government from negotiating with drug companies. Of course, the federal government already negotiates directly with drug makers and receives deep discounts for

FIGURE 1
2006 OUT-OF-POCKET SPENDING WITH STANDARD PART D BENEFIT PACKAGE

Annual Drug Costs	Out of Pocket Spending (Including Premiums)	Percent of Drug Costs Paid By Enrollee
$500	$699	140%
$1,000	$824	82%
$2,250	$1,136	51%
$3,000	$1,886	63%
$4,000	$2,886	72%
$5,100	$3,986	78%
$6,000	$4,031	67%
$8,000	$4,131	52%
$10,000	$4,231	42%

Spending calculations were based on the standard Part D benefit package.

Source for percent of enrollees: Actuarial Research Corp. and the Kaiser Family Foundation, Estimates of Medicare Beneficiaries Out-of-Pocket Drug Spending in 2006, November 2004.

drugs purchased by the Department of Defense and the Veterans Administration. According to a study done by the staff of Rep. Henry Waxman (D-Calif.), the price of a month's supply of the top ten drugs under Medicare D is 80% higher than the negotiated price the VA pays for those same drugs (see Figure 2). Rather than using the government's purchasing power to provide seniors with a better benefit, Congress, citing fears of "price controls," has essentially cut a blank check to the drug industry.

3. Less Consumer Protection

Enrollees who sign up after the May 15, 2006, deadline will incur a 1% per month penalty for every month they delay enrollment, with no limitation. For example, someone who signs up three years after the deadline will be charged an additional 36% on their premium, *forever.* This is designed to prevent people from signing up only when they know they will need expensive medications.

Once enrolled, consumers cannot change plans for a year. Insurance companies, however, are free to drop drugs from their coverage lists at any time, as long as they cover two drugs within each class of drugs used to treat similar conditions—for example, two statin drugs for high cholesterol. Consumers are stuck, even if their medical needs or the drugs offered by their plan change. There is an appeal process, but the law gives plans the power to decide whether or not to grant exceptions—and even allows them to overrule a patient's doctor.

4. Intoxication with Markets

Conservatives have been dying to privatize Medicare for years, and they got their way with Part D. Instead of being handled directly through Medicare, the prescription drug benefit will be delivered by private insurance companies through competing Prescription Drug Plans. The justification is that competitive markets will cut out government inefficiency and lower prices for consumers. (This justification is questionable from the start, of course, given that traditional Medicare, a government-run, single-payer system, has a super-low overhead of less than 4% *and* a high level of beneficiary satisfaction.)

However, unless insurance companies can screen patients or set higher prices

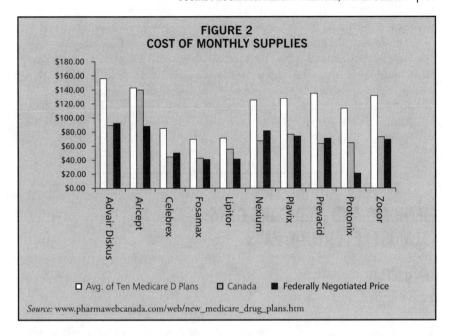

FIGURE 2
COST OF MONTHLY SUPPLIES

Legend: ☐ Avg. of Ten Medicare D Plans   ☐ Canada   ■ Federally Negotiated Price

Source: www.pharmawebcanada.com/web/new_medicare_drug_plans.htm

for sicker people, they are reluctant to enter the market for providing drug insurance. So Congress packed the law with sweeteners to reduce the risk borne by companies. During the first two years, the government will pay 50% of the losses for plans whose costs are more than 2.5% higher than expected, and will also pay 80% of the costs of very expensive patients through a "reinsurance" provision. Insurers quickly realized that these terms make it nearly impossible to lose money, so many more than expected have chosen to participate.

The huge number of plans worsens another problem with the insurance market: consumer confusion. With so many competing offers, it's hard for seniors to tell which plan is right for them. In many regions more than 40 plans are available, each with its own benefit and pricing structure. With limited time to choose, and with the financial and medical stakes high, seniors understandably feel overwhelmed. Republicans refer to this as "empowering the consumer." The rest of us call it stress.

5. Undermining Social Insurance

Part D is part of a larger effort to transform the health care system through market-based "reforms." These strategies, which include health savings accounts, high-deductible health plans, and tax credits for the purchase of individual insurance, are designed to reduce health spending by placing more financial burden on patients.

A public plan, like the enormously popular traditional Medicare program, would have provided more benefit to more people at lower cost, and would not have required any of the backwards market fixes that make the Part D program so complex. In reality, private markets for individual health insurance do not work well—except for enriching corporations—and relying more heavily upon them will only further impoverish and destabilize our health care system.

Sources: Geraldine Dalleck, "Consumer Protection Issues Raised by the Medicare Prescription Drug, Improvement, and Modernization Act of 2003," July 2004; Kaiser Family Foundation, "The Medicare Prescription Drug Benefit," September 2005; Actuarial Research Corp. and Kaiser Family Foundation, "Estimates of Medicare Beneficiaries Out-of-Pocket Drug Spending in 2006, Modeling the Impact of the MMA," November 2004, all available at www.kff.org/medicare/upload/; "Falling Short: Medicare Prescription Drug Plans Offer Meager Savings," Families USA Special Report, December 2005; "Health Plans Undaunted By Medicare Part D," *Managed Care,* May 2005; "New Medicare Plan to Cut Off Free Drugs," *Philadelphia Inquirer,* 11/17/05.

MEDICAID AND MEDICARE CUTS: (ALMOST) EVERYONE PAYS

SAM URETSKY
July/August 2006

U nless you belong to the select and dwindling group of those with fully employer-paid health coverage—or to the 40-million-and-counting with no health insurance at all—you've probably noticed your health insurance premiums rising at a frightening pace. In 2005, premiums for family coverage rose by an average of 9.2%, six percentage points more than the rate of inflation, according to the Kaiser Family Foundation's Annual Survey Of Employer Health Benefits. The cost of health insurance has increased by 73% since 2000, with an average family plan costing $10,880 in 2005; the average monthly premium contribution paid by employees with family plans rose from $135 in 2000 to $226 in 2005.

There is plenty of blame to go around for rising health insurance costs. But an under-recognized part of the story lies in the shifting of costs from public to private insurers. This May, Premera Blue Cross, a Washington state insurer, released a study of public versus private reimbursements to hospitals and doctors. The study found that "employers and consumers are paying billions of dollars more a year for medical care to compensate for imbalances in the nation's health care system resulting from tight Medicare and Medicaid budgets" and pointed to "a rapid acceleration in higher costs to private payers in Washington state, for example, as hospitals and doctors grapple with constraints in the federal health insurance programs," as the *New York Times* summed it up.

The Premera study found that in 2004, Washington state hospitals had losses of 15.4% for services to Medicare beneficiaries, compared to profits of 2.9% for these services in 1997. Over the same period, hospitals' profit margins for patients with employer-sponsored health plans rose, from 5% to 16.4%. As the report put it, "This phenomenon can be thought of as a cost shift from the public programs to commercial payers. That is, if Medicare and Medicaid had paid higher hospital rates, commercial payer rates could have been lower with hospitals still achieving the same ... operating margins." The study found a similar trend for doctors' offices. Medicare pays physicians 25% to 31% less than private insurers do in Washington, and Medicaid pays about 30% less than private insurers for children's office visits and up to 54% less for adults' office visits.

In sum, the study found that hospitals in Washington state charged private insurers an additional $738 million in 2004 to compensate for losses incurred by treating patients under Medicare and Medicaid. Through the 1990s, by contrast, treatment of Medicare and Medicaid patients was profitable for both hospitals and physicians. The percentage profit was small—about 2% in Washington state—but it meant that Medicare and Medicaid were covering all direct expenses for their patients.

What accounts for this sharp reversal? The simple answer: the Bush tax cuts. In 2001, Bush inherited a 10-year budget surplus of around $5.6 trillion, according to Congressional Budget Office projections. "We can proceed with tax relief without fear of budget deficits, even if the economy softens. ... The projections for the surplus in my budget are cautious and conservative," the president claimed. But 2000 was the last year the United States ran a budget surplus. Between 2001 and 2003, the federal government saw that projected $5.6 trillion 10-year surplus turn into a projected 10-year deficit of $378 billion. And the 2001 and 2003 tax cuts, primarily benefiting the wealthiest families, were the single most important cause of the new deficits, according to analyses by the Congressional Budget Office and the Center on Budget and Policy Priorities, among others.

Between 2001 and 2005, Medicare and Medicaid spending per beneficiary did grow, but only very slightly—far less than the rise in health care costs. So the gap between how much hospitals and doctors were spending to provide care and how much they were being reimbursed under the two programs grew. And the situation is about to get even worse. To deal with the growing deficits, last year Congress passed the Deficit Reduction Act of 2005. The new law did nothing to restore earlier tax levels, but did make major cuts in Medicare and Medicaid funding. For instance, the law cuts Medicaid spending by $4.8 billion over the next five years and by $26.1 billion over the next 10 years. The direct effects of these cuts will be to reduce reimbursements to hospitals and physicians—more of the income shortfalls described in the Premera report. No doubt these shortfalls will result in more cost shifting onto those with private coverage, who will continue to face steep increases in their premiums.

Of course, Medicare and Medicaid recipients are hurt by the cuts too. Under the 2005 law, states will be allowed to tighten restrictions on Medicaid eligibility and impose higher co-payments for some drugs and services. The law cuts spending on acute care health services for children by 15% and on acute care for the elderly poor by 8%. Elderly people who require nursing home care will be less able to protect their assets, although 84% of nursing home residents have assets of less than a single year's nursing home costs.

So, tax cuts for the wealthy are paid for in part by cuts in services to the elderly and poor, and by making private health insurance costs even more burdensome for employees who have coverage and employers who provide it.

But there's one group not burdened at all by these difficulties: top health insurance executives. In 2003, the nonprofit watchdog group FamiliesUSA issued a report on executive pay in the 11 for-profit, publicly-traded health insurance companies that offer so-called Medicare+Choice plans, under which Medicare beneficiaries receive their coverage through a private insurer rather than directly from Medicare. Annual CEO compensation ranged from $1.6 million at Humana to $76 million at Oxford, with an average of $15.1 million. And these figures do not include the average of $57.6 million in unexercised stock options these top dogs held. Since executive pay is part of the overhead cost of running an insurance company, it's no wonder that traditional Medicare, which paid its chief executive $130,000 in 2002—and with no stock options—is able to operate with overhead costs of around 1%, while the private sector has overhead costs of 10% to 15%.

To the credit of Premera Blue Cross, which paid for the Washington state study on cost-shifting, in 1999 its CEO was paid a relatively modest $736,650. On the other hand, Premera has applied to change from a nonprofit to a for-profit corporation, in spite of opposition from consumer groups who believe a for-profit company will increase rates and reduce services.

Top insurance executives are among the super-high-income elite, and as such, prime beneficiaries of the Bush tax cuts. (Not to mention that their role in the design of Medicare's new prescription drug benefit, which cuts private insurers in on the program, is also contributing to the budget deficit.) When the federal government tried to make up the revenue lost to tax cuts by cutting benefits and reimbursements under Medicare and Medicaid, these same insurance companies cried foul. It is good to see CEOs advocating for increased funding of social programs. Now maybe they could offer to give back part of their tax-cut bonus to help pay the bill.

Sources: Milt Freudenheim, "Low Payments by U.S. Raise Medical Bills Billions a Year," *New York Times*, 6/1/06; Premera Blue Cross, "Payment Level Comparison between Public Programs and Commercial Health Plans for Washington State Hospitals and Physicians," (Milliman Consultants & Actuaries, May 2006); Families USA, "Top Dollar: CEO Compensation in Medicare's Private Insurance Plans," June 2003; John Holahan and Mindy Cohen, "Understanding the Recent Changes in Medicaid Spending and Enrollment Growth," (Kaiser Commission on Medicaid and the Uninsured, May 2006).

THE OPPOSITE OF INSURANCE
Unless you're rich, healthy, or both, Health Savings Accounts are bad news.

JAMES WOOLMAN
November/December 2006

Congress created Health Savings Accounts (HSAs) in 2003 as tax-advantaged savings accounts linked to the purchase of a high-deductible health plan. But the scheme is not a new idea. HSA proponents, including many health economists, have long argued that standard "comprehensive" insurance policies are too generous, sheltering consumers from the true cost of medical care. "Empowering" consumers to decide for themselves how much money to save for medical expenses, the theory goes, will unleash the magic of the market; costs will decline and quality will improve as doctors, hospitals, and other providers compete for discriminating customers.

New research on consumer and employer experiences with HSAs, however, confirms many of the fears cited by critics of the plans. The evidence shows that these plans attract relatively high-income, healthy people who are attracted to the tax benefits, while they place other consumers—including those with families, health problems, or low incomes—at risk for steep increases in out-of-pocket spending.

FIGURE 1
THE HEALTH SAVINGS ACCOUNT/HIGH DEDUCTIBLE HEALTH PLAN SCHEME: WORKERS PAY MORE, EMPLOYERS PAY LESS

Annual Worker Contribution Comparison

	Single		Family	
	All Plans	HDHP	All Plans	HDHP
Worker Premium Contribution	$624	$467	$2,976	$2,115
Deductible	$508	$2,011	$1,099	$4,008
Employer HSA Contribution	☐	($988)	☐	($1,139)
Total Potential Out-of-Pocket*	$1,132	$1,490	$4,075	$4,984

Annual Employer Contribution Comparison

	Single		Family	
	All Plans	HDHP	All Plans	HDHP
Employer Premium Contribution	$4,248	$2,709	$7,756	$6,400
Employer HSA Contribution	☐	$988	☐	$1,139
Total Employer Spending	$4,248	$3,697	$7,756	$7,539

* Totals do not include coinsurance.
Source: The Kaiser Family Foundation and The Health Research and Education Trust 2006 Employer Benefits Survey.

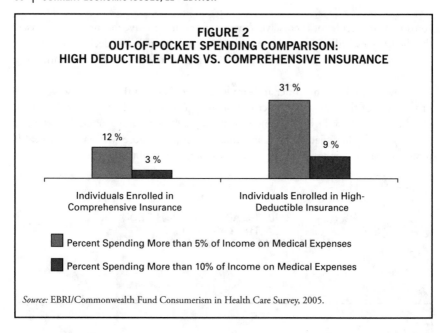

FIGURE 2
OUT-OF-POCKET SPENDING COMPARISON:
HIGH DEDUCTIBLE PLANS VS. COMPREHENSIVE INSURANCE

Individuals Enrolled in Comprehensive Insurance — 12 %, 3 %
Individuals Enrolled in High-Deductible Insurance — 31 %, 9 %

■ Percent Spending More than 5% of Income on Medical Expenses

■ Percent Spending More than 10% of Income on Medical Expenses

Source: EBRI/Commonwealth Fund Consumerism in Health Care Survey, 2005.

The Mechanics of HSAs

Workers can contribute pre-tax income to an HSA and can withdraw from it at any time for health-related spending. Employers may also contribute to employees' HSAs. Any money remaining at the end of the year stays in the account, enjoys tax benefits, and can be invested just like money in an Individual Retirement Account.

To open an HSA, however, you must have a high-deductible health insurance plan, and you cannot have ordinary health coverage. To qualify, a plan must have a deductible of at least $1,050 for an individual or $2,100 for a family. (HSA-qualified plans are allowed to cover some preventive care without a deductible.) Actual deductibles are much higher: in 2006 HSA-qualified plans had average deductibles of around $2,000 (individual) or $4,000 (family). Under the HSA scheme, in other words, a family typically has to pay the first $4,000 in medical bills each year out of pocket; their insurance plan kicks in—with all of the usual co-pays, exclusions, etc.—only after annual medical expenses exceed that amount.

The funds in the HSA are supposed to cover a portion of these out-of-pocket expenses, but workers are wholly responsible for any gap between the amount in their HSA and the amount of the deductible. The gap can be sizeable. A national survey by the Kaiser Family Foundation found the average deductible for a family HSA plan was $4,008, while the average employer HSA contribution was $1,139. Enrollees are fully responsible for the $2,869 gap, in addition to their premium payments and additional co-pays (see Figure 1).

By reducing employers' premium costs, limiting the amount of services employees are likely to use, and increasing the likelihood that employees will pay more out of pocket for health care, high-deductible plans shift financial risk from employers onto employees. Monthly premiums are lower under these plans than for comprehensive insurance, but high-deductible plan enrollees are still much more likely to spend a substantial amount of their income on health expenses than people enrolled in comprehensive plans. For instance, 31% of enrollees in HSA-type plans spent over 5% of their income on medical expenses, including premiums, compared with only 12% of enrollees in comprehensive plans, according to a recent survey conducted by the Employee Benefits Research Institute and the Commonwealth Fund (see Figure 2).

Flawed Plan

Proponents of HSAs would say this shifting of risk is a good thing: a market-based reform to address escalating health care costs. But this is a deeply flawed view.

For one thing, high-deductible plans are unlikely to have much impact on overall health care spending, most of which results from expensive treatments for serious illnesses whose costs exceed the high deductibles. One recent study found that more than 95% of medical expenditures by working-age households with health insurance were made by those who spend above the minimum HSA deductibles, and that overall, nearly 79% of total medical expenditures occurred above the minimum HSA deductibles. In fact, the only type of spending HSAs are likely to reduce is the kind we want to encourage: primary and preventive care. According to the Commonwealth Fund, enrollees with deductibles over $1,000 were twice as likely as enrollees with deductibles under $500 to avoid seeing the doctor for a medical problem, avoid seeing a specialist, or skip a recommended treatment due to cost.

Moreover, people do not and cannot shop for health care services as they do for other goods. Most people do not have adequate information on the cost and quality of care to make informed purchasing decisions. Nor are they inclined to do so when they are sick or in distress, which is when health care decisions are typically made. Most people enrolled in high-deductible plans do not, in fact, shop for less expensive care, although many shop for better prescription drug prices, according to a 2006 Government Accountability Office (GAO) report.

The GAO found that current HSA participants are disproportionately high-income, healthy people who will benefit from the tax advantages and are unlikely to need much health care. Although generally satisfied with their own experience, HSA enrollees polled by the GAO said they would not recommend high-deductible plans for people with families, health problems, maintenance medications, or moderate incomes—in other words, most people.

So HSAs represent a double-edged sword. If large numbers of people are forced to switch from comprehensive health coverage to high-deductible plans, they will likely face significantly higher out-of-pocket costs. On the other hand, if HSAs continue to attract the healthiest enrollees, the exit of this healthy segment from the comprehensive coverage pool will likely drive up health insurance costs for everyone else.

HSAs and high-deductible plans appeal to employers looking to cut health care costs, high-income earners looking for more tax breaks, and younger workers willing to gamble they won't get sick. For most people, however, they are the opposite of insurance: they concentrate the financial risk of illness instead of spreading it, and they increase the likelihood of incurring medical debt instead of reducing it.

Sources: "Consumer-Directed Health Plans: Early Enrollee Experiences with Health Savings Accounts and Eligible Health Plans," GAO, 8/06; Kaiser Family Foundation and Health Research and Educational Trust, "Employer Health Benefits: 2006 Annual Survey," 9/06; Paul Fronstin and Sara R. Collins, "Early Experience With High-Deductible and Consumer-Driven Health Plans," Employee Benefits Research Institute and the Commonwealth Fund, 12/05; Edwin Park and Robert Greenstein, "Latest Enrollment Data Still Fail to Dispel Concerns about Health Savings Accounts," Center on Budget and Policy Priorities, 1/30/06.

SCHOOL FINANCE: INEQUALITY PERSISTS

MICHAEL ENGEL
January/February 2007

In his groundbreaking 1991 book on U.S. public school finance, *Savage Inequalities,* Jonathan Kozol painted a stark picture of conditions in some of the public schools that poor children—mostly children of color—attend. After visiting elementary and secondary schools in East Saint Louis and Chicago, in New York City, in Camden and Paterson, N.J., in Washington, D.C., and in San Antonio, Kozol described decrepit school buildings with leaky roofs and sewage flowing in; overcrowded classrooms where 35 or 40 students shared 30 chairs and 25 copies of the textbook; classes taught month after month by a rapid turnover of underpaid substitutes; science labs with no equipment, schoolyards with no jungle gyms, and football fields with no goalposts. He concluded with this plea for educational equality:

> *Surely there is enough for everyone in this country. It is a tragedy that these good things are not more widely shared. All our children ought to be allowed a stake in the enormous richness of America ... [w]hether they were born to poor white Appalachians or to wealthy Texans, to poor black people in the Bronx or to rich people in Manhattan or Winnetka ...*

As Kozol points out, the chief policy roadblock to this goal is the uniquely American system of paying for public schools by relying primarily on local property taxes. Twenty years before *Savage Inequalities* was published, the California Supreme Court had broken new legal ground by issuing the first of three decisions in the *Serrano v. Priest* case. These rulings struck down California's public school funding system for violating constitutional guarantees of equal protection under the law. The U.S. Supreme Court rejected that argument with respect to the federal constitution in the *San Antonio v. Rodriguez* case two years later. Nonetheless, over the next three decades courts around the country issued rulings, typically based on state constitutional language, that required or prompted legislatures to reform school finance.

In 2005, Kozol revisited the issue with his book *The Shame of the Nation*. The intervening years had witnessed a virtual frenzy of "school reform" activity at both the state and federal levels; observers like Kozol might have expected to discover that the situation had improved. Instead, his new book describes a racially segregated American public school system with financial and educational inequalities as bad—or worse—than those he had written about 15 years earlier. At about the same time, the nonprofit research and advocacy group Education Trust issued a report, *The Funding Gap* 2005, confirming this judgment: "Instead of organizing our educational systems to make things better for children, we organize our systems of public education in ways that make things worse ... by simply spending less in schools serving high concentrations of low-income and minority children than we do on schools serving more affluent and White children."

What is the nature and extent of these persistent inequalities? What have the states done—or not done—to mitigate or eliminate them? What methods might work best to build a system of school finance that begins to fulfill the promise of equal education for all children?

Unequal Funding: The Numbers

The states vary widely among themselves in terms of support for public education, and there are multiple ways of measuring that variation. According to the federal government's National Center for Education Statistics (NCES), median per pupil expenditure in 2003-2004 ranged from $5,862 in Utah to $14,667 in Alaska; the national median was $7,860. A more significant statistic, calculated by the Census Bureau, is the amount spent by each state per $1,000 of personal income. This measures spending against how much the state's population can potentially afford. In 2003-2004, Florida was at the bottom with $34.36, and Alaska was at the top with $62.92. The figure for the nation as a whole was $43.68.

Perhaps more important is the inequality in spending among school districts *within* each state. The "federal range ratio" for school spending, as reported by the NCES, compares per pupil expenditure in districts spending the least and those spending the most. In Montana, for example, districts at the fifth percentile (those that spend less per pupil than 95% of the districts in the state) spend $5,526 per pupil, versus $19,400 per pupil at the 95th percentile; thus Montana's federal range ratio is 2.51, the highest in the country. (A federal range ratio of zero would denote equal spending across all districts; a federal range ratio of one describes a state where districts at the 95th percentile spend twice as much per pupil as districts at the 5th percentile.) States with relatively low range ratios—for instance, Maryland at 0.32 and Florida at 0.38—are the most "egalitarian."

Putting these three sets of figures together offers a detailed picture of educational inequality in the United States (see Table 1). Interestingly, West Virginia, one of the poorest states in the union, spends more than the median amounts *and* has the lowest federal range ratio in the country. The state's school districts are countywide, which may explain its relatively equitable school funding: wealthier suburban towns cannot fund their own schools well without also supporting the schools in nearby cities.

TABLE 1
PROFILE OF PUBLIC SCHOOL SPENDING IN SELECTED STATES, 2004

MEDIAN PER PUPIL EXPENDITURE

		Below the National Median	Above the National Median
FEDERAL RANGE RATIO	0.5 or under (Relatively Equal)	Florida Georgia Louisiana	Maryland North Carolina Wisconsin
	0.51 – 0.99 (Moderately Unequal)	Michigan Virginia	Kansas New Jersey New York Pennsylvania Vermont
	1.00 and up (Highly Unequal)	Arizona California Colorado Illinois Oregon Texas Washington	Montana New Mexico

Source: National Center for Education Statistics, "Current Expenditures for Public Elementary and Secondary Education: School Year 2003-04," Table 4, July 2006.

So far, these data reveal the wide spreads between high- and low-budget school districts. But *which* children are getting the short end of the stick? Here we can look to the Education Trust, whose analysts have calculated the state and local dollars per pupil available to the highest- versus the lowest-poverty school districts and to the districts with the highest versus the lowest minority populations in each state (for 2004). They found that in about half of the states, the one-fourth of school districts with the highest share of poor students had less in state and local dollars to spend per pupil than the one-fourth of districts with the lowest share of poor students.

The variation from one state to another is striking. At the more egalitarian end of the spectrum are states such as New Mexico, Massachusetts, Minnesota, and New Jersey, where the highest-poverty districts have between $1,000 and $2,000 *more* to spend per pupil than the lowest-poverty districts. At the other end are Illinois, New Hampshire, New York, and Pennsylvania, where the highest-poverty districts have between $1,000 and $2,000 *less* to spend per pupil than the lowest-poverty districts.

As the Education Trust analysts note, though, it costs more—not the same—to provide an equal education to poor children. So these figures actually understate the disparity. The report offers the same comparisons cost-adjusted by 40% to account for the higher expense of educating poor children. (See Figure 2.) Using the cost-adjusted figures, the highest-poverty districts have less to spend per pupil than the lowest-poverty district in two-thirds of the states. The adjusted figures show a funding gap in Illinois and New York that exceeds $2,000 per pupil. (Just imagine

TABLE 2
FUNDING GAPS FOR SCHOOL DISTRICTS
WITH THE HIGHEST POOR AND MINORITY ENROLLMENTS
(WITH 40% ADJUSTMENT FOR LOW-INCOME STUDENTS)

	Gap between Spending per Student in the Highest- and Lowest-Poverty Districts	Gap between Spending per Student in the Highest- and Lowest-Minority Districts
United States	−$1,307	−$1,213
States that Shortchange (Gap of $600 or more in per pupil spending favoring the lowest-poverty or lowest-minority districts)	New York (−$2,927) Illinois (−$2,355) Pennsylvania (−$1,511) New Hampshire (−$1,297) Montana (−$1,148) Michigan (−$1,072) Vermont (−$894) Kansas (−$885) Texas (−$757) Wisconsin (−$742) Arizona (−$736) Alabama (−$656)	New York (−$2,636) New Hampshire (−$2,392) Montana (−$1,838) Kansas (−$1,630) Illinois (−$1,524) Nebraska (−$1,374) North Dakota (−$1,290) Wisconsin (−$1,270) Texas (−$1,167) South Dakota (−$1,140) Wyoming (−$1,041) Colorado (−$1,032) Maine (−$874) Idaho (−$849) Pennsylvania (−$709) Arizona (−$680) Rhode Island (−$639) Vermont (−$613) Connecticut (−$602
States that Help (Gap of $600 or more in per pupil spending favoring the highest-poverty or highest-minority districts)	Alaska ($2,054) New Jersey ($1,069) Minnesota ($950) Massachusetts ($694) New Mexico ($679)	Massachusetts ($1,139) Indiana ($1,096) New Jersey ($1,087) Ohio ($942) Missouri ($662) Minnesota ($623)

Note: Dollar amounts have been adjusted to account for regional cost differences and for the additional cost of educating students with disabilities.

Source: Education Trust, *Funding Gaps 2006,* Tables 3 & 4.

how an additional $60,000 a year could transform the educational environment for a class of 30 fourth graders!) In terms of discrimination against both the poor and minorities, the worst offenders are Arizona, Illinois, Montana, New Hampshire, New York, Texas, and Wyoming. States that rank high in shortchanging minority districts include Kansas, Nebraska, North Dakota, South Dakota, and Wisconsin.

In states with large urban centers surrounded by wealthy suburbs, the differences in school funding can be especially dramatic. Among the 69 school districts within 15 miles of downtown Chicago, for instance, the city itself ranks 50th in per-pupil spending, according to NCES data. Chicago spends $8,356 per pupil; compare that to $18,055 for Evanston and $15,421 for Oak Park, both wealthy suburbs. In fact, Illinois has a terrible record in every respect, but the state Supreme Court has twice explicitly rejected any judicial responsibility for reform. Among the 41 school districts in New York state within 20 miles of downtown Manhattan, New York City ranks 37th, with spending of $13,131 per pupil, compared with Great Neck at $20,995, Lawrence at $22,499, and Manhasset at $22,199. Even among suburbs, poorer ones with larger minority populations such as Mount Vernon fall far behind whiter and more prosperous communities. In New York, court battles continue while the legislature stalls, ignoring deadlines for reform already set by the courts.

These inequalities extend even to differences in funding within school districts, mostly in the form of teacher salary differentials. A 2005 report by the Education Trust-West *California's Hidden Teacher Spending Gap* concluded that "the concentration of more experienced and more highly credentialed teachers (along with their corresponding high salaries) in whiter and more affluent schools drives huge funding gaps between schools—even between schools within the very same school district."

Financial inequality in U.S. public schools is not an anomaly, nor is it the result of a lack of possible remedies. States have undertaken countless so-called reforms over the past 20 years—to little effect. Only a few states, however, have taken any *serious* steps to guarantee even an adequate, much less an equal, education for all their children.

Courtroom Remedies

As of 2003, cases challenging the constitutionality of education finance systems had been heard in the courts of 44 states; in 18 of those states, the systems were declared unconstitutional. In 12 states the courts refused to act at all. The court decisions are all over the map in terms of setting standards of adequacy, equity, or equality, requiring legislative action, or prescribing specific remedies. Often it has taken a series of decisions over a number of years to force any change at all. The main overall effect of these rulings has been to push reluctant state legislatures, including those in some states where courts had not yet issued decisions, to modify their educational finance systems.

The outcomes, again, are all over the map, but very few have enacted serious and thorough reforms. For the most part, states have merely tinkered with the existing methods of aiding local schools. The most prevalent method—used in forty-one states—is foundation aid, which sets a statewide minimum per- pupil expenditure and appropriates state funds to make up the difference between that amount and the amounts localities are able (or required) to raise from property taxes. Each state uses a different formula, some so complex as to defy comprehension. Most reforms have involved a change in that formula to benefit poor districts, or a higher foundation level financed by increased state appropriations, or separate and additional grant programs.

A less common and even more complex method is known as "district power equalizing", which essentially guarantees a minimum property tax base to each community. In other words, the state determines the amount of revenue that is to be raised by any given local property tax rate and offers aid to communities whose property tax base is too poor to reach that level. Thus if the state determines a 5% rate should raise $10 million, a community that can only raise $7 million at that tax rate will receive $3 million in state aid. A more radical version, such as the one enacted in Vermont (see below), provides for "recapturing" and redistributing the excess revenues raised by wealthier communities.

Some states combine both methods. In any case, although several states, such as New Jersey and Massachusetts, have managed to improve their formulas to the benefit of poorer communities, none of these adjustments address the basic cause of inequality, namely, reliance on local funding. Overall, in that regard there has been no improvement in twenty years. The state share of public school funding across the nation peaked at 49% in 1985; the federal share peaked at 9% in 1980. Federal aid to elementary and secondary education was $41 billion in 2003, a paltry 2% of the entire federal budget. To the extent that communities continue to have to rely on local property taxes to fund their schools, there is no question that serious inequities will persist.

At least four states, however, have gone beyond the norm. It is instructive to examine their experience with devising school funding systems that ostensibly aim for equality, that is, making sure that no district has a significant financial advantage over any other.

Hawaii is unique in the nation in that the whole state is one school district, and the state government is responsible for appropriating funds to the individual schools. On the surface, this appears to be a perfect example of equal education. Unfortunately, it is not. Until quite recently, funds were appropriated on an enrollment basis, without allowing for the extra costs involved in educating students in high-poverty areas or those with special needs. Moreover, Hawaii ranks 50th in terms of the percent of total state and local government revenues allocated for public education. Per pupil expenditure is just slightly above the national median, and the state ranks 35th in spending per $1,000 of personal income. Thus Hawaii resembles a number of southern states in uniformly underfunding all its public schools.

Kansas adopted a new school finance system in 1992, prompted by a lower court decision invalidating the existing one. The School District Finance and Quality Performance Act set a uniform statewide property tax rate, and established a $3,600 foundation funding level per pupil. The pupil count was weighted to take into account factors such as poverty. State aid was to make up the difference between that foundation level and what each community could raise with the property tax. But an escape hatch was provided by allowing a "local option budget" for communities to raise additional monies, up to 25% over the foundation level. The subsequent failure of the state to fully fund this reform led to widespread use of the local option budget. Richer communities were thus able to raise more money, so pre-existing inequalities continued. According to the Education Trust report, Kansas had one of the largest minority funding gaps in the country in 2003, and the poverty gap increased substantially between 1997 and 2003. The Kansas courts are thus still involved in the issue of educational finance.

Michigan's reforms were not inspired by any court actions. Rather, facing widespread anger over high property taxes, in 1993 Republican governor John Engler bit the bullet by getting the legislature to eliminate the property tax as the basis for school funding. He then forced the issue further by slashing the state education budget, creating a financial crisis for the schools. As a result, voters in 1994 approved a 2% sales tax increase to fund education. Reform legislation set a statewide property tax rate, and localities were not allowed to exceed that rate. State aid would be based on a foundation plan. The result was that the state share of school spending more than doubled. But property taxes still accounted for one-third of school budgets, and with the rate frozen by state mandate, communities with low property values still fell behind. Combined with insufficient state funding (per pupil spending is below the national median), this means that although progress was achieved, Michigan still has a way to go to provide equal and adequate funding to the schools serving its poorest children.

Vermont's Act 60 came closest to bringing schools toward the ideal of educational equality. In 1995, the state's supreme court ruled that the existing finance system violated the state constitution. Two years later the legislature responded with Act 60, the most radical reform in the country. The new law set a statewide property tax rate and foundation spending level. Localities were allowed to levy additional property taxes, but if revenues from a locality exceeded the foundation amount, that excess reverted to the state and was put into a "sharing pool" used to aid poorer communities. This was essentially a district power equalizing program with a socialist twist. Rich communities were hit hard, and their budget process became guesswork since they had no way of knowing in a timely way how much property tax revenue they would be able to keep for the following year. A political uproar ensued; Act 60 was succeeded by Act 68 in 2004, which kept the statewide property tax and increased the state sales tax, but ended the sharing pool. How this will play out is as yet not clear, but as of 2003-2004, Vermont ranked 2nd in per $1000 spending and 8th in per pupil spending with a relatively low poverty gap.

Prospects for Change

The complexity and confusion of school finance systems and of all of the efforts to reform them obscure a simple and obvious solution, which no state has chosen: progressive taxation. If public schools were funded entirely by state and local taxes whose effective rates increase with income and wealth, if state aid was weighted sharply in favor of districts with higher educational costs, if federal aid was increased and similarly appropriated, and if strict limits were placed on local supplementation, financial inequality among schools would be history.

To free-market ideologues and neoclassical economists, these alternatives are obviously anathema. But they are rarely mentioned even by liberal or progressive politicians concerned about educational inequality. For they involve confronting two of the most sensitive issues in American politics: taxes and race. All state and local revenue systems in the United States are regressive to one extent or another. And as Jonathan Kozol points out, racial segregation makes it easy for the majority of public officials, and of whites in general, to ignore the disastrous conditions in predominantly-black schools.

It would thus take enormous public pressure to force the government to choose a new course and pursue financial equality. If that were done, we could build a system of public schools that would offer all students genuinely equal opportunity to learn, and the false promise of the Bush administration—"No Child Left Behind"—could actually become a reality.

Sources: Jonathan Kozol, *Savage Inequalities* (Crown, 1991); *The Shame of the Nation* (Crown, 2005); John Yinger, ed., *Helping Children Left Behind* (MIT Press, 2004); Education Trust, *The Funding Gap 2005, The Funding Gap 2006*; Education Trust—West, *California's Hidden Teacher Spending Gap* (2005); US Census Bureau, Survey of Local Government Finances (www.census. gov/govs/www/estimate.html); U.S. Dept. of Education, National Center for Education Statistics, Education Finance Statistics Center (www.nced.ed.gov/edfin); National Conference of State Legislatures, Education Finance Database (www.ncsl.org/programs/educ/ed_finance); Hawaii Superintendent of Education, 16th Annual Report (2005); Teachers College, Columbia University, National Access Network (www.schoolfunding.info/).

Chapter 4

SOCIAL SECURITY AND PENSIONS

WHEN BAD THINGS HAPPEN TO GOOD PENSIONS

TERESA GHILARDUCCI
May/June 2005

February was a momentous month for American workers' retirement security. Just days after President Bush called for the partial privatization of Social Security, his administration proposed major modifications to the system that guarantees employer-sponsored defined-benefit pensions. Both initiatives break with longstanding "insurance" models of old-age income security and accelerate the use of individual accounts.

Defined-benefit pensions, like Social Security, provide a modest but steady stream of income for the duration of a retiree's life. Both systems are based on collective risk sharing: they gather premium contributions from populations facing similar risks—such as old age or disability—and provide a guaranteed stream of income to individuals when those risks befall them.

Much as the administration is using a financing problem in the Social Security system as an excuse to demand big changes that would endanger Social Security itself, it's using a deficit in the agency that insures defined-benefit pensions to call for "reforms" that would imperil those very pensions.

Both of Bush's proposals would undermine the retirement security of working people and their families. But the two proposals also deeply contradict each other. By making the puzzling claim that the Social Security trust fund, which holds only U.S. Treasury bonds, owns no "real money," the Social Security proposal urges younger workers to divert Social Security contributions into individual accounts. On the other hand, most independent analysts believe the administration's proposed pension reform would lead corporations to load up on bonds in order to stabilize their asset portfolios—and their credit ratings—and over time drive them out of the defined-benefit system altogether. The Social Security proposal is based on the premise that individuals don't own enough stock; the pension proposal is based on the premise that pension funds fall short because they own too much.

The administration's proposals place us at a crossroads. We can either hasten the end of group and social insurance and move toward individual accounts—personal savings accounts and 401(k)s—or we can save Social Security and expand incentives for employers to provide defined-benefit pensions to workers.

Why Defined-Benefit Plans Should Be Strengthened—Not Undermined

Unlike defined-contribution plans like 401(k)s, which yield benefits—or losses—based on the contributions and investment prowess of the individual worker, defined benefits are predictable; they're usually based on a worker's pay rate and length of employment. For the median worker, defined-benefit wealth is higher than defined-contribution account wealth, and because the former is paid as an annuity, workers collect for as long as they live. (See Table 1 for the risks associated with defined-benefit versus defined-contribution plans.)

Defined-benefit plans offer another, frequently overlooked, benefit to society: they serve as an equalizing force. For over 40 years, American retirement policies have reduced income inequality between the top tier and the rest, narrowing consumption gaps as people age. Social Security and defined-benefit plans set an income floor underneath the working class that does not fluctuate with the financial markets. Among current retirees (Americans born between 1926 and 1935), the ratio of the income that goes to the top 20% versus the middle 20% of the income distribution is 234%. For retired boomers (workers born between 1946 and 1956), the gap will be 285%, and it will continue to rise for subsequent generations. This growth in inequality is tied to the decline of defined-benefit pensions and the rise of defined-contribution plans as shares of the income of elderly households. Current retirees have 20% of their income coming from defined-benefit plans while future retirees are projected to have only 11%.

Under the current system, companies with defined-benefit pensions pay insurance premiums to the Pension Benefit Guaranty Corporation (PBGC), a government corporation created in 1974 to insure pension assets. If a pension plan fails, the PBGC takes control of it and continues to pay covered workers' retirement benefits up to a cap. The PBGC receives no federal tax dollars, relying instead primarily on insurance premiums paid by employers and unions who sponsor defined-benefit pensions.

Bush's Pension Proposal

On February 7 [2005], the Bush administration unveiled a sweeping rewrite of federal pension law in the form of a proposal it calls "Strengthen Funding for Single-Employer Pension Plans." The administration claims to want to strengthen pensions by fixing the problem of "underfunded plan terminations"—which, it argues, "are placing an increasing strain on the pension insurance system."

The proposal is tailored to an imagined reality where most companies grossly underfund their plans, and it ignores fundamental problems caused by the rise of risky defined-contribution plans and the one-time contraction of the steel and airline industries. If enacted, it would destroy the very system the administration claims it wants to save.

Federal Policy for Defined-Benefit Plans

For almost a century, the U.S. government has promoted defined-benefit pension plans because they increase productivity and reinforce the employment relationship while stabilizing retirement income. In 1919, the federal government was faced with a melt-down of the defined-benefit plans of legacy railroads that struggled in competition with small, low-cost start-ups that didn't provide pensions to their young workers. This is analogous to regional air carriers like Jet Blue decimating United Airlines and other legacy airlines today. In response, the mandatory, industry-wide Railroad Retirement system was established in 1935, a decade before Social Security, requiring all railroads to pay into a multi-employer pension fund.

During World War II and in the post-war period, court cases and tax laws favored rapid growth in defined-benefit plans. An unusually large pension default at the Studebaker automobile corporation in South Bend, Ind., in 1964, led Congress to pass comprehensive pension regulatory legislation, the Employee Retirement Income Security Act (ERISA), in 1974. ERISA established the PBGC to insure firms' defined-benefit pensions in the event of bankruptcy (which, even before 1974, happened infrequently; one out of 1,000 defined-benefit sponsors had defaulted in 10 years). Since its creation in 1974, the PBGC has operated without ever missing a payment it owes, despite having an overall balance-sheet deficit in most years, using the premium income that every plan sponsor (single employers, multiple employers, or unions) pays to carry the agency through normal cyclical downturns.

In creating an insurance structure, the legislation required companies to fund their defined-benefit promises over time, anticipating "moral hazard" problems (when an insured entity becomes lax, relying on another body to bail it out). ERISA intended companies to have flexibility, contributing more in good times and less in bad. Originally, companies had 40 years to reach 100% funding, using wage, investment returns, and interest-rate projections. In the late 1980s and 1990s, faster funding was required of plans that were less than 70% funded. (A pension's funded status refers to its ratio of assets to liabilities. If a plan is more than 90% funded, that is, if its current assets amount to 90% of the present value of promises, including expected future promises, made to its participants, it is considered fully funded.)

The plan dramatically increases PBGC premiums for single-employer defined-benefit sponsors, doubling premiums for "at risk" firms (those with unfunded liabilities that are likely to default) and tripling premiums for healthy firms (see Table 2). Whereas today, healthy firms pay premiums equal to 66% of their "expected losses" (meaning the amount they would owe to current and future retirees if they defaulted), the Bush plan would raise healthy firms' premiums to 340% of their expected losses. It thus penalizes healthy companies for sponsoring defined-benefit pensions.

For the first time, a company's ability to provide such pensions to its workers would be linked to the company's own creditworthiness. The plan divides companies into two groups: those above and those below "investment grade." Companies that fall below investment grade face large premium rate hikes and have just five years to reach a 90% pension-funding level. (See "Federal Policy for Defined-Benefit Plans" for more on pension funding requirements.) An estimated one-fourth of the nation's largest firms, including Delta Air Lines, Goodyear Tire and Rubber, United States Steel, and Lucent Technologies, are currently below investment grade. In this way, the plan intensifies the funding obligations of companies already experiencing financial difficulties. At the same time, it prohibits firms from building up a cushion of credit during flush periods. For decades, companies have contributed more during boom years so as to lighten their funding obligations during slow periods. The

Bush plan takes away that flexibility.

What's more, firms would be required to value their plan assets according to their market value, rather than using an average or smoothed valuation of assets, as they do now. This change will produce greater year-to-year volatility in asset prices and funding obligations. Measures of liability (the amount a plan owes to current and future beneficiaries) would also become more volatile: The plan requires firms to use a complex method to calculate the present value of future liabilities. Firms now use a single interest rate in the calculations; under the Bush plan their interest rates would be pegged to when their workers are expected to retire. Firms with younger employees would use a higher interest rate tied to a long-term bond, while firms with older employees would use a low rate, which would make their liabilities soar. These accounting changes will hurt older plans in blue-collar manufacturing and make contributions more uncertain.

Bush claims the changes would result in "increased accuracy." But he fails to mention that they will make defined-benefit plans more expensive for companies to offer, required contributions less predictable, and valuations much more complicated to compute—something companies, especially small and medium sized ones, complain about.

The volatility produced by the new accounting framework would force firms to shift their pension investments from stocks to bonds. In fact, bonds, with their predictable rates of return, would become the only reasonable investment to include in a corporate pension fund. But bonds' low yields would drive up the cost of providing a plan—and hasten the elimination of the defined-benefit pension.

The Bush proposal starts from the wrong premise. It assumes that many firms purposefully underfund their plans because they know that the PBGC will pick up the shortfall if they go bankrupt. (Economists call this the "moral hazard" problem.) Similarly, it reduces employer flexibility in the belief that firms will use the flexible rules to "game the system." It anticipates bad faith behavior rather than mixing protections against bad behavior with positive incentives for promoting and strengthening the system, which, in reality, most companies deal with in good faith and want to keep strong.

Why the Shortfall?

There's no question that the PBGC is facing a serious shortfall. In 2004, its budget plummeted into a $23 billion hole from a 2000 (stock-swollen) surplus of $10 billion. The dramatic fall was caused by crippling mass bankruptcies and defaults in the steel and airline industries. The agency was designed to cope with isolated cases of default, not sector-wide crises. Since 2002, about 70% of the $8 billion the PBGC has absorbed in pension losses was related to steel and airline defaults. It is expected to absorb another $6.6 billion from United Airlines. The independent monitoring organization Center for Federal Financial Institutions (COFFI) projects a program deficit of $16.2 billion in 2013. According to its founder, former Treasury staffer Douglas Elliot, the PBGC might require a program bailout of $56 to $100 billion by 2020 under certain scenarios.

The Bush proposal may have been prompted by the PBGC's deficit, but it does not address the two most fundamental causes of the agency's financing troubles: First, its premium base is shrinking thanks to the financial industry and to government regulations that privilege defined-contribution plans over defined-benefit plans; second, two industries recently caused unusual PBGC outlays. (In 2004 less than 5% of all defined-benefit participants constituted over two-thirds of the claims—see Table 3.) Underfunding of plans, the problem the Bush plan targets, is rare; a minority of companies underfund, and most are not at risk of defaulting.

Fewer DB Plans   The number of private defined-benefit plans peaked in the mid-1980s at 112,000, when they covered 40% of the U.S. work force. By 2004, just 31,000 remained, covering only 20% of workers. New economy companies like Microsoft and Wal-Mart never adopted the plans and old economy companies such as GE and IBM (along with 18% to 20% of other long-time sponsors) are freezing and terminating their plans.

When I served on the PBGC advisory board during the Clinton administration, we used to say "pension plans aren't created—they're sold." Vendors, brokers, money management firms, and mutual funds charge more for individual account management than defined-benefit management, so they actively market 401(k)-type programs to employers. Employers find these plans attractive because they can subcontract record keeping and paperwork to vendors while passing administration costs on to their workers. Under employer-sponsored defined-benefit plans, employers bear the administrative costs—and the long-term liability. Moreover, the decline of unions, the shrinking of the manufacturing sector, and the erosion of durable employment relationships more generally have all combined to cut the number of defined-benefit pensions.

As more companies replace their guaranteed defined-benefit pensions with defined-contribution plans, the PBGC's financial position erodes because defined-contribution sponsors don't pay premiums to the PBGC. For a while, the effects of these long-term problems were masked by the stock market bubble, but no longer.

A glimmer of evidence suggests the decline is slowing. Four major companies, SBC, UMC, UK Barclays, and TransCanada, adopted defined-benefit plans in 2004. And public-sector employees are fending off muscular attempts, the latest one by California Governor Arnold Schwarzenegger, to convert their defined-benefit plans to defined-contribution plans.

External Industry Factors   The second threat to the defined-benefit pension has nothing to do with the pension system's internal flaws, but with outside economic and political events and trends, namely the dramatic acceleration in the offshoring of U.S. manufacturing; strong dollar policies that boosted cheap imports; the 9/11 attacks; and fuel price hikes. These combined factors have pummeled the airline and steel sectors. Bethlehem Steel, Delta Airways, US Airways, and the giant United Airlines, plus one large company in another sector, Polaroid, have all offloaded some of their pension liabilities onto the PBGC within the past few years. In doing so, the steel and airline sectors brought down some of America's largest pension plans. The pension losses in these two industries have overwhelmed the PBGC. Given the exceptional confluence of factors at work here, Congress should not expect the PBGC to absorb the impacts of two major industry collapses with its own premium revenues.

The Bush administration is simply wrong in assuming that corporate moral hazard and poor funding lie behind the PBGC's woes. Most firms actually behave as though they are committed to their plans. My survey of over 700 firms over a 19-year period (1981–1998) shows that when rates of return of defined-benefit pension funds were high—in good times—firms contributed more to both their defined-benefit and defined-contribution plans, just as the 1974 pension law known as ERISA intended. The airline and steel industries alone stopped contributing recently when both industries, facing crises, altered course and cut back their contributions when the defined-benefit plans were earning high rates of return. (There are two explanations, not mutually exclusive, for this reversal. One is that these industries decided to offload their liabilities onto the PBGC and workers; the other is that when the rest of the economy was doing all right, these industries were experiencing their own sector-specific recessions.) This is an unusual behavior pattern—the exception, not the rule. Beyond these sectors, far fewer firms withhold contributions to the PBGC during flush periods than the Bush administration contends.

Toward Secure Retirement Income

Raising pension funding standards as aggressively as the Bush administration proposes tightens the rules to the point where plan sponsors could no longer afford or want to afford most of the defined-benefit pensions they now offer. According to Pensions and Investments, Ron Gebhardtsbauer, senior pension fellow at the American Academy of Actuaries, predicts, "Instead of investing their pension assets in stocks, companies will simply shut down their pension plans, set up defined-contribution plans and let the employees invest in stocks." Surveys show that when asked what poses a threat to defined-benefit plans, firms point to market downturns and volatility caused by eliminating actuarial smoothing in favor of "mark to market" funding schemes (exactly what Bush plans to implement). Standard & Poor's Ratings Services agrees. Credit ratings would likely fall for defined-benefit sponsors because of increased pension costs and volatility. Given the specter of lowered credit ratings, companies will use bonds to stabilize their fund pension contributions, and their reputation in the finance community, at the same time that the new regulations push them to drop their defined-benefit plans altogether.

There are three chief ways to truly advance defined-benefit pensions. They all involve strengthening the PBGC. The first is to promote cash balance plans, a form of defined-benefit pension typically distributed in some form of annuity for the life of a retiree and spouse. Employers appreciate cash balance plans because, like in a 401(k), the employer contribution is predictable: the employer contributes a defined amount of money to an account every year. But unlike in a 401(k), individuals don't have to manage their own money and they bear no risk—the employer guarantees the rate of return. Because they are a form of defined-benefit pension, cash balance plans are insured by the PBGC. More defined-benefit plans of any type would bring fresh revenues to the PBGC, yet the Bush administration has dragged its feet in forming regulatory rules to make firms feel comfortable with providing them.

Second, Congress should infuse the PBGC with revenue, perhaps from taxes on goods and services tied to the airline and steel industries that have most strained the system. The PBGC's recent losses coincided with windfalls of low prices for steel-made products and air travel. Consumers could help pay some portion of the price of industry dislocation and workers' retirements if Congress imposed a modest tax on airline tickets and tons of steel (domestically produced or imported), and dedicated the revenue to the PBGC. More broadly, reforms to strengthen rather than destroy the defined-benefit system and the PBGC will have to deal with the health of the airline industry and steel industry—like we did almost a 100 years ago with railroads. (See "Federal Policy for Defined-Benefit Plans.")

Third, the PBGC is modeled as insurance; strengthening it requires applying insurance principles. Any proper insurance system distinguishes between catastrophic events and normal ones. Other insurance companies have "reinsurance" to cover catastrophes, recognizing that larger-than-usual claims, if absorbed only by premium payers, can severely damage an entire insurance system. But the PBGC itself currently has no insurance. The need for a bailout should be avoided by correcting this mistake.

Government policy makers recognized long ago that in a competitive capitalist economy, some employers might be driven out of business before they had fully funded the pension benefits they had promised their workers. Congress knew that mandating plan sponsors to back up their benefit promises by requiring them to fund their pension trusts according to a prescribed payment schedule was not enough. It recognized that business failure is a possibility and wisely added the PBGC as a backstop for retirees, should their company fail. It also knew that the defined-benefit system had to renew itself by attracting new sponsors to adopt such plans, and mandated, by statute, that the PBCG encourage and maintain the defined-benefit system and keep premiums as low as possible.

Even as it's lobbying to dismantle the nation's only form of social insurance, Social Security, and drive workers into individual accounts, the Bush administration is taking aim at the only other source of guaranteed retirement income available to millions of working people, the defined-benefit pension. The defined-benefit pension system needs to be strengthened and expanded—not undermined. The president, and officials at the PBGC who are now supporting the president's proposals, are in an awkward position: they are purportedly saving an agency by eliminating its reason to exist.

Resources: American Academy of Actuaries, "Analysis of the president's proposals to strengthen the single employer pension funding," 2005, <www.actuary.org/pdf/pension/funding–single. pdf>; Vineeta Anand, "Pension Reform: White House might be in the mood to deal," Pensions and Investments, January 2005; Julia L. Coronado and Sylvester J. Schieber, "Saving Private Pension Insurance: An Evaluation of Current Proposal to Shore up the PBGC," Watson – Wyatt Worldwide, 2005; Center on Federal Financial Institutions, "PBGC Updated Cash Flow Model from COFFI, November 18, 2004; T. Ghilarducci and Weis Sun, "Pension Regulation and Destabilization: Are firms forced to decrease pension funding in an upturn and to contribute in a recession?" University of Notre Dame, Faculty of Economics, 2005; Scott Sprinzen, "Pension Plans and Credit Ratings," Business Week, March 31, 2005; Fay Hansen, "Rethinking Employee

Benefits," Business Finance, 2005; Department of Labor, "The administration's single employer defined benefit pension reform proposal," <www.dol.gov/ebsa/pensionreform.html>; James Wooten, The Employee Retirement Income Security Act of 1974: A Political History, California/ Milbank Books on Health and the Public Policy.

SOCIAL SECURITY ISN'T BROKEN
So why the rush to "fix" it?

DOUG ORR
November/December 2004

Federal Reserve Chairman Alan Greenspan told Congress earlier this year that everyone knows there's a Social Security crisis. That's like saying "everyone knows the earth is flat."

Starting with a faulty premise guarantees reaching the wrong conclusion. The truth is there is no Social Security crisis, but there is a potential crisis in retirement income security and there may be a crisis in the future in U.S. financial markets. It's this latter crisis that Greenspan actually is worried about.

Social Security is the most successful insurance program ever created. It insures millions of workers against what economists call "longevity risk," the possibility they will live "too long" and not be able to work long enough, or save enough, to provide their own income. Today, about 10% of those over age 65 live in poverty. Without Social Security, that rate would be almost 50%.

Social Security was originally designed to supplement, and was structured to resemble, private-sector pensions. In the 1930s, all private pensions were defined-benefit plans. The retirement benefit was based on a worker's former wage and years of service. In most plans, after 35 years of service the monthly benefit, received for life, would be at least half of the income received in the final working year.

Congress expected that private-sector pensions eventually would cover most workers. But pension coverage peaked at 40% in the 1960s. Since then, corporations have systematically dismantled pension systems. Today, only 16% of private-sector workers are covered by defined-benefit pensions. Rather than supplementing private pensions, Social Security has become the primary source of retirement income for almost two-thirds of retirees. Thus, Congress was forced to raise benefit levels in 1972.

What has happened to private-sector defined benefit pensions? They've been replaced with defined-contribution (DC) savings plans such as 401(k)s and 403(b)s. These plans provide some retirement income but offer no real protection from longevity risk. Once a retiree depletes the amount saved in the plan, their retirement income is gone.

In a generous DC plan, a firm might match the worker's contribution up to 3% of his or her pay. With total contributions of 6%, average wage growth of 2% a year, and an average return on the investment portfolio of 5%, after 35 years of work, a retiree would exhaust the plan's savings in just 8.5 years even if her annual spending is only half of her final salary. If she restricts spending to just one-third of the final salary, the savings can stretch to 14 years.

At age 65, life expectancy for women today is about 20 years, and for men about 15 years, so DC savings plans will not protect the elderly from longevity risk. The conversion of defined-benefit pensions to defined-contribution plans is the source of the real potential crisis in retirement income. Yet Greenspan did not mention this in his testimony to Congress.

No Crisis

Opponents of Social Security have hated it since its creation in 1935. The first prediction of a Social Security crisis was published in 1936! The Heritage Foundation and Cato Institute are home to many of the program's opponents today, and they fixate on the concept of a "demographic imperative." In 1960, the United States had 5.1 workers per retiree, in 1998 we had 3.4, and by 2030 we will have only 2.1. Opponents claim that with these demographic changes, revenues will eventually be insufficient to pay Social Security retirement benefits.

The logic is appealingly simple, but wrong for two reasons. First, this "old-age dependency" ratio in itself is irrelevant. No amount of financial manipulation can change this fact: all current consumption must come from current physical output. The consumption of all dependents (non-workers) must come from the output produced by current workers. It's the overall dependency ratio——the number of workers relative to all non-workers, including the aged, the young, the disabled, and those choosing not to work—that determines whether society can "afford" the baby boomers' retirement years. In the 1960s we had only 0.62 workers for each dependent, and we were building new schools and the interstate highway system and getting ready to put a man on the moon. No one bemoaned a demographic crisis or looked for ways to cut the resources allocated to children; in fact, the living standards of most families rose rapidly. In 2030, we will have 0.98 workers per dependent. We'll have more workers per dependent in the future than we did in the past. While it is true a larger share of total output will be allocated to the aged, just as a larger share was allocated to children in the 1960s, society will easily produce adequate output to support all workers and dependents, and at a higher standard of living.

Second, the "demographic imperative" ignores productivity growth. Average worker productivity has grown by about 2% per year, adjusted for inflation, for the past half-century. That means real output per worker doubles every 36 years. This productivity growth is projected to continue, so by 2040, each worker will produce twice as much as today. Suppose each of three workers today produces $1,000 per week and one retiree is allocated $500 (half of his final salary)—then each worker gets $833. In 2040, two such workers will produce $2,000 per week each (after adjusting for inflation). If each retiree gets $1,000, each worker still gets $1,500. The incomes of both workers and retirees go up. Thus, paying for the baby boomers' retirement need not decrease their children's standard of living. A larger share of output going to retirees does not imply that the standard of living of those still working will be lower. Those still working will have a slightly smaller share of a much larger pie.

So why the talk of a Social Security crisis? Social Security always has been a pay-as-you-go system. Current benefits are paid out of current tax revenues. But in the 1980s, a commission headed by Greenspan recommended raising payroll taxes to expand the trust fund in order to supplement tax revenues when the baby boom generation retires. Congress responded in 1984 by raising payroll taxes significantly. As a result, the Social Security trust fund, which holds government bonds as assets, has grown every year since. As the baby boom moves into retirement, these assets will be sold to help pay their retirement benefits.

Each year, Social Security's trustees must make projections of the system's status for the next 75 years. In 1996, they projected the trust fund balance would go to zero in 2030. In 2000, they projected a zero balance in 2036 and today they project a zero balance in 2042. The projection keeps changing because the trustees continue to make unrealistic assumptions about future economic conditions. The current projections are based on the assumption that annual GDP growth will average 1.8% for the next 75 years. In no 20-year period, even including the Great Depression, has the U.S. economy grown that slowly. Each year the economy grows faster than 1.8%, the zero balance date moves further into the future. But the trustees continue to suggest that if we return to something like the Great Depression, the trust fund will go to zero.

Opponents of Social Security claim the system will then be "bankrupt." Bankruptcy implies ceasing to exist. But if the trust fund goes to zero, Social Security will not shut down and stop paying benefits. It will simply revert to the pure pay-as-you-go system that it was before 1984 and continue to pay current benefits using current tax revenues. Even if the trustees' worst-case assumptions come true, the payroll tax paid by workers would need to increase by only about 2% points, and only in 2042, not today.

If the economy grows at 2.4%—which is still slower than the stagnant growth of the 1980s—the trust fund never goes to zero. The increase in real output and real incomes will generate sufficient revenues to pay promised benefits. By 2042, we will need to lower payroll taxes or raise benefits to reduce the surplus.

The claim that benefits of future retirees must be reduced in order to not reduce the standard of living of future workers is simply wrong. It is being used to drive a wedge between generations and panic younger workers into supporting Bush's plan to destroy Social Security. Under the most likely version of his privatization proposal, according to Bush's own Social Security Commission, the guaranteed benefits from Social Security of a 20-year-old worker joining the labor force today would be reduced by 46%. That Commission also admitted that private accounts are unlikely to make up for this drop in benefits. An estimate made by the Goldman-Sacks brokerage firm suggests that even with private accounts, retirement income of younger workers would be reduced by 42% compared to what they would receive if nothing is done to change the Social Security system. Private accounts are a losing proposition for younger workers.

The Real Fear: An Oversupply of Bonds

So why did Greenspan claim cutting benefits would become necessary? To understand the answer, we need to take a side trip to look at how bonds and the financial markets affect each other. It turns out that rising interest rates reduce the selling price of existing financial assets, and falling asset prices push up interest rates (see box "How Does the Bond Market Work?").

For example, in the 1980s, President Reagan cut taxes and created the largest government deficits in history up to that point. This meant the federal government had to sell lots of bonds to finance the soaring government debt; to attract enough buyers, the Treasury had to offer very high interest rates. During the 1980s, real interest rates (rates adjusted for inflation) were almost four times higher than the historic average. High interest rates slow economic growth by making it more expensive for consumers to buy homes or for businesses to invest in new infrastructure. The GDP growth rate in the 1980s was the slowest in U.S. history apart from the Great Depression.

But high interest rates also depress financial asset prices. A five percentage point rise in interest rates reduces the selling price of a bond (loan) that matures in 10 years by 50%. It was the impact of the record-high interest rates of the 1980s on the value of the loan portfolios of the savings and loan industry that caused the S&L crisis and the industry's collapse.

Greenspan is worried because he sees history repeating itself in the form of President Bush's tax cuts. In his testimony, Greenspan expressed concern over a potentially large rise in interest rates. This is his way of warning about an excess supply of bonds. Starting in 2020, Social Security will have to sell about $150 billion (in 2002 dollars) in trust fund bonds each year for 22 years. At the same time, private-sector pension funds will be selling $100 billion per year of financial assets to make their pension payments. State and local governments will be selling $75 billion per

---

How Does the Bond Market Work?

A bond is nothing more than an IOU. A company or government borrows money and promises to pay a certain amount of interest annually until it repays the loan. When you buy a newly issued bond, you are making a loan. The amount of the loan is the "face value" of the bond. The initial interest rate at which the bond is issued, the "face rate," multiplied by this face value determines the amount of interest paid each period. Until the debt is paid back, events in the financial markets affect the bond's value.

If market interest rates fall, prices of existing bonds rise. Why? Suppose you buy a bond with a face value of $100 that pays 10%. You then collect $10 per year. If the current interest rate falls to 5%, newly issued bonds will pay that new rate. Since your bond pays 10%, people would rather buy that one than one paying 5%. They are willing to pay more than the face value to get it, so the price will be bid up until interest rates equalize. The price at which you could sell your bond will rise to $200, since $10 is 5% of $200.

But changes in bond prices also affect interest rates. If more people are selling bonds than buying them, an excess supply exists, and prices will fall. If you need to sell your bond to get money to pay your rent, you might have to lower the price of the bond you hold to $50. Because the bond still pays $10 per year to the owner, the new owner gets a 20% return on the $50 purchase. Anyone trying to issue new bonds will have to match that return, so the new market interest rate becomes 20%.

year to cover their former employees' pension expenses, and holdings in private mutual funds will fall by about $50 billion per year as individual retirees cash in their 401(k) assets. Private firms will still need to issue about $100 billion of new bonds a year to finance business expansion. Combined, these asset sales could total $475 billion per year.

This level of bond sales is more than double the record that was set in the 1980s following the Reagan tax cuts. But back then, the newly issued bonds were being purchased by "institutional investors" such as private-sector pension funds and insurance companies. After 2020, these groups will be net sellers of bonds. The financial markets will strain to absorb this level of asset sales. It's unlikely they will be able to also absorb the extra $400 billion per year of bond sales needed to cover the deficit spending that will occur if the new Bush tax cuts are made permanent. This oversupply of bonds will drive down the value of all financial assets.

In a 1994 paper, Sylvester Schieber, a current advisor to President Bush on pension and Social Security reform, predicted this potential drop in asset prices. After 2020, the value of assets held in 401(k) plans, already inadequate, will be reduced even more. More importantly, at least to Greenspan, the prices of assets held by corporations to fund their defined benefit pension promises will fall. Thus, pension payments will need to come out of current revenues, reducing corporate profits and, in turn, driving down stock prices.

It's this potential collapse in the prices of financial assets that worries Greenspan most. In order to reduce the run-up of long-term interest rates, some asset sales must be eliminated. Greenspan said, "You don't have the resources to do it all." But rather than rescinding Bush's tax cuts, Greenspan favors reducing bond sales by the Social Security trust fund. Doing that requires a reduction in benefits and raising payroll taxes even more.

Framing a question incorrectly makes it impossible to find a solution. The problem is not with Social Security, but rather with blind reliance on financial markets to solve all economic problems. If the financial markets are likely to fail us, what is the solution? The solution is simple once the question is framed correctly: where will the real output that baby boomers are going to consume in retirement come from?

The federal budget surplus President Bush inherited came entirely from Social Security surpluses resulting from the 1984 payroll tax increase. Bush gave away revenues meant to provide for workers' retirement as tax cuts for the wealthiest 10% of the population.

We should rescind Bush's tax cuts and use the Social Security surpluses to really prepare for the baby boom retirement. Public investment or targeted tax breaks could be used to encourage the building of the hospitals, nursing homes, and hospices that aging baby boomers will need. Such investment in public and private infrastructure would also stimulate the real economy and increase GDP growth. Surpluses could be used to fund the training of doctors, nurses and others to staff these facilities, and of other high skilled workers more generally. The higher wages of skilled labor will help generate the payroll tax revenues needed to fund future benefits. If baby boomers help to fund this infrastructure expansion through their payroll taxes while they are still working, less output will need to be allocated when they retire. These expenditures will increase the productivity of the real economy, which will help keep the financial sector solvent to provide for retirees. Destroying Social Security in order to "save" it is not a solution.

Sources: Dean Baker and Mark Weisbrot, *Social Security: The Phony Crises*, University of Chicago Press, 1999; William Wolman and Anne Colamosca, *The Great 401(k) Hoax*, Perseus Publishing, 2002; Sylvester J. Schieber and John B. Shoven, "The Consequences of Population Aging on Private Pension Fund Saving and Asset Markets," National Bureau of Economic Research, Working Paper No. 4665, 1994.

AFRICAN AMERICANS AND SOCIAL SECURITY
Why the privatization advocates are wrong.

WILLIAM E. SPRIGGS
November/December 2004

Proponents of Social Security privatization are trying to claim that the current program is unfair to African Americans and that a privatized program would serve African Americans better. This argument lends support to the privatization agenda while at the same time giving its advocates a compassionate gloss. But the claims about African Americans and Social Security are wrong.

The Old Age Survivors and Disability Insurance Program (OASDI), popularly known as Social Security, was put in place by Franklin Roosevelt to establish a solid bulwark of economic rights for the public—specifically, as he put it, "the right to adequate protection from the economic fears of old age, sickness, accident, and unemployment." Most Americans associate Social Security only with the retirement—or old age—benefit. Yet it was created to do much more, and it does.

As its original name suggests, Social Security is an insurance program that protects workers and their families against the income loss that occurs when a worker retires, becomes disabled, or dies. All workers will eventually either grow too old to compete in the labor market, become disabled, or die. OASDI insures all workers and their families against these universal risks, while spreading the costs and benefits of that insurance protection among the entire workforce. Currently, 70% of Social Security funds go to retirees, 15% to disabled workers, and 15% to survivors.

Social Security is a "pay as you go" system, which means the taxes paid by today's workers are not set aside to pay their own benefits down the road, but rather go to pay the benefits of current Social Security recipients. It's financed using the Federal Insurance Contribution Act (or FICA) payroll tax, paid by all working Americans on earnings of less than about $90,000 a year. While the payroll tax is not progressive, Social Security benefits are—that is, low-wage workers receive a greater percentage of pre-retirement earnings from the program than higher-wage workers.

In the 1980s, recognizing that the baby boom generation would strain this system, Congress passed reforms to raise extra tax revenues above and beyond the current need and set up a trust fund to hold the reserve. Trustees were appointed and charged with keeping Social Security solvent. Today's trustees warn that their projections, which are based on modest assumptions about the long-term growth of the U.S. economy, show the system could face a shortfall around 2042, when either benefits would have to be cut or the FICA tax raised.

Those who oppose the social nature of the program have pounced on its projected shortfall in revenues to argue that the program cannot—or ought not—be fixed, but should instead be fundamentally changed (see "Privatization Advocates.") Privatization proponents are seeking to frame the issue as a matter of social justice, as if Social Security "reform" would primarily benefit low-income workers, blue-collar workers, people of color, and women. Prompted by disparities in life expectancy between whites and African Americans and the racial wealth gap, a growing chorus within the privatization movement is claiming that privatizing Social Security would be beneficial to African Americans.

Opponents attack the program on the basis of an analogy to private retirement accounts. Early generations of Social Security beneficiaries received much more in benefits than they had paid into the system in taxes. Privatization proponents argue those early recipients received a "higher rate of return" on their "investment" while current and future generations are being "robbed" because they will see "lower rates of return." They argue the current system of social insurance—particularly the retirement program—should be privatized, switching from the current "pay-as-you-go" system to one in which individual workers claim their own contribution and decide where and how to invest it.

But this logic inverts the premise of social insurance. Rather than sharing risk across the entire workforce to ensure that all workers and their families are protected from the three inevitabilities of old age, disability, and death, privatizing Social Security retirement benefits would enable high-wage workers to reap gains from private retirement investment without having to help protect lower-wage workers from their (disproportionate) risks of disability and death. High-wage workers, who are more likely to live long enough to retire, could in fact do better on average if they

Privatization Advocates

Powerful advocates for privatization include libertarian and conservative think tanks and advocacy groups such as the Cato Institute, the Heritage Foundation, Americans for Tax Reform, and Citizens for a Sound Economy, all driven by an ideological commitment to the abolition of federal social programs.

Wall Street too is thirsty for the $1.4 trillion that privatization would funnel into equities if the taxes collected to support the Social Security system were invested privately rather than reinvested in federal government bonds. That's not to mention the windfall of fees privatization would deliver for banks, brokerage houses, and investment firms.

Just after he took office, President Bush appointed a commission to examine privatizing the Social Security system. The commission could not figure out how to maintain payments to current recipients while diverting tax dollars to the savings of current workers, nor could it resolve how to cover the benefits of the disabled or resolve issues surrounding survivors' benefits. Although the president did not succeed in carrying out Social Security privatization in his first term, he has made the partial privatization of Social Security retirement accounts the top priority of his second-term domestic agenda.

opt out of the general risk pool and devote all their money to retirement without having to cover the risk of those who may become disabled or die, although they would of course be subjecting their retirement dollars to greater risk. But low-wage workers, who are far more likely to need disability or survivors' benefits to help their families and are less likely to live long enough to retire, would then be left with lower disability and survivors' benefits, and possibly no guaranteed benefits. This is what the Social Security privatization movement envisions. But you wouldn't know it from reading their literature.

And when the myths about Social Security's financial straits meet another American myth—race—even more confusion follows. Here is a look at three misleading claims by privatization proponents about African Americans and Social Security.

Myth #1

Several conservative research groups argue that Social Security is a bad deal for African Americans because of their lower life expectancies. "Lifetime Social Security benefits depend, in large part, on longevity," writes the Cato Institute's Michael Tanner in his briefing paper "Disparate Impact: Social Security and African Americans." "At every age, African-American men and women both have shorter life expectancies than do their white counterparts. ... As a result, a black man or woman earning exactly the same lifetime wages, and paying exactly the same lifetime Social Security taxes, as his or her white counterpart will likely receive a far lower rate of return." Or as the Americans for Tax Reform web site puts it: "A black male born today has a life expectancy of 64.8 years. But the Social Security retirement age for that worker in the future will be 67 years. That means probably the majority of black males will never even receive Social Security retirement benefits."

The longevity myth is the foundation of all the race-based arguments for Social Security privatization. There are several problems with it.

First, the shorter life expectancy of African Americans compared to whites is the result of higher morbidity in mid-life, and is most acute for African-American men. The life expectancies of African-American women and white men are virtually equal. So the life expectancy argument can really only be made about African-American men.

Second, the claim that OASDI is unfair to African Americans because their expected benefits are less than their expected payments is usually raised and then answered from the perspective of the retirement (or "old age") benefit alone. That is an inaccurate way to look at the problem. Because OASDI also serves families of workers who become disabled or die, a correct measure would take into account the probability of all three risk factors—old age, disability, and death. Both survivor benefits and disability benefits, in fact, go disproportionately to African Americans.

While African Americans make up 12% of the U.S. population, 23% of children receiving Social Security survivor benefits are African American, as are about 17% of disability beneficiaries. On average, a worker who receives disability benefits or a family that receives survivor benefits gets far more in return than the worker paid in FICA taxes, notwithstanding privatizers' attempts to argue that Social Security is a bad deal.

Survivors' benefits also provide an important boost to poor families more generally. A recent study by the National Urban League Institute for Opportunity and Equality showed that the benefit lifted 1 million children out of poverty and helped another 1 million avoid extreme poverty (living below half the poverty line).

Finally, among workers who do live long enough to get the retirement benefit, life expectancies don't differ much by racial group. For example, at age 65, the life expectancies of African-American and white men are virtually the same.

President Bush's Social Security commission proposed the partial privatization of Social Security retirement accounts, but cautioned that it could not figure out how to maintain equal benefits for the other risk pools. The commission suggested that disability and survivor's benefits would have to be reduced if the privatization plan proceeds.

This vision is of a retirement program designed for the benefit of the worker who retires—only. A program with that focus would work against, not for, African Americans because of the higher morbidity rates in middle age and the smaller share of African Americans who live to retirement.

Myth #2

African Americans have less education, and so are in the work force longer than whites, and yet Social Security only credits 35 years of work experience in figuring benefits. Tanner says, "benefits are calculated on the basis of the highest 35 years of earnings over a worker's lifetime. Workers must still pay Social Security taxes during years outside those 35, but those taxes do not count toward or earn additional benefits. Generally, those low-earnings years occur early in an individual's life. That is particularly important to African Americans because they are likely to enter the workforce at an earlier age than whites...."

This claim misinterprets the benefit formula for Social Security. Yes, African Americans on average are slightly less educated than whites. The gap is mostly because of a higher college completion rate for white men compared to African-American men. But the education argument fails to acknowledge that white teenagers have a significantly higher labor force participation rate (at 46%) than do African-American teens (29%). The higher labor force participation of white teenagers helps to explain why young white adults do better in the labor market than young African-American adults. (The racial gaps in unemployment are considerably greater for teenagers and young adults than for those over 25.)

These differences in early labor market experiences mean that African-American men have more years of zero earnings than do whites. So while the statement about education is true, the inference from education differences to work histories is false. By taking only 35 years of work history into account in the benefit formula, the Social Security formula is progressive. It in effect ignores years of zero or very low earnings. This levels the playing field among long-time workers, putting African Americans with more years of zero earnings on par with whites. By contrast, a private system based on total years of earnings would exacerbate racial labor market disparities.

Myth #3

A third claim put forward by critics of Social Security is that African-American re-tirees are more dependent on Social Security than whites. Tanner writes: "Elderly African Americans are much more likely than their white counterparts to be dependent on Social Security benefits for most or all of their retirement income." Therefore, he concludes, "African Americans would be among those with the most to gain from the privatization of Social Security—transforming the program into a system of individually owned, privately invested accounts." Law professor and senior policy advisor to Americans for Tax Reform Peter Ferrara adds, "the personal accounts would produce far higher returns and benefits for lower-income workers, African Americans, Hispanics, women and other minorities."

It's true that African-American retirees are more likely than whites to rely on Social Security as their only income in old age. It's the sole source of retirement income for 40% of elderly African Americans. This is a result of discrimination in the labor market that limits the share of African Americans with jobs that offer pension benefits. Privatizing Social Security would not change labor market discrimination or its effects.

Privatizing Social Security would, however, exacerbate the earnings differences between African Americans and whites, since benefits would be based solely on individual savings. What would help African-American retirees is not privatization, but rather changing the redistributive aspects of Social Security to make it even more progressive.

The current formula for Social Security benefits is progressive in two ways: low earners get a higher share of their earnings than do higher wage earners and the lowest years of earning are ignored. Changes in the formula to raise the benefits floor enough to lift all retired Social Security recipients out of poverty would make it still more progressive. Increasing and updating the Supplemental Security Income payment, which helps low earners, could accomplish the same goal for SSI recipients. (SSI is a program administered by Social Security for very low earners and the poor who are disabled, blind, or at least 65 years old.)

The proponents of privatization argue that the heavy reliance of African-American seniors on Social Security requires higher rates of return—returns that are only possible by putting money into the stock market. Yet given the lack of access to private pensions for African-American seniors and their low savings from lifetimes of low earnings, such a notion is perverse. It would have African Americans gamble with their only leg of retirement's supposed three-legged stool—pension, savings, and Social Security. And, given the much higher risk that African Americans face of both death before retirement and of disability, it would be a risky gamble indeed to lower those benefits while jeopardizing their only retirement leg.

Privatizing the retirement program, and separating the integrated elements of Social Security, would split America. The divisions would be many: between those more likely to be disabled and those who are not; between those more likely to die before retirement and those more likely to retire; between children who get survivors' benefits and the elderly who get retirement benefits; between those who retire with high-yield investments and those who fare poorly in retirement. The "horizontal equity" of the program (treating similar people in a similar way) would be lost, as volatile stock fluctuations and the timing of retirement could greatly affect individuals' rates of return. The "vertical equity" of the program (its progressive nature, insuring a floor for benefits) would be placed in greater jeopardy with the shift from social to private benefits.

Social Security works because it is "social." It is America's only universal federal program. The proposed changes would place Social Security in the same political space as the rest of America's federal programs—and African Americans have seen time and again how those politics work.

THE SOCIAL SECURITY ADMINISTRATION'S CRACKED CRYSTAL BALL

JOHN MILLER
November/December 2004

2042. That's the year the Social Security Trust Fund will run out of money, according to the Social Security Administration (SSA). But its doomsday prophesy is based on overly pessimistic assumptions about our economic future: The SSA expects the U.S. economy to expand at an average annual rate of just 1.8% from 2015 to 2080—far slower than the 3.0% average growth rate the economy posted over the last 75 years.

What's behind the gloomy growth projections? Is there anything to them—or has the SSA's economic crystal ball malfunctioned?

Flawed Forecast

The Social Security Administration foresees a future of sluggish economic growth in which labor productivity, or output per worker, improves slowly; total employment barely grows; and workers put in no additional hours on the job. (It reasons that economic growth, or growth of national output, must equal the sum of labor productivity increases, increases in total employment, and increases in the average hours worked.)

In its widely cited "intermediate" 1.8% growth scenario, labor productivity improves by just 1.6% a year and workforce growth slows almost to a standstill at 0.2% a year—rates well below their historical averages. (See Table 1.) Under these assumptions, and if average work time holds steady, Social Security exhausts its trust fund in the year 2042, at which point it faces an initial shortfall of 27% of its obligations. After that, Social Security would be able to pay out just 70% of the benefits it owes to retirees.

TABLE 1
SOCIAL SECURITY ADMINISTRATION'S PRINCIPAL
ECONOMIC ASSUMPTIONS[a]
Annual Percentage Increase

Year	Real Gross Domestic Product[b]	Productivity (Total U.S. Economy)	Total Employment[c]	Average Hours Worked
2004	4.4%	2.7%	1.7%	0.0%
2005	3.6%	1.8%	1.7%	0.0%
2006	3.2%	1.9%	1.3%	0.0%
2007	3.0%	1.9%	1.1%	0.0%
2008	1.0%	1.8%	2.8%	0.0%
2009	2.7%	1.8%	0.9%	0.0%
2010	2.6%	1.7%	0.8%	0.0%
2011	2.4%	1.7%	0.8%	0.0%
2012	2.3%	1.6%	0.6%	0.0%
2013	2.2%	1.6%	0.6%	0.0%
Average Annual Percentage Increase				
2010 to 2015	2.2%	1.6%	0.6%	0.0%
2015 to 2080	1.8%	1.6%	0.2%	0.0%

[a] These are the "intermediate economic assumptions" that the Social Security Administration regards as most plausible. The SSA also reports a "low cost" forecast that projects a 2.6% real growth rate from 2015 to 2080 and a "high cost" forecast that projects a 1.1% real growth rate from 2015 to 2080.

[b] Real Gross Domestic Product is calculated in constant 1996 dollars.

[c] Total employment is the total of civilian and military employment in the U.S. economy.

Source: Social Security Administration, 2004 *Annual Report of the Board of Trustees* (March 23, 2004), Table V.B.1 and Table V.B.2, pp. 89 and 94.

The problem is not with the logic of the method the Social Security Administration uses to make its projections, but rather with its demographic and economic assumptions. Its forecast of 1.6% annual labor productivity growth is especially suspect. When the nonpartisan Congressional Budget Office (CBO) assessed the financial health of Social Security earlier this year, it assumed that productivity would improve at a rate of 1.9% per year. In the CBO forecast, faster productivity growth, along with a lower unemployment rate, boosts wages—the tax base of the system—allowing Social Security to remain solvent until 2052, 10 years longer than the SSA had projected just a few months earlier.

One doesn't have to buy into the hype about the magic of the new economy to conclude that the CBO came closer to getting the projected productivity growth rates right than the SSA did. The federal government's own Bureau of Labor Statistics estimates that productivity rates in the nonfarm sector improved at a 2.3% average pace from 1947 through 2003. Adjusting for the gap of 0.2 percentage points between the productivity growth of the nonfarm business sector and the economy as a whole still leaves productivity across the economy growing by a healthy 2.1% over the postwar period. That historical record convinces economist Dean Baker, from the Washington-based Center for Economic and Policy Research, that a productivity growth rate of 2.0% a year is a "very reasonable" assumption.

The drastic deceleration of employment growth, from its historic (1960 to 2000)

average of 1.78% to 0.2% per year, is also overstated. As the trustees see it, employment will grow far more slowly as the baby-boomers leave the labor force. That is
true as far as it goes. But if their projections are correct, the country will soon face a
chronic labor shortage. And in that context, the immigration rate is unlikely to slow,
as they assume, to 900,000 a year. Rather, future immigration rates would likely
be at least as high as they were in the 1990s, when 1.3 million people entered the
United States annually, and possibly even higher if immigration laws are relaxed in
response to a labor shortage. Faster immigration would boost employment growth
and add workers, who would pay into Social Security, helping to relieve the financial
strain on the system created by the retirement of the baby-boom generation.

In its own optimistic or "low cost" scenario, the SSA erases the shortfall in the
trust fund by assuming a faster productivity growth rate (of 1.9%), a lower unemployment rate (of 4.5% per year), and higher net immigration (of 1.3 million people
per year). The still rather sluggish 2.6% average growth rate that results would wipe
out the rest of the imbalance in the system and leave a sizeable surplus in the trust
fund—0.15% of GDP over the next 75 years.

Making Short Work of the Shortfall

Even in the unlikely event that the pessimistic predictions the SSA has conjured up
actually do come to pass, the Social Security imbalance could be easily remedied.

The Social Security Trust Fund needs $3.7 trillion to meet its unfunded obliga-
tions over the next 75 years. That is a lot of money—about 1.89% of taxable payroll
and about 0.7% of GDP over that period. But it's far less than the 2.0% of GDP the
2001 to 2003 tax cuts will cost over the next 75 years if they are made permanent.
(Many of the tax cuts are currently scheduled to sunset in 2010.) The portion of the
Bush tax cuts going to the richest 1% of taxpayers alone will cost 0.6% of GDP—
more than the CBO projected shortfall of 0.4% of GDP.

Here are a few ways to make short work of any remaining shortfall without cutting retirement benefits or raising taxes for low- or middle-income workers. First,
newly hired state and local government workers could be brought into the system.
(About 3.5 million state and local government workers are not now covered by Social
Security.) That move alone would eliminate about 30% of the projected deficit.

In addition, we could raise the cap on wages subject to payroll taxes. Under current law, Social Security is funded by a payroll tax on the first $87,900 of a person's
income. As a result of this cap on covered income, the tax applies to just 84.5% of
all wages today—but historically it applied to 90%. Increasing the cap for the next
decade so that the payroll tax covers 87.3% of all wages, or halfway back to the 90%
standard, would eliminate nearly one-third of the SSA's projected deficit.

Finally, stopping the repeal of the estate tax, a tax giveaway that benefits only the
richest taxpayers, would go a long way toward closing the gap. Economists Peter Dia-
mond and Peter Orszag, writing for The Century Fund, advocate dedicating the revenues generated by renewing the estate tax to the Social Security Trust Fund. They
suggest an estate tax set at its planned 2009 level, which would exempt $3.5 million
of an individual's estate. The tax would fall exclusively on the wealthiest 0.3% of taxpayers. That alone would close another one-quarter of the SSA's projected shortfall.

Returning the estate tax to its 2001 (pre-tax cut) level (with a $675,000 exemption for individuals) would do yet more to relieve any financial strain on Social Security.

Any way you look at it, Social Security can remain on sound financial footing even in the dreariest of economic futures, so long as alarmist reports like those of its trustees don't become an excuse to corrupt the system.

Sources: Congressional Budget Office, *The Outlook for Social Security* (June 2004); Social Security Administration, *2004 Annual Report of the Board of Trustees* (March 23, 2004); "What the Trustees' Report Indicates About the Financial Status of Social Security," Robert Greenstein, Center on Budget and Policy Priorities (March 31, 2004); "The Implications of the Social Security Projections Issued By the Congressional Budget Office" Robert Greenstein, Peter Orszag, and Richard Kogan, Center on Budget and Policy Priorities (June 24, 2004); "Letter to Rudolph G. Penner" from Dean Baker, co-director of the Center For Economic and Policy Research (January 26, 2004); *Countdown to Reform: The Great Social Security Debate*, Henry Aaron and Robert Reischauer, The Century Foundation Press, 1998.

Chapter 5

PRIVATE SAVING, DEBT, AND ECONOMIC SECURITY

THE GREAT STOCK ILLUSION

ELLEN FRANK
November/December 2002

During the 1980s and 1990s, the Dow Jones and Standard & Poor's indices of stock prices soared ten-fold. The NASDAQ index had, by the year 2000, sky-rocketed to 25 times its 1980 level. Before the bubble burst, bullish expectations reached a feverish crescendo. Three separate books—Dow 36,000, Dow 40,000 and Dow 100,000—appeared in 1999 forecasting further boundless growth in stock prices. Bullish Wall Street gurus like Goldman's Abby Cohen and Salomon's Jack Grubman were quoted everywhere, insisting that prices could go nowhere but up.

But as early as 1996, skeptics were warning that it couldn't last. Fed chair Alan Greenspan fretted aloud about "irrational exuberance." Yale finance professor Robert Shiller, in his 2001 book titled Irrational Exuberance, insisted that U.S. equities prices were being driven up by wishful thinking and self-fulfilling market sentiment, nourished by a culture that championed wealth and lionized the wealthy. Dean Baker and Marc Weisbrot of the Washington-based Center for Economic and Policy Research contended in 1999 that the U.S. stock market looked like a classic speculative bubble—as evidence they cited the rapidly diverging relationship between stock prices and corporate earnings and reckoned that, to justify the prices at which stocks were selling, profits would have to grow at rates that were frankly impossible.

In 1999 alone, the market value of U.S. equities swelled by an astounding $4 trillion. During that same year, U.S. output, on which stocks represent a claim, rose by a mere $500 billion. What would have happened if stockholders in 1999 had all tried to sell their stock and convert their $4 trillion into actual goods and services? The answer is that most would have failed. In a scramble to turn $4 trillion of paper gains into $500 billion worth of real goods and services, the paper wealth was bound to dissolve, because it never existed, save as a kind of mass delusion.

The Illusion of Wealth Creation

Throughout the 1990s, each new record set by the Dow or NASDAQ elicited grateful cheers for CEOs who were hailed for "creating wealth." American workers, whose retirement savings were largely invested in stocks, were encouraged to buy more stock—even to bet their Social Security funds in the market—and assured that stocks always paid off "in the long run," that a "buy-and-hold" strategy couldn't lose. Neither the financial media nor America's politicians bothered to warn the public about the gaping disparity between the inflated claims on economic output that stocks represented and the actual production of the economy. But by the end of the decade, insiders saw the writing on the wall. They rushed to the exits, trying to realize stock gains before the contradictions inherent in the market overwhelmed them. Prices tumbled, wiping out trillions in illusory money.

The case of Enron Corp. is the most notorious, but it is unfortunately not unique. When Enron filed for bankruptcy protection in November of 2001 its stock, which had traded as high as $90 per share a year before, plummeted to less than $1. *New York Times* reporter Jeffrey Seglin writes that the elevators in Enron's Houston headquarters sported TV sets tuned to CNBC, constantly tracking the firm's stock price and acclaiming the bull market generally. As Enron stock climbed in the late 1990s, these daily market updates made employees— whose retirement accounts were largely invested in company shares—feel quite wealthy, though most Enron workers were not in fact free to sell these shares. Enron's contributions of company stock to employee retirement accounts didn't vest until workers reached age 50. For years, Enron had hawked its stock to employees, to pension fund managers, and to the world as a surefire investment. Many employees used their own 401(k) funds, over and above the firm's matching contributions, to purchase additional shares. But as the firm disintegrated amid accusations of accounting fraud, plan managers froze employee accounts, so that workers were unable to unload even the stock they owned outright. With employee accounts frozen, Enron executives and board members are estimated to have dumped their own stock and options, netting $1.2 billion cash—almost exactly the amount employees lost from retirement accounts.

Soon after Enron's collapse, telecommunications giant Global Crossing imploded amid accusations of accounting irregularities. Global Crossing's stock, which had traded at nearly $100 per share, became virtually worthless, but not before CEO Gary Winnick exercised his own options and walked away with $734 million. Qwest Communications director Phil Anschutz cashed in $1.6 billion in the two years before the firm stumbled under a crushing debt load; the stock subsequently lost 96% of its value. The three top officers of telecom equipment maker JDS Uniphase collectively raked in $1.1 billion between 1999 and 2001. The stock is now trading at $2 per share. An investigation by the *Wall Street Journal* and Thompson Financial analysts estimates that top telecommunications executives captured a staggering $14.2 billion in stock gains between 1997 and 2001. The industry is now reeling, with 60 firms bankrupt and 500,000 jobs lost. The Journal reports that, as of August 2002, insiders at 38 telecom companies had walked away with gains greater than the current market value of their firms. "All told, it is one of the greatest transfers of wealth from investors—big and small—in American history," reporter

Dennis Berman writes. "Telecom executives ... made hundreds of millions of dollars, while many investors took huge, unprecedented losses."

Executives in the energy and telecom sectors were not the only ones to rake in impressive gains. Michael Eisner of Disney Corp. set an early record for CEO pay in 1998, netting $575 million, most in option sales. Disney stock has since fallen by two-thirds. Lawrence Ellison, CEO of Oracle Corp., made $706 million when he sold 29 million shares of Oracle stock in January 2001. Ellison's sales flooded the market for Oracle shares and contributed, along with reports of declining profits, to the stock's losing two-thirds of its value over the next few months. Between 1999 and 2001, Dennis Kozlowski of Tyco International sold $258 million of Tyco stock back to the company, on top of a salary and other compensation valued near $30 million. Kozlowski defended this windfall with the claim that his leadership had "created $37 billion in shareholder wealth." By the time Kozlowski quit Tyco under indictment for sales tax fraud in 2002, $80 billion of Tyco's shareholder wealth had evaporated.

Analyzing companies whose stock had fallen by at least 75%, Fortune magazine discovered that "executives and directors of the 1035 companies that met our criteria took out, by our estimate, roughly $66 billion."

The Illusion of Retirement Security

During the bull market, hundreds of U.S. corporations were also stuffing employee savings accounts with corporate equity, creating a class of captive and friendly shareholders who were in many cases enjoined from selling the stock. Studies by the Employee Benefit Research Council found that, while federal law restricts holdings of company stock to 10% of assets in regulated, defined-benefit pension plans, 401(k)-type plans hold an average 19% of assets in company stock. This fraction rises to 32% when companies match employee contributions with stock and to 53% where companies have influence over plan investments. Pfizer Corporation, by all accounts the worst offender, ties up 81% of employee 401(k)s in company stock, but Coca-Cola runs a close second with 76% of plan assets in stock. Before the firm went bankrupt, WorldCom employees had 40% of their 401(k)s in the firm's shares. Such stock contributions cost firms virtually nothing in the short run and, since employees usually aren't permitted to sell the stock for years, companies needn't worry about diluting the value of equity held by important shareholders—or by their executive option-holders. Commenting on recent business lobbying efforts to gut legislation that would restrict stock contributions to retirement plans, Marc Machiz, formerly of the Labor Department's retirement division, told the *Wall Street Journal*, "business loves having people in employer stock and lobbied very hard to kill this stuff."

Until recently, most employees were untroubled by these trends. The market after all was setting new records daily. Quarterly 401(k) statements recorded fantastic returns year after year. Financial advisers assured the public that stocks were and always would be good investments. But corporate insiders proved far less willing to bank on illusory stock wealth when securing their own retirements.

Pearl Meyer and Partners, an executive compensation research firm, estimates that corporate executives eschew 401(k) plans for themselves and instead negotiate sizable cash pensions—the average senior executive is covered by a defined-benefit plan promising 60% of salary after 30 years of service. Under pressure from the board, CEO Richard McGinn quit Lucent at age 52 with $12 million in severance and a cash pension paying $870,000 annually. Lucent's employees, on the other hand, receive a 401(k) plan with 17% of its assets invested in Lucent stock. The stock plunged from $77 to $10 after McGinn's departure. Today it trades at around $1.00. Forty-two thousand Lucent workers lost their jobs as the firm sank.

When Louis Gerstner left IBM in 2002, after receiving $14 million in pay and an estimated $400 million in stock options, he negotiated a retirement package that promises "to cover car, office and club membership expenses for 10 years." IBM's employees, in contrast, have been agitating since 1999 over the firm's decision to replace its defined benefit pension with a 401(k)-type pension plan that, employee representatives estimate, will reduce pensions by one-third to one-half and save the firm $200 million annually. Economist Paul Krugman reports in the *New York Times* that Halliburton Corp. eliminated its employee pensions; first, though, the company "took an $8.5 million charge against earnings to reflect the cost of its parting gift" to CEO Dick Cheney. *Business Week*, surveying the impact of 401(k)s on employee retirement security, concludes that "CEOs deftly phased out rich defined-benefit plans and moved workers into you're-on-your-own 401(k)s, shredding a major safety net even as they locked in lifetime benefits for themselves."

Since 401(k)s were introduced in the early 1980s their use has grown explosively, and they have largely supplanted traditional defined-benefit pensions. In 2002, three of every four dollars contributed to retirement accounts went into 401(k)s. It is thanks to 401(k)s and other retirement savings plans that middle-income Americans became stock-owners in the 1980s and 1990s. It is probably also thanks to 401(k)s, and the huge demand for stocks they generated, that stock prices rose continuously in the 1990s. And it will almost certainly be thanks to 401(k)s that the problems inherent in using the stock market as a vehicle to distribute income will become glaringly apparent once the baby-boom generation begins to retire and liquidate its stock.

If stocks begin again to rise at historical averages—something financial advisors routinely project and prospective retirees are counting on—the discrepancy between what the stock market promises and what the economy delivers will widen dramatically. Something will have to give. Stocks cannot rise faster than the economy grows, not if people are actually to live off the proceeds.

Or rather, stock prices can't rise that fast unless corporate profits—on which stocks represent a legal claim—also surpass GDP gains. But if corporate earnings outpace economic growth, wages will have to stagnate or decline.

Pension economist Douglas Orr believes it is no accident that 401(k)s proliferated in a period of declining earnings and intense economic insecurity for most U.S. wage-earners. From 1980 until the latter half of the 1990s, the position of the typical American employee deteriorated noticeably. Wages fell, unemployment rose, benefits were slashed, stress levels and work hours climbed as U.S. firms "downsized" and "restructured" to cut costs and satiate investor hunger for higher profits. Firms like General Electric cut tens of thousands of jobs and made remaining jobs far less secure in order to generate earnings growth averaging 15% each year. Welch's ruthless union-busting and cost-cutting earned him the nickname "Neutron Jack" among rank-and-file employees. GE's attitude towards its employees was summed up by union negotiator Steve Tormey: "No matter how many records are broken in productivity or profits, it's always 'what have you done for me lately?' The workers are considered lemons and they are squeezed dry." Welch was championed as a hero on Wall Street, his management techniques widely emulated by firms across the nation. During his tenure, GE's stock price soared as the firm slashed employment by nearly 50%.

The Institute for Policy Studies, in a recent study, found that rising stock prices and soaring CEO pay packages are commonly associated with layoffs. CEOs of firms that "announced layoffs of 1000 or more workers in 2000 earned about 80 percent more, on average, than the executives of the 365 firms surveyed by Business Week."

Throughout the 1980s and 1990s, workers whose jobs were disappearing and wages collapsing consoled themselves by watching the paper value of their 401(k)s swell. With labor weak and labor incomes falling, wage and salary earners chose to cast their lot with capital. In betting on the stock market, though, workers are in reality betting that wage incomes will stagnate and trying to offset this by grabbing a slice from the profit pie. This has already proved a losing strategy for most.

Even at the peak of the 1990s bull market, the net wealth—assets minus debts—of the typical household fell from $55,000 to $50,000, as families borrowed heavily to protect their living standards in the face of stagnant wages. Until or unless the nation's capital stock is equitably distributed, there will always be a clash of interests between owners of capital and their employees. If stocks and profits are routinely besting the economy, then either wage-earners are lagging behind or somebody is cooking the books.

Yet surveys show that Americans like 401(k)s. In part, this is because savings accounts are portable, an important consideration in a world where workers can expect to change jobs several times over their working lives. But partly it is because savings plans provide the illusion of self-sufficiency and independence. When retirees spend down their savings, it feels as if they are "paying their own way." They do not feel like dependents, consuming the fruits of other people's labor. Yet they are. It is the nature of retirement that retirees opt out of production and rely on the young to keep the economy rolling. Pensions are always a claim on the real economy—they represent a transfer of goods and services from working adults to non-working retirees, who no longer contribute to economic output. The shift from defined-benefit pensions to 401(k)s and other savings plans in no way changes the fact that pensions transfer resources, but it does change the rules that will govern how those transfers take place—who pays and who benefits.

Private defined-benefit pensions impose a direct claim on corporate profits. In promising a fixed payment over a number of years, corporations commit to transfer a portion of future earnings to retirees. Under these plans, employers promise an annual lifetime benefit at retirement, the amount determined by an employee's prior earnings and years of service in the company. How the benefit will be paid, where the funds will come from, whether there are enough funds to last through a worker's life—this is the company's concern. Longevity risk—the risk that a worker will outlive the money put aside for her retirement—falls on the employer. Retirees benefit, but at a cost to shareholders. Similarly, public pension programs, whether through Social Security or through the civil service, entail a promise to retirees at the expense of the taxpaying public.

Today, the vast majority of workers, if they have pension coverage at all, participate in "defined-contribution" plans, in which they and their employer contribute a fixed monthly sum and invest the proceeds with a money management firm. At retirement, the employee owns whatever funds have accrued in the account and must make the money last until she dies. Defined-contribution plans are a claim on nothing. Workers are given a shot at capturing some of the cash floating around Wall Street, but no promise that they will succeed. 401(k)s will add a huge element of chance to the American retirement experience. Some will sell high, some will not. Some will realize gains. Some will not.

Pearl Meyer and Partners estimate that outstanding, unexercised executive stock options and employee stock incentives today amount to some $2 trillion. Any effort to cash in this amount, in addition to the stock held in retirement accounts, would have a dramatic impact on stock prices. American workers and retirees, in assessing their chances for coming out ahead in the competition to liquidate stock, might ponder this question: If, as employees in private negotiations with their corporate employers, they have been unable to protect their incomes or jobs or health or retirement benefits, how likely is it that they will instead be able to wrest gains from Wall Street where corporate insiders are firmly in control of information and access to deals?

ILL AND INSOLVENT

Illness and medical bills trigger half of all personal bankruptcies, and private insurance offers little protection.

KAYTY HIMMELSTEIN
July/August 2005

This spring, Congress voted overwhelmingly to pass the Bankruptcy Abuse Prevention and Consumer Protection Act, which makes it harder for people to declare bankruptcy. President Bush hurriedly added his signature on April 20, saying, "America is a nation of personal responsibility where people are expected to meet their obligations." The law, a gift to the banking and credit card industries, imposes new restrictions on bankruptcy filing, including rigid rules for setting repayment schedules, mandatory credit counseling, and a predetermined formula (dubbed a "means test") that takes away judges' discretion in determining whether a person may file for bankruptcy at all.

The means test provision has alarmed legal scholars because it does not allow judges to take individual circumstances into consideration. As Harvard Law School Professor Elizabeth Warren testified to the Senate Judiciary Committee, "The means test as written … treats all families alike. … If Congress is determined to sort the good from the bad, then begin by sorting those who have been laid low by medical debts, those who lost their jobs, those whose breadwinners have been called to active duty and sent to Iraq, those who are caring for elderly parents and sick children from those few who overspend on frivolous purchases."

The new rule is especially worrisome in light of a recent study that found health care costs contributed to about half of America's 1.5 million bankruptcy filings in 2001. The study was coauthored by Elizabeth Warren, David Himmelstein, Deborah Thorne, and Steffie Woolhandler, and published in February 2005 on the website of the journal *Health Affairs*. The authors surveyed 1,771 people who filed for personal bankruptcy, conducting interviews with 931 of them. Nearly half (46.2%) of those surveyed met the authors' criteria for "major medical bankruptcy," and more than half (54.5%) met their broader criteria for "any medical bankruptcy" (see figure). Assuming the data are representative, 1.9 to 2.2 million Americans (filers and dependents) experienced some type of medical bankruptcy in 2001.

These are not by and large the uninsured. Three-fourths of medical debtors interviewed had health insurance at the onset of the illness. Many, however, faced lapses in coverage. One-third of those who had private insurance at first lost their coverage during the course of the illness. These gaps in coverage, tied primarily to unaffordable premiums and loss of employment, left debtors with enormous out-of-pocket expenses. Patients who lost private insurance racked up medical costs averaging $18,005 from hospital bills, prescription medicines, and doctor visits. Some who kept their insurance sank into debt nonetheless thanks to copayments and deductibles. In sum, private health insurance offers surprisingly little protection from bankruptcy, given involuntary interruptions in coverage and privately borne costs.

Illness triggered financial problems both directly, through medical costs, and indirectly, through lost income. Three-fifths (59.9%) of families bankrupted by medical problems said that bills from medical-care providers contributed to bankruptcy; 47.6% cited drug costs. Thirty-five percent had to curtail employment because of an illness, often to care for someone else. In the interviews, filers described the compounding effects of direct medical costs and indirect employment-related costs—for example, when an illness caused a job loss, which led to the loss of employment-based health coverage, or when parents of chronically ill children had to take time off from work, only to find that the simultaneous costs of the child's medical care and the loss of their income proved catastrophic.

The congressional debate over the bankruptcy bill focused on debtors who cheat the bankruptcy system and pass costs on to more responsible consumers, but the *Health Affairs* study paints a different picture. It shows that about half of those who file for bankruptcy do so because they or their family members have fallen ill or become injured in the context of a shredded health safety net. The new bankruptcy law wrongly treats all debtors as careless spendthrifts. It will make it far more difficult for hundreds of thousands forced by circumstance into overwhelming medical debt to regain their financial footing.

AMERICA'S GROWING FRINGE ECONOMY

HOWARD KARGER
November/December 2006

Financial services for the poor and credit-challenged are big business.

Ron Cook is a department manager at a Wal-Mart store in Atlanta. Maria Guzman is an undocumented worker from Mexico; she lives in Houston with her three children and cleans office buildings at night. Marty Lawson works for a large Minneapolis corporation.* What do these three people have in common? They are all regular fringe economy customers.

The term "fringe economy" refers to a range of businesses that engage in financially predatory relationships with low-income or heavily indebted consumers by charging excessive interest rates, superhigh fees, or exorbitant prices for goods or services. Some examples of fringe economy businesses include payday lenders, pawnshops, check-cashers, tax refund lenders, rent-to-own stores, and "buy-here/pay-here" used car lots. The fringe economy also includes credit card companies that charge excessive late payment or over-the-credit-limit penalties; cell phone providers that force less creditworthy customers into expensive prepaid plans; and subprime mortgage lenders that gouge prospective homeowners.

The fringe economy is hardly new. Pawnshops and informal high-interest lenders have been around forever. What we see today, however, is a fringe-economy sector that is growing fast, taking advantage of the ever-larger part of the U.S. population whose economic lives are becoming less secure. Moreover, in an important sense the sector is no longer "fringe" at all: more and more, large mainstream financial corporations are behind the high-rate loans that anxious customers in run-down storefronts sign for on the dotted line.

The Payday Lending Trap

Ron and Deanna Cook have two children and a combined family income of $48,000—more than twice the federal poverty line but still $10,000 below Georgia's median income. They are the working poor.

To make ends meet, the Cooks borrow from payday lenders. When Ron and Deanna borrow $300 for 14 days they pay $60 in interest—an annual interest rate of 520%! If they can't pay the full $360, they pay just the $60 interest fee and roll over the loan for another two weeks. The original $300 loan now costs $120 in interest for 30 days. If they roll over the loan for another two-week cycle, they pay $180 in interest on a $300 loan for 45 days. If the payday lender permits only four rollovers, the Cooks sometimes take out a payday loan from another lender to repay the original loan. This costly cycle can be devastating. The Center for Responsible Lending tells the tale of one borrower who entered into 35 back-to-back payday loans over 17 months, paying $1,254 in fees on a $300 loan.

The Cooks take out about ten payday loans a year, which is close to the national average for payday loan customers. Although the industry claims payday loans are intended only for emergencies, a 2003 study of Pima County, Ariz., by the Southwest Center for Economic Integrity found that 67% of borrowers used their loans for general non-emergency bills. The Center for Responsible Lending found that 66% of borrowers initiate five or more loans a year, and 31% take out twelve or more loans yearly. Over 90% of payday loans go to borrowers with five or more loans a year. Customers who take out 13 or more loans a year account for over half of payday lenders' total revenues.

The Unbanked

Maria Guzman and her family are part of the 10% of U.S. households—more than 12 million—that have no relationship with a bank, savings institution, credit union, or other mainstream financial service provider. Being "unbanked," the Guzmans turn to the fringe economy for check cashing, bill payment, short-term pawn or payday loans, furniture and appliance rentals, and a host of other financial services. In each case, they face high user fees and exorbitant interest rates.

Without credit, the Guzmans must buy a car either for cash or through a "buy-here/pay-here" (BHPH) used car lot. At a BHPH lot they are saddled with a 28% annual percentage rate (APR) on a high-mileage and grossly overpriced vehicle. They also pay weekly, and one missed payment means a repossession. Since the Guzmans have no checking account, they use a check-casher who charges 2.7% for cashing their monthly $1,500 in payroll checks, which costs them $40.50 a month or $486 a year.

Like many immigrants, the Guzmans send money to relatives in their home country. (Money transfers from the United States to Latin America are expected to reach $25 billion by 2010.) If they sent $500 to Mexico on June 26, 2006, using Western Union's "Money in Minutes," they would have paid a $32 transfer fee. Moreover, Western Union's exchange rate for the transaction was 11.12 pesos for the U.S. dollar, while the official exchange rate that day was 11.44. The difference on $500 was almost $14, which raised the real costs of the transaction to $46, or almost 10% of the transfer amount.

Without a checking account, the Guzmans turn to money orders or direct bill pay, both of which add to their financial expenses. For example, ACE Cash Express charges 79 cents per money order and $1 or more for each direct bill payment. If the Guzmans use money orders to pay six bills a month, the fees total nearly $57 a year; using direct bill pay, they would pay a minimum of $72 in fees per year.

All told, the Guzmans spend more than 10% of their income on alternative financial services, which is average for unbanked households. To paraphrase James Baldwin, it is expensive to be poor and unbanked in America.

The Cooks and the Guzmans, along with people like Marty Lawson caught in a cycle of credit card debt (see sidebar on next page), may not fully appreciate the economic entity they are dealing with. Far from a mom-and-pop industry, America's fringe economy is largely dominated by a handful of large, well-financed multinational corporations with strong ties to mainstream financial institutions. It is a comprehensive and fully formed parallel economy that addresses the financial needs of the poor and credit-challenged in the same way as the mainstream economy meets the needs of the middle class. The main difference is the exorbitant interest rates, high fees, and onerous loan terms that mark fringe economy transactions.

The Scope of the Fringe Economy

The unassuming and often shoddy storefronts of the fringe economy mask the true scope of this economic sector. Check-cashers, payday lenders, pawnshops, and rent-to-own stores alone engaged in at least 280 million transactions in 2001, according to Fannie Mae Foundation estimates, generating about $78 billion in gross revenues. By comparison, in 2003 combined state and federal spending on the core U.S. social welfare programs—Temporary Aid to Needy Families (AFDC's replacement), Supplemental Security Income, Food Stamps, the Women, Infants and Children (WIC) food program, school lunch programs, and the U.S. Department of Housing and Urban Development's (HUD) low-income housing programs—totaled less than $125 billion. Revenues in the combined sectors of the fringe economy—including subprime home mortgages and refinancing, and used car sales—would in-

Credit Cards, College Students, and the Fringe Economy

Marty Lawson is one of the growing legions of the credit poor. Although he earns $65,000 a year, his $50,000 credit card debt means that he can buy little more than the essentials. This cycle of debt began when Marty received his first credit card in college.

Credit cards are the norm for today's college students. A 2005 Nellie Mae report found that 55% of college students get their first credit card during their freshman year; by senior year, 91% have a credit card and 56% carry four or more cards.

College students are highly prized credit card customers because of their high future earnings and lifetime credit potential. To ensnare them, credit card companies actively solicit on campus through young recruiters who staff tables outside university bookstores and student centers. Students are baited with free t-shirts, frisbees, candy, music downloads, and other come-ons. Credit card solicitations are stuffed into new textbooks and sent to dormitories, electronic mailboxes, and bulletin boards. According to Junior Achievement, the typical college freshman gets about eight credit card offers in the first week of the fall semester. The aggressiveness of credit card recruiters has led several hundred colleges to ban them from campus.

Excited by his newfound financial independence, Marty overlooked the fine print explaining that cash advances carried a 20% or more APR. He also didn't realize how easily he could reach the credit limit, and the stiff penalties incurred for late payments and over-the-credit-limit transactions. About one-third of credit card company profits come from these and other penalties.

Marty applied for a second credit card after maxing out his first one. The credit line on his second card was exhausted in only eight months. Facing $4,000 in high-interest credit card bills, Marty left college to pay off his debts. He never returned. Dropping out to repay credit card debt is all too common, and according to former Indiana University administrator John Simpson, "We lose more students to credit card debt than academic failure." Not coincidentally, by graduation the average credit card debt for college seniors is almost $3,000. Credit card debt worsens the longer a student stays in school. A 2004 Nellie Mae survey found the average credit card debt for graduate students was a whopping $7,831, a 59% increase over 1998. Fifteen percent of graduate students carry credit card balances of $15,000 or more.

flate the $78 billion several times over and eclipse federal and state spending on the poor.

There can be no doubt that the scope of the fringe economy is enormous. The Community Financial Services Association of America claims that 15,000 payday lenders extend more than $25 billion in short-term loans to millions of households each year. According to Financial Service Centers of America, 10,000 check-cashing stores process 180 million checks with a face value of $55 billion.

The sheer number of fringe economy storefronts is mind-boggling. For example, ACE Cash Express—only one of many such corporations—has 68 locations within 10 miles of my Houston zip code. Nationwide there are more than 33,000 check-cashing and payday loan stores, just two parts of the fringe economy. That's more than the all the McDonald's and Burger King restaurants and all the Target, J.C. Penney, and Wal-Mart retail stores in the United States combined.

ACE Cash Express is the nation's largest check-casher and exemplifies the growth and profitability of the fringe economy. In 1991 ACE had 181 stores; by 2005 it had 1,371 stores with 2,700 employees in 37 states and the District of Columbia. ACE's revenues totaled $141 million in 2000 and by 2005 rose to $268.6 million. In 2005 ACE:

—cashed 13.3 million checks worth approximately $5.3 billion (check cashing fees totaled $131.6 million);

—served more than 40 million customers (3.4 million a month or 11,000 an hour) and processed $10.3 billion in transactions;

—processed over 2 million loan transactions (worth $640 million) and generated interest income and fees of $91.8 million;

—added a total of 142 new locations (in 2006 the company anticipates adding 150 more);

—processed over $410 million in money transfers and 7.6 million money orders with a face value of $1.3 billion;

—processed over 7.8 million bill payment and debit card transactions, and sold approximately 172,000 prepaid debit cards.

Advance America is the nation's leading payday lender, with 2,640 stores in 36 states, more than 5,500 employees, and $630 million this year in revenues. Dollar Financial Corporation operates 1,106 stores in 17 states, Canada, and the United Kingdom. Their 2005 revenues were $321 million. Check-into-Cash has more than 700 stores; Check N' Go has 900 locations in 29 states. Almost all of these are publicly traded NASDAQ corporations.

There were 4,500 pawnshops in the United States in 1985; now there are almost 12,000, including outlets owned by five publicly traded chains. In 2005 the three big chains—Cash America International (a.k.a Cash America Pawn and SuperPawn), EZ Pawn, and First Cash—had combined annual revenues of nearly $1 billion. Cash America is the largest pawnshop chain, with 750 locations; the company also makes payday loans through its Cash America Payday Advance, Cashland, and Mr. Payroll stores. In 2005, Cash America's revenues totaled $594.3 million.

The Association of Progressive Rental Organizations claims that the $6.6 billion a year rent-to-own (RTO) industry serves 2.7 million households through 8,300 stores in 50 states. Many RTOs rent everything from furniture, electronics,

A Glossary of the Fringe Economy

- **Payday loans** are small, short-term loans, usually of no more than $1,500, to cover expenses until the borrower's next payday. These loans come with extremely high interests rates, commonly equivalent to 300% APR. The Center for Responsible Lending conservatively estimates that predatory payday lending practices cost American families $3.4 billion annually.
- **Refund anticipation loans (RALs)**, provided by outlets of such firms as H&R Block, Western Union, and Liberty Tax Service, are short-term loans, often with high interest rates or fees, secured by an expected tax refund. Interest rates can reach over 700% APR-equivalent.
- **Check cashing stores** (ACE Cash Express is the biggest chain) provide services for people who don't have checking accounts. These stores are most often located in low-income neighborhoods and cash checks for a fee, which can vary greatly but is typically far higher than commercial banks charge for the same service. Check cashing fees have steadily increased over the past ten years.
- **Money Transfer companies** (outlets of such companies as Western Union, Moneygram, and Xoom) allow people to make direct bill payments and send money either to a person or bank account for a fee, typically 10% of the amount being sent, not including the exchange rate loss for money sent internationally. the total cost can reach up to 25% of the amount sent.
- **Pawnshops** give loans while holding objects of value as collateral. The pawnbroker returns the object when the loan is repaid, usually at a high interest rates. If the borrower doesn't repay the loan within a specified period, the pawnbroker sells the item. For example, the interest charge on a 30-day loan of $10 could be $2.20, equivalent to a 264% APR. Most pawnshops are individually owned but regional chains are now appearing.
- **Rent-to-own (RTO) stores**—two leading chains are Rent-A-Center and Aaron Rents—rent furniture, electronics, and other consumer goods short-term or long-term. The consumer can eventually own the item after paying many times the standard retail price through weekly rental payments with an extremely high interest rate, commonly around 300% APR. If the consumer misses a payment, the item is repossessed.
- **Buy here/pay here (BHPH) car lots** offer car loans on used cars on-site, with interest rates much higher than auto loans issued by commercial banks. Customers are often saddled with high-interest loans for high-mileage, overpriced vehicles. If a customer misses one payment, the car is repossessed. The largest BHPH company is the J.D. Byrider franchise, with 124 dealerships throughout the country.

—Barbara Sternal

major appliances, and computers to jewelry. Rent-A-Center is the largest RTO corporation in the world. In 2005 it employed 15,000 people; owned or operated 3,052 stores in the United States and Canada; and had revenues of $2.4 billion. Other leading RTO chains include Aaron Rents (with 1,255 stores across the United States and Canada and gross revenues of $1.1 billion in 2005) and RentWay (with 788 stores in 34 states and revenues of almost $516 million in 2005).

These corporations represent the tip of the iceberg. Low-income consumers spent $1.75 billion for tax refund loans in 2002. Many lost as much as 16% of their tax refunds because of expensive tax preparation fees and/or interest incurred in tax refund anticipation loans. The interest and fees on such loans can translate into triple-digit annualized interest rates, according to the Consumer Federation of

America, which has also reported that 11 million tax filers received refund anticipation loans in 2000, almost half through H&R Block. According to a Brookings Institution report, the nation's largest tax preparers earned about $357 million from fringe economy "fast cash" products in 2001, more than double their earnings in 1998. All for essentially lending people their own money!

The fringe economy plays a big role in the housing market, where subprime home mortgages rose from 35,000 in 1994 to 332,000 in 2003, a 25% a year growth rate and a tenfold increase in just nine years. (A subprime loan is a loan extended to less creditworthy customers at a rate that is higher than the prime rate.) According to Edward Gramlich, former member of the Board of Governors of the Federal Reserve System, subprime mortgages accounted for almost $300 billion or 9% of all mortgages in 2003.

While the fringe economy squeezes its customers, it is generous to its CEOs. According to Forbes, salaries in many fringe economy corporations rival those in much larger companies. In 2004 Sterling Brinkley, chairman of EZ Corp, earned $1.26 million; ACE's CEO Jay Shipowitz received $2.1 million on top of $2.38 million in stocks; Jeffrey Weiss, Dollar Financial Group's CEO, earned $1.83 million; Mark Speese, Rent-A-Center's CEO, made $820,000 with total stock options of $10 million; and Cash America's CEO Daniel Feehan was paid almost $2.2 million in 2003 plus the $9 million he had in stock options.

Fringe-economy corporations argue that the high interest rates and fees they charge reflect the heightened risks of doing business with an economically unstable population. While fringe businesses have never made their pricing criteria public, some risks are clearly overstated. For example, ACE assesses the risk of each check-cashing transaction and reports losses of less than 1%. Since tax preparers file a borrower's taxes, they are reasonably assured that refund anticipation loans will not exceed refunds. To further guarantee repayment, they often establish an escrow account into which the IRS directly deposits the tax refund check. Pawnshops lend only about 50% of a pawned item's value, which leaves them a large buffer if the pawn goes unclaimed (industry trade groups claim that 70% of customers do redeem their goods). The rent-to-own furniture and appliance industry charges well above the "street price" for furniture and appliances, which is more than enough to offset any losses. Payday lenders require a post-dated check or electronic debit to assure repayment. Payday loan losses are about 6% or less, according to the Center for Responsible Lending.

Much of the profit in the fringe economy comes from financing rather than the sale of a product. For example, if a used car lot buys a vehicle for $3,000 and sells it for $5,000 cash, their profit is $2,000. But if they finance that vehicle for two years at a 25% APR, the profit jumps to $3,242. This dynamic is true for virtually every sector of the fringe economy. A customer who pays off a loan or purchases a good or service outright is much less profitable for fringe economy businesses than customers who maintain an ongoing financial relationship with the business. In that sense, profit in the fringe economy lies with keeping customers continually enmeshed in an expensive web of debt.

Funding and Exporting America's Fringe Economy

Fringe economy corporations require large amounts of capital to fund their phenomenal growth, and mainstream financial institutions have stepped up to the plate. ACE Cash Express has a relationship with a group of banks including Wells Fargo, JP Morgan Chase Bank, and JP Morgan Securities to provide capital for acquisitions and other activities. Advance America has relationships with Morgan Stanley, Banc of America Securities LLC, Wachovia Capital Markets, and Wells Fargo Securities, to name a few. Similar banking relationships exist throughout the fringe economy.

The fringe economy is no longer solely a U.S. phenomenon. In 2003 the HSBC Group purchased Household International (and its subsidiary Beneficial Finance) for $13 billion. Headquartered in London, HSBC is the world's second largest bank and serves more than 90 million customers in 80 countries. Household International is a U.S.-based consumer finance company with 53 million customers and more than 1,300 branches in 45 states. It is also a predatory lender. In 2002, a $484 million settlement was reached between Household and all 50 states and the District of Columbia. In effect, Household acknowledged it had duped tens of thousands of low-income home buyers into loans with unnecessary hidden costs. In 2003, another $100 million settlement was reached based on Household's abusive mortgage lending practices.

HSBC plans to export Household's operations to Poland, China, Mexico, Britain, France, India, and Brazil, for starters. One shudders to think how the fringe economy will develop in nations with even fewer regulatory safeguards than the United States. Presumably, HSBC also believes that predatory lending will not tarnish the reputation of the seven British lords and one baroness who sit on its 20-member board of directors.

What Can be Done?

The fringe economy is one of the few venues that credit-challenged or low-income families can turn to for financial help. This is especially true for those facing a penurious welfare system with a lifetime benefit cap and few mechanisms for emergency assistance. In that sense, enforcing strident usury and banking laws to curb the fringe economy while providing no legal and accessible alternatives would hurt the very people such laws are intended to help by driving these transactions into a criminal underground. Instead of ending up in court, non-paying debtors would wind up in the hospital. Simply outlawing a demand-driven industry is rarely successful.

One strategy to limit the growth of the fringe economy is to develop more community-based lending institutions modeled on the Grameen Bank or on local cooperatives. Although community banks might charge a higher interest rate than commercial banks charge prime rate customers, the rates would still be significantly lower than in the existing fringe sector.

Another policy option is to make work pay, or at least make it pay better. In other words, we need to increase the minimum wage and the salaries of the lower middle class and working poor. One reason for the rapid growth of the fringe economy is the growing gap between low and stagnant wages and higher prices, especially for necessities like housing, health care, pharmaceuticals, and energy.

Stricter usury laws, better enforcement of existing banking regulations, and a more active federal regulatory system to protect low-income consumers can all play a role in taming the fringe economy. Concurrently, federal and state governments can promote the growth of non-predatory community banking institutions. In addition, commercial banks can provide low-income communities with accessible and inexpensive banking services. As the "DrillDown" studies conducted in recent years by the Washington, D.C., non-profit Social Compact suggest, low-income communities contain more income and resources than one might think. If fringe businesses can make billions in low-income neighborhoods, less predatory economic institutions should be able to profit there too. Lastly, low and stagnant wages make it difficult, if not impossible, for the working poor to make ends meet without resorting to debt. A significant increase in wages would likely result in a significant decline in the fringe economy. In the end, several concerted strategies will be required to restrain this growing and out-of-control economic beast.

Sources: "2003 Credit Card Usage Analysis" (2004) and "Undergraduate Students and Credit Cards in 2004" (2005) (Nellie Mae); Alan Berube, Anne Kim, Benjamin Forman, and Megan Burns, "The Price of Paying Taxes: How Tax Preparation and Refund Loan Fees Erode the Benefits of the EITC" (Brookings Institution and Progressive Policy Institute, May 2002); James H. Carr and Jenny Shuetz, "Financial Services in Distressed Communities: Framing the Issue, Finding Solutions," Financial Services in Distressed Communities: Issues and Answers (2001, Fannie Mae Foundation); "Making the Case for Financial Literacy: A Collection of Current Statistics Regarding Youth and Money" (Junior Achievement); Amanda Sapir and Karen Uhlich, "Pay Day Lending in Pima County Arizona" (Southwest Center for Economic Integrity, 2003); Keith Urnst, John Farris, and Uriah King, "Quantifying the Economic Cost of Predatory Payday Lending" (Center for Responsible Lending, 2004).

Organizations working on these issues include U.S. Public Interest Research Group, www.uspirg.org; Association of Community Organizations for Reform Now (ACORN), www.acorn.org; Coalition for Responsible Credit Practices, www.responsible-credit.net; Community Financial Services Association of America, www.cfsa.net; Consumer Federation of America, www.consumerfed.org; Harvard University, Joint Center for Housing Studies, www.jchs.harvard.edu; National Consumer Law Center, www.consumerlaw.org.

THE HOMEOWNERSHIP MYTH

HOWARD KARGER
May/June 2007

Anyone who has given the headlines even a passing glance this winter knows the subprime mortgage industry is in deep trouble. Since 2006 more than 20 subprime lenders have quit the business or gone bankrupt. Many more are in serious trouble, including the nation's number two subprime lender, New Century Financial. The subprime crisis is also hitting Wall Street brokerages that invested in these loans, with reverberations from Tokyo to London. And the worst may be yet to come. At least $300 billion in subprime adjustable-rate mortgages will reset this year to higher interest rates. CNN reports that one in five subprime mortgages issued in 2005-2006 will end up in foreclosure. If these dire predictions come true, it will be the equivalent of a nuclear meltdown in the mortgage and housing industries.

What's conspicuously absent from the news reports is the effect of the subprime lending debacle on poor and working class families who bought into the dream of homeownership, regardless of the price. Sold a false bill of goods, many of these families now face foreclosure and the loss of the small savings they invested in their homes. It's critical to examine the housing crisis not only from the perspective of the banks and the stock market, but also from the perspective of the families whose homes are on the line. It is also critical to uncover the systemic reasons for the recent burst of housing-market insanity that saw thousands upon thousands of families getting signed up for mortgage loans that were highly likely to end in failure and foreclosure.

Like most Americans, I grew up believing that buying a home represents a rite of passage in U.S. society. Americans widely view homeownership as the best choice for everyone, everywhere and at all times. The more people who own their own homes, the common wisdom goes, the more robust the economy, the stronger the community, and the greater the collective and individual benefits. Homeownership is the ticket to the middle class through asset accumulation, stability, and civic participation.

For the most part, this is an accurate picture. Homeowners get a foothold in a housing market with an almost infinite price ceiling. They enjoy important tax benefits. Owning a home is often cheaper than renting. Most important, homeownership builds equity and accrues assets for the next generation, in part by promoting forced savings. These savings are reflected in the data showing that, according to the National Housing Institute's Winton Picoff, the median wealth of low-income homeowners is 12 times higher than that of renters with similar incomes. Plus, owning a home is a status symbol: homeowners are seen as winners compared to renters.

Homeownership may have positive effects on family life. Ohio University's Robert Dietz found that owning a home contributes to household stability, social involvement, environmental awareness, local political participation and activism, good health, low crime, and beneficial community characteristics. Homeowners are better citizens, are healthier both physically and mentally, and have children who achieve more and are better behaved than those of renters.

Johns Hopkins University researchers Joe Harkness and Sandra Newman looked at whether homeownership benefits kids even in distressed neighborhoods. Their study concluded that "[h]omeownership in almost any neighborhood is found to benefit children. ... Children of most low-income renters would be better served by programs that help their families become homeowners in their current neighborhoods instead of helping them move to better neighborhoods while remaining renters." (Harkness and Newman also found, however, that the positive effects of homeownership on children are weaker in unstable low-income neighborhoods. Moreover, the study cannot distinguish whether homeownership leads to positive behaviors or whether owners were already predisposed to these behaviors.)

Faith in the benefits of homeownership—along with low interest rates and a range of governmental incentives—have produced a surge in the number of low-income homeowners. By 2003, 48% of black households owned their own homes, up from 34.5% in 1950. In 1994 Bill Clinton set—and ultimately surpassed—a goal to raise the nation's overall homeownership rate to 67.5% by 2000. There are now 71 million U.S. homeowners, representing close to 68% of all households. Much of this gain has been among low-income families.

Government efforts to increase homeownership for low-income families include both demand-side (e.g., homeowner tax credits, housing cost assistance programs) and supply-side (e.g., developer incentives) strategies. Federal housing programs insure more than a million loans a year to help low-income homebuyers. Fannie Mae and Freddie Mac—the large, federally chartered but privately held corporations that buy mortgages from lenders, guarantee the notes, and then resell them to investors—have increasingly turned their attention to low-income homebuyers as the upper-income housing market becomes more saturated. Banking industry regulations such as the Community Reinvestment Act and the Home Mortgage Disclosure Act encourage homeownership by reducing lending discrimination in underserved markets.

The Housing and Urban Development department (HUD) has adapted some of its programs originally designed to help renters to focus on homeownership. For instance, cities and towns can now use the federal dollars they receive through HOME (the Home Investment Partnerships Act) and Community Development Block Grants to provide housing grants, down payment loans, and closing cost assistance. The American Dream Downpayment Initiative, passed by Congress in 2003, authorized up to $200 million a year for down payment assistance to low-income families. Private foundations have followed suit. The Ford Foundation is currently focusing its housing-related grants on homeownership rather than rental housing; the foundation views homeownership as an important form of asset-building and the best option for low-income people.

While homeownership has undeniable benefits, that doesn't mean it is the best option for everyone. For many low-income families, buying a home imposes burdens that end up outweighing the benefits. It is time to re-assess the policy emphasis on homeownership, which has been driven by an honest belief in the advantages of homeownership, but also by a wide range of business interests who stand to gain when a new cohort of buyers is brought into the housing market.

The Downsides of Homeownership

Low-income families can run into a range of pitfalls when they buy homes. These pitfalls may stem from the kinds of houses they can afford to buy (often in poor condition, with high maintenance costs); the neighborhoods they can afford to buy in (often economically distressed); the financing they can get (often carrying high interest rates, high fees, and risky gimmicks); and the jobs they work at (often unstable). Taken together, these factors can make buying a home a far riskier proposition for low-income families than it is for middle- and upper-income households.

Most low-income families only have the financial resources to buy rundown houses in distressed neighborhoods marked by few jobs, high crime rates, a dearth of services, and poor schools. Few middle-class homebuyers would hitch themselves to 30-year mortgages in these kinds of communities; poor families, too, have an interest in making the home-buying commitment in safe neighborhoods with good schools.

Homeownership is no automatic hedge against rising housing costs. On the contrary: lower-end affordable housing stock is typically old, in need of repair, and expensive to maintain. Low-income families often end up paying inflated prices for homes that are beset with major structural or mechanical problems masked by cosmetic repairs. A University of North Carolina study sponsored by the national nonprofit organization NeighborWorks found that almost half of low-income homebuyers experienced major unexpected costs due to the age and condition of their homes. If you rent, you can call the landlord; but a homeowner can't take herself to court because the roof leaks, the plumbing is bad, or the furnace or hot water heater quits working.

Besides maintenance and repairs, the expenses of homeownership also include property taxes and homeowners insurance, both of which have skyrocketed in cost in the last decade. Between 1997 and 2002 property tax rates rose nationally by more than 19%. Ten states (including giants Texas and California) saw their property tax rates rise by 30% or more during that period. In the suburbs of New York City, property tax rates grew two to three times faster than personal income from 2000 to 2004.

Nationally, the average homeowner's annual insurance premiums rose a whopping 62% from 1995 to 2005—twice as fast as inflation. Low-income homeowners in distressed neighborhoods are hit especially hard by high insurance costs. According to a Conning and Co. study, 92% of large insurance companies run credit checks on potential customers. These credit checks translate into insurance scores that are used to determine whether the carrier will insure an applicant at all, and if so, what they will cover and how much they will charge. Those with poor or no credit are denied coverage, while those with limited credit pay high premiums. Needless to say, many low-income homeowners do not have stellar credit scores. Credit scoring may also partly explain why, according to HUD, "Recent studies have shown that, compared to homeowners in predominantly white-occupied neighborhoods, homeowners in minority neighborhoods are less likely to have private home insurance, more likely to have policies that provide less coverage in case of a loss, and are likely to pay more for similar policies."

With few cash reserves, low-income families are a heartbeat away from financial disaster if their wages decline, property taxes or home insurance rates rise, or expensive repairs are needed. With most—or all—of their savings in their homes, these families have no cushion for emergencies. HUD data show that between 1999 and 2001, the only group whose housing conditions worsened—by HUD's definition, the only group which saw a larger share of households paying over 30% of gross household income for housing in 2001 than in 1999) were low- and moderate-income homeowners. The National Housing Conference reports that 51% of working families with critical housing needs (i.e., those paying more than 50% of gross household income for housing) are owners.

Most people who buy a home imagine they will live there for a long time, benefiting from a secure and stable housing situation. For many low-income families this is not what happens. Nationwide data from 1976 to 1993 reveal that 36% of low-income homeowners gave up or lost their homes within two years and 53% exited within five years, according to a 2005 study by Carolina Katz Reid of the University of Washington. Reid found that very few low-income families ever bought another house after returning to renting. A 2004 HUD research study by Donald Haurin and Stuart Rosenthal reached similar conclusions. Following a national sample of African Americans from youth (ages 14 to 21) in 1979 to middle age in 2000, the researchers found that 63% of the sample owned a home at some point, but only 34% still did in 2000.

Low-income homeowners, often employed in unstable jobs with stagnant incomes, few health care benefits, limited or no sick days, and little vacation time, may find it almost impossible to keep their homes if they experience a temporary job loss or a change in family circumstances, such as the loss of a wage earner. Homeownership can also limit financial opportunities. A 1999 study by economists Richard Green (University of Wisconsin) and Patric Hendershott (Ohio State University) found that states with the highest homeownership rates also had the highest unemployment rates. Their report concluded that homeownership may constrain labor mobility since the high costs of selling a house make unemployed homeowners reluctant to relocate to find work.

Special tax breaks have been a key selling point of homeownership. If mortgage interest and other qualifying expenses come to less than the standard deduction ($10,300 for joint filers in 2006), however, there is zero tax advantage to owning. That is one reason why only 34% of taxpayers itemize their mortgage interest, local property taxes, and other deductions. Even for families who do itemize, the effective tax saving is usually only 10 to 35 cents for every dollar paid in mortgage interest. In other words, the mortgage deduction benefits primarily those in high income brackets who have a need to shelter their income; it means little to low-income homeowners.

Finally, homeownership promises growing wealth as home prices rise. But the homes of low-income, especially minority, homeowners generally do not appreciate as much as middle-class housing. Low-income households typically purchase homes in distressed neighborhoods where significant appreciation is unlikely. Among other reasons, if financially-stressed property owners on the block can't afford to maintain their homes, nearby property values fall. For instance, Reid's longitudinal study surveyed low-income minority homeowners from 1976 to 1994 and found that they realized a 30% increase in the value of their homes after owning for 10 years, while middle- and upper-income white homeowners enjoyed a 60% jump.

"Funny Money" Mortgages And Other Travesties

Buying a home and taking on a mortgage are scary, and people often leave the closing in a stupor, unsure of what they signed or why. My partner and I bought a house a few years ago, and like many buyers, we didn't retain an attorney. The title company had set aside one hour for the closing. During that time more than 125 single-spaced pages (much of it in small print) were put in front of us. More than 60 required our signature or initials. It would have been difficult for us to digest these documents in 24 hours, much less one. When we asked to slow down the process, we were met with impatience. After the closing, Anna asked, "What did we sign?" I was clueless.

Yet buying a home is the largest purchase most families will make in their life-

---

The New World of Home Loans

The new home loan products, widely marketed in recent years but especially to low- and moderate-income families, are generally adjustable-rate mortgages (ARMs) with some kind of twist. Here are a few of these "creative" (read: confusing and risky) mortgage options.

Option ARM: *With this loan, borrowers choose each month which of three or four different—and fluctuating—payments to make:*

- full (principal + interest) payment based on a 30-year or 15-year repayment schedule.

- interest-only payment—does not reduce the loan principal or build homeowner equity. Borrowers who pay only interest for a period of time then face a big jump in the size of monthly payments or else are forced to refinance.

- minimum payment—may be lower than one month's interest; if so, the shortfall is added to the loan balance. The result is "negative amortization": over time, the principal goes up, not down. Eventually the borrower may have an "upside down" mortgage where the debt is greater than the market value of the home. According to the credit rating firm Fitch Ratings, up to 80% of all option ARM borrowers choose the minimum monthly payment option. So it's no surprise that in 2005, 20% of option ARMs were "upside down." When a negative amortization limit is reached, the minimum payment jumps up to fully amortize the loan for the remaining loan term. In other words, borrowers suddenly have to start paying the real bill.

- Even borrowers who pay more than the monthly minimums can face payment shocks. Option ARMs often start with a temporary super-low teaser rate (and correspondingly low monthly payments) that allows borrowers to qualify for "more house." The catch? Since the low initial monthly payment, based on interest rates as low as 1.25%, is not enough to cover the real interest rate, the borrower eventually faces a sudden increase in monthly payments.

times, the largest expenditure in a family budget, and the single largest asset for two-thirds of homeowners. It's also the most fraught with danger.

For low-income families in particular, homeownership can turn out to be more a crushing debt than an asset-building opportunity. The primary reason for this is the growing chasm between ever-higher home prices and the stagnant incomes of millions of working-class Americans. The last decade has seen an unprecedented surge in home prices, which have risen 35% nationally. While the housing bubble is largely confined to specific metropolitan areas in the South, the Southwest, and the two coasts (home prices rose 50% in the Pacific states and 60% in New England), there are also bubbles in Midwestern cities like Chicago and Minneapolis. And although the housing bubble is most pronounced in high-end properties, the prices of low-end homes have also spiked in many markets.

Current incomes simply do not support these inflated home prices. For example, only 18% of Californians can afford the median house in the state using traditional loan-affordability calculations. Even the fall in mortgage interest rates in the 1990s and early 2000s was largely neutralized by higher property taxes, higher

---

Balloon Loan: This loan is written for a short 5- to 7-year term during which the borrower pays either interest and principal each month or, in a more predatory form, interest only. At the end of the loan term, the borrower must pay off the entire loan in a lump sum—the "balloon payment." At that point, buyers must either refinance or lose their homes. Balloon loans are known to real estate pros as "bullet loans," since if the loan comes due during a period of high interest rates, it's like getting a bullet in the heart. According to the national organizing and advocacy group ACORN, about 10% of all subprime loans are balloons.

Balloon loans are sometimes structured with monthly payments that fail to cover the interest, much less pay down the principal. Although the borrower makes regular payments, her loan balance increases each month: negative amortization. Many borrowers are unaware that they have a negative amortization loan until they have to refinance.

Shared Appreciation Mortgages (SAM): These are fixed-rate loans for up to 30 years that have easier credit qualifications and lower monthly payments than conventional mortgages. In exchange for a lower interest rate, the borrower relinquishes part of the future value of the home to the lender. Interest rate reductions are based on how much appreciation the borrower is willing to give up. SAMs discourage "sweat equity" since the homeowner receives only some fraction of the appreciation resulting from any remodeling. Not surprisingly, these loans have been likened to sharecropping.

Stated-Income Loan: Aimed at borrowers who do not draw regular wages from an employer but live on tips, casual jobs that pay under-the-table, commissions, or investments, this loan does not require W-2 forms or other standard wage documentation. The trade-off: higher-interest rates.

No-Ratio Loan: The debt-income ratio (the borrower's monthly payments on debt, including the planned mortgage, divided by her monthly income) is a standard benchmark that lenders use to determine how large a mortgage they will write. In return for a higher interest rate, the no-ratio loan abandons this benchmark; it is aimed at borrowers with complex financial lives or those who are experiencing divorce, the death of a spouse, or a career change.

—Amy Gluckman

insurance premiums, and rising utility costs.

This disparity might have put a dent in the mortgage finance business. But no: in 2005, Americans owed $5.7 trillion in mortgages, a 50% increase in just four years. Over the past decade the mortgage finance industry has developed creative schemes designed to squeeze potential homebuyers, albeit often temporarily, into houses they cannot afford. It is a sleight of hand that requires imaginative and risky financing for both buyers and financial institutions.

Most of the "creative" new mortgage products fall into the category of sub-prime mortgages—those offered to people whose problematic credit drops them into a lower lending category. Subprime mortgages carry interest rates ranging from a few points to ten points or more above the prime or market rate, plus onerous loan terms. The subprime mortgage industry is growing: lenders originated $173 billion in subprime loans in 2005, up from only $25 billion in 1993. By 2006 the subprime market was valued at $600 billion, one-fifth of the $3 trillion U.S. mortgage market.

Subprime lending can be risky. In the 37 years since the Mortgage Bankers Association (MBA) began conducting its annual national mortgage delinquency survey, 2006 saw the highest share of home loans entering foreclosure. According to the MBA, in early 2007 13.5% of subprime mortgages were delinquent (compared to 4.95% of prime-rate mortgages) and 4.5% were in foreclosure. By all accounts, this is just the tip of the iceberg. However, before the current collapse the rate of return for subprime lenders was spectacular. Forbes claimed that subprime lenders could realize returns up to six times greater than the best-run banks.

In the past there were two main kinds of home mortgages: fixed-rate loans and adjustable-rate loans (ARMs). In a fixed-rate mortgage, the interest rate stays the same throughout the 15- to 30-year loan term. In a typical ARM the interest rate varies over the course of the loan, although there is usually a cap. Both kinds of loans traditionally required borrowers to provide thorough documentation of their finances and a downpayment of at least 10% of the purchase price, and often 20%.

Adjustable-rate loans can be complicated, and a Federal Reserve study found that fully 25% of homeowners with ARMs were confused about their loan terms. Nonetheless, ARMs are attractive because in the short run they promise a home with an artificially low interest rate and affordable payments.

Even so, traditional ARMs proved inadequate to the tasks of ushering low-income families into the housing market and generally keeping home sales up in the face of skyrocketing home prices. So in recent years the mortgage industry created a whole range of "affordability" products with names like "no-ratio loans," "option ARMS," and "balloon loans" that it doled out like candy to people who were never fully apprised of the intricacies of these complicated loans. (See sidebar for a glossary of the new mortgage products.) These new mortgage options have opened the door for almost anyone to secure a mortgage, whether or not their circumstances auger well for repayment. They also raise both the costs and risks of buying a home— sometimes steeply—for the low- and moderate-income families to whom they're largely marketed.

Beyond the higher interest rates (at some point in the loan term if not at the start) that characterize the new "affordability" mortgages, low-income homebuyers face other costs as well. For instance, predatory and subprime lenders often require credit life insurance, which pays off a mortgage if the homeowner dies, to be added to the loan. This insurance is frequently sold either by the lender's subsidiary or else by a company that pays the lender a commission. Despite low pay-outs, lenders frequently charge high premiums for credit life insurance.

As many as 80% of subprime loans include prepayment penalties if the borrower pays off or refinances the loan early, a scam that costs low-income borrowers about $2.3 billion a year and increases the risk of foreclosure by 20%. Prepayment penalties lock borrowers into a loan by making it difficult to sell the home or refinance with a different lender. And while some borrowers face penalties for paying off their loans ahead of schedule, others discover that their mortgages have so-called "call provisions" that permit the lender to accelerate the loan term even if payments are current.

And then there are all of the costs outside of the mortgage itself. Newfangled mortgage products are often sold not by banks directly, but by a rapidly growing crew of mortgage brokers who act as finders or "bird dogs" for lenders. There are approximately 53,000 mortgage brokerage companies in the United States employing an estimated 418,700 people, according to the National Association of Mortgage Brokers; *BusinessWeek* notes that brokers now originate up to 80% of all new mortgages.

Largely unregulated, mortgage brokers live off loan fees. Their transactions are primed for conflicts of interest or even downright corruption. For example, borrowers pay brokers a fee to help them secure a loan. Brokers may also receive kickbacks from lenders for referring a borrower, and many brokers steer clients to the lenders that pay them the highest kickbacks rather than those offering the lowest interest rates. Closing documents use arcane language ("yield spread premiums," "service release fees") to hide these kickbacks. And some hungry brokers find less-than-kosher ways to make the sale, including fudging paperwork, arranging for inflated appraisals, or helping buyers find co-signers who have no intention of guaranteeing the loan.

Whether or not a broker is involved, lenders can inflate closing costs in a variety of ways: charging outrageous document preparation fees; billing for recording fees in excess of the law; "unbundling," whereby closing costs are padded by duplicating charges already included in other categories.

All in all, housing is highly susceptible to the predations of the fringe economy. Unscrupulous brokers and lenders have considerable latitude to ply their trade, especially with vulnerable low-income borrowers.

Time to Change Course

Despite the hype, homeownership is not a cure-all for low-income families who earn less than a living wage and have poor prospects for future income growth. In fact, for some low-income families homeownership only leads to more debt and financial misery. With mortgage delinquencies and foreclosures at record levels, especially among low-income households, millions of people would be better off today if they had remained renters. Surprisingly, rents are generally more stable than housing prices. From 1995 to 2001 rents rose slightly faster than inflation, but not as rapidly as home prices. Beginning in 2004 rent increases began to slow—even in hot markets like San Francisco and Seattle—and fell below the rate of inflation.

In the mid-1980s, low- and no-downpayment mortgages led to increased foreclosures when the economy tanked. Today, these mortgages are back, along with a concerted effort to drive economically marginal households into homeownership and high levels of unsustainable debt. To achieve this goal, the federal government spends $100 billion a year for homeownership programs (including the $70+ billion the mortgage interest deduction costs the Treasury).

Instead of focusing exclusively on homeownership, a more progressive and balanced housing policy would address the diverse needs of communities for both homes and rental units, and would facilitate new forms of ownership such as community land trusts and cooperatives. A balanced policy would certainly aim to expand the stock of affordable rental units. Unfortunately, just the opposite is occurring: rental housing assistance is being starved to feed low-income homeownership programs. From 2004 to 2006, President Bush and the Congress cut federal funding for public housing alone by 11%. Over the same period, more than 150,000 rental housing vouchers were cut. And, of course, policymakers must act to protect those consumers who do opt to buy homes: for instance, by requiring mortgage lenders to make certain not only that a borrower is eligible for a particular loan product, but that the loan is suitable for the borrower.

The reason the United States lacks a sound housing policy is obvious if we follow the money. Overheated housing markets and rising home prices produce lots of winners. Real estate agents reap bigger commissions. Mortgage brokers, appraisers, real estate attorneys, title companies, lenders, builders, home remodelers, and everyone else with a hand in the housing pie does well. Cities raise more in property taxes, and insurance companies enroll more clients at higher premiums. Although housing accounts for only 5% of GDP, it has been responsible for up to 75% of all U.S. job growth in the last four years, according to the consulting firm Oxford Analytica. Housing has buffered the economy, and herding more low-income families into homes, regardless of the consequences, helps keep the industry ticking. The only losers? Renters squeezed by higher rents and accelerating conversion of rental units into condos. Young middle-income families trying to buy their first house. And, especially, the thousands of low-income families for whom buying a home turns into a financial nightmare.

Sources: Carolina Katz Reid, Studies in Demography and Ecology: Achieving the American Dream? A Longitudinal Analysis of the Homeownership Experiences of Low-Income Households. Univ. of Washington, CSDE Working Paper No. 04-04; Dean Baker, "The Housing Bubble: A Time Bomb in Low-Income Communities?" Shelterforce Online, Issue #135, May/June 2004, http://www.nhi.org/online/issues/135/bubble.html; Howard Karger, Shortchanged: Life and Debt in the Fringe Economy (Berrett-Koehler, 2005); National Multi Housing Council (www.nmhc. org).

Chapter 6

WINDFALLS FOR THE WEALTHY
Tax Cuts and Corporate Welfare

CORPORATE TAX CUT BONANZA
Without fanfare, Congress gives big tax breaks to U.S. corporations.

AMY GLUCKMAN
November/December 2004

Today, U.S. corporations are sitting on unusually large piles of cash and not investing much, their profits are rising much faster than workers' wages, and they're paying a smaller share of taxes, by any reckoning, than they have in decades. *And* the 2004 federal budget deficit is over $400 billion. So what's Congress to do? Pass a large corporate tax cut, of course.

Dubbed the American Jobs Creation Act, the megalith tax bill, which the *Wall Street Journal* termed "the most sweeping rewrite of corporate tax law in nearly two decades," passed in October. The original impetus for the bill was the need for a relatively minor fix: ending a tax subsidy for U.S. exporters that the World Trade Organization had ruled to be an illegal trade barrier.

Ending this tax subsidy would have raised $49 billion in federal revenue over 10 years. Congress could have taken the $49 billion and either applied it against rising federal deficits or used it to stem cutbacks in housing, environmental protection, or other important programs. Or, legislators could have given the $49 billion back to U.S. companies in the form of alternative tax breaks, creating a "revenue-neutral" bill.

Instead, legislators took the opportunity to lavish what will likely turn out to be about $210 billion over 10 years in tax breaks on a wide swath of U.S. corporations. (The actual sum of the tax breaks in the bill as written is about $138 billion. However, this figure assumes that those tax breaks which are supposed to last for only one or a few years will actually sunset when specified. Experience suggests this is unlikely. An analysis by the Center on Budget and Policy Priorities of provisions likely to be extended suggests the true 10-year total will be about $80 billion more.)

The biggest tax break, at $76.5 billion over 10 years, is a deduction for a share of profits from manufacturing; bolstering domestic manufacturing was the bill's main selling point. The "manufacturing" being bolstered is defined broadly, though; oil and gas producers, architecture and engineering firms, and large farming operations, for example, are all included.

Dozens of provisions in the bill are designed to benefit specific corporations and industries. Among them:

- A one-year tax holiday for companies that repatriate profits from overseas operations. The bill drops the tax rate on these profits from 35% to 5.25%. The biggest likely beneficiaries are technology and pharmaceutical firms including Johnson & Johnson, Hewlett Packard, Schering-Plough, and Oracle. All belong to the patriotically-named Homeland Investment Coalition, which has lobbied for the provision, claiming it would create jobs in the United States. Even the president's Council of Economic Advisers, however, concluded easing repatriation "would not produce any substantial economic benefits," the *Wall Street Journal* reports.
- A change in the depreciation rules governing certain aircraft outside of the transportation industry. Citizens for Tax Justice (CTJ) suggests this provision is designed to aid GE, which stands to benefit from other provisions in the bill as well, such as those dealing with interest costs and foreign tax credits. The interest allocation and foreign tax credit changes alone will reduce federal revenues by an estimated $22.3 billion over 10 years.
- Higher tax write-offs for certain film and television productions. Likely beneficiaries are entertainment companies such as Disney and TimeWarner.
- A modification in the tax treatment of some pipeline property in Alaska. According to CTJ, this provision affects one particular project; partners in the project include ExxonMobil, Conoco Phillips, and BP.
- Other beneficiaries of specific provisions in the new law, according to the *Wall Street Journal,* include defense giants General Dynamics and Northrup Grumman, importers of Chinese ceiling fans, and NASCAR race track owners.

The law does manage to shrink a few tax loopholes; for example, it reduces the ability of companies to avoid taxes by reincorporating in tax havens like Barbados. However, House leaders stripped out of the final bill a number of Senate provisions aimed at stopping other forms of corporate tax evasion.

Before its final passage in October, the *Washington Post* reported that the Bush administration had doubts about the bill and was trying to slow it down "until at least after the election." Perhaps the president just wanted to avoid signing a huge corporate giveaway a few weeks before November 2. In any case, Treasury Secretary John Snowe wrote the House-Senate conference committee that the bill included "a myriad of special interest tax provisions that benefit few taxpayers." For once, a Bush administration economic policy official got it right.

Sources: "Bush Signs $138 Billion Corporate Tax Cut Bill," *Wall Street Journal Online*, 10/22/04; Joel Friedman, "Temporary Provisions in the Corporate Tax Bill Mask its Likely Long-term Impact," Center on Budget and Policy Priorities, 10/7/04; "Congress Passes $210

Billion in New Corporate Tax Breaks," Citizens for Tax Justice, 10/13/04; J. Weisman and M. Kaufman, "Tax Cut Bill Draws White House Doubts," *Washington Post*, 10/5/04; G. Simpson and G. Zuckerman, "Tax Windfall May Not Boost Hiring Despite Claims," *WSJ*, 10/13/04.

WAL-MART WELFARE
How taxpayers subsidize the world's largest retailer.

JENNA WRIGHT
January/February 2005

W al-Mart has released its expansion plans for 2005, and Americans can expect up to 230 new supercenters to open in their communities. The company plans to open 50 million square feet of retail space this year. President and CEO Lee Scott is confident the expansion will boost Wal-Mart's bottom line. But it takes money to make money, and Wal-Mart is getting a surprising amount of that seed money, along with massive subsidies to its existing operations, from U.S. taxpayers.

A raft of studies show that millions of taxpayer dollars are flowing to new and existing Wal-Mart stores around the country. In many instances, individual Wal-Mart facilities have received either direct or indirect subsidies from states and localities. Last May, Good Jobs First (GJF), a research and advocacy group that seeks to hold corporations accountable when they receive public subsidies, released a report detailing subsidies Wal-Mart has received to build both retail stores and the network of nearly 100 distribution centers the company has created to facilitate its expansion. The group found that over 90% of the company's distribution centers have been subsidized. It also uncovered 91 instances when the retail stores received public funds, and believes "the real total is certainly much higher."

GJF investigators documented 244 Wal-Mart subsidy deals with a total value of $1.008 billion. Taxpayer dollars have helped individual stores and distribution centers with everything from free or cut-price land to general grants. One example: in Sharon Springs, N.Y., a distribution center made a deal with an industrial development agency for the agency to hold the legal title to the facility so the corporation could evade property taxes. Good Jobs First estimates that Wal-Mart will save about $46 million over the life of this one agreement.

Subsidizing Low Wages

Wal-Mart's low-road labor policies give the corporation access to a less obvious taxpayer subsidy: government benefits to its employees. The company's policies by now are notorious: wages at or close to poverty level, managers discouraged from awarding overtime, employees forced to work off the clock without pay and repeatedly denied their right to organize. The result is that many Wal-Mart employees are eligible for myriad forms of public assistance. In other words, by providing financial assistance in various forms to Wal-Mart employees, the federal and state governments are essentially subsidizing the corporation for its substandard wages and benefits.

Health care benefits represent one such subsidy. Wal-Mart's employee health coverage is minimal and expensive; little of the company's vast low-wage workforce is covered. Nationally, two-thirds of workers at large firms get health insurance from their employer. But at Wal-Mart, only 41% to 46% of employees use the company's health insurance, in large part because many of Wal-Mart's low-wage workers simply cannot afford to pay the high premium the company charges. In 2001, Wal-Mart workers paid 42% of the total cost of the company's health plan. In contrast, the typical large business expects employees to pay only 16% of the total cost for individual coverage, or 25% for family coverage. At discount retailer Costco, which competes directly with Wal-Mart's Sam's Club stores, employees pay less than 10%; as a result, 82% of them are covered through the company.

Instead of providing affordable health insurance, Wal-Mart encourages its employees to sign up for publicly funded programs, dodging its health care costs and passing them on to taxpayers. The company is the poster child for a problem outlined in a 2003 AFL-CIO report on Wal-Mart's role in the health care crisis: "federal, state and local governments—American taxpayers—must pick up the multi-billion-dollar tab for employees and dependents, especially children, of large and profitable employers who are forced to rely on public hospitals and other public health programs for care and treatment they need but cannot obtain under their employers' health plans."

In Georgia, one of every four Wal-Mart employees has a child in the state's PeachCare health program, according to a recent survey. Over 10,000 of the 166,000 children covered by PeachCare have a parent working for Wal-Mart; no other employer in the state has a comparable share of its employees in the program.

In California, the families of Wal-Mart employees use an estimated 40% more in publicly funded health care than the average for families of employees at other large retail firms, according to an August 2003 study by University of California, Berkeley's Institute for Industrial Relations. Providing health care to Wal-Mart families costs California taxpayers an estimated $32 million annually.

Thanks to their poverty-level wages, Wal-Mart workers are often eligible for other kinds of government assistance as well. The same study found that California Wal-Mart employees and their families utilize an additional $54 million in non-health related federal assistance, including food stamps, the Earned Income Tax Credit, subsidized school lunches, and subsidized housing.

The Democratic staff of the House Committee on Education and the Workforce estimated the breakdown of costs for one 200-employee Wal-Mart store:

- $36,000 a year for free or reduced school lunches, assuming that 50 families of employees qualify.
- $42,000 a year for Section 8 rental assistance, assuming that 3% of the store employees qualify.
- $125,000 a year for federal tax credits and deductions for low-income families, assuming that 50 employees are heads of households with a child, and 50 employees are married with two children.

- $108,000 a year for the additional federal contribution to state children's health insurance programs, assuming that 30 employees with an average of two children qualify.
- $100,000 a year for additional Title I expenses, assuming 50 families with two children qualify.
- $9,750 a year for the additional costs of low-income energy assistance.

Overall, the committee estimates that one 200-person Wal-Mart store may result in an excess cost of $420,750 a year for federal taxpayers.

The effects of Wal-Mart's free-loader policies radiate beyond Wal-Mart itself; Wal-Mart employees are not the only victims. Firms large and small are forced to cut their own costs in order to compete, creating a "race to the bottom, in which everyone suffers," according to the AFL-CIO report. Employers that provide adequate pay and benefits to their employees are under pressure from companies like Wal-Mart that do not. The result: a growing low-wage sector and ever-greater need for government benefits (funded, incidentally, by an increasingly regressive tax structure).

As an economic power, Wal-Mart is in a class by itself, with over $8 billion in net income last year—it's about five times the size of the second-largest retailer in the United States. Wal-Mart's sheer size means it can drag whole sectors with millions of workers both in the United States and abroad down its low-road path. Taxpayers are feeding this giant corporate monster, and at a very high price.

Sources: Democratic Staff of the Committee on Education and the Workforce, U.S. House of Representatives, "Everyday Low Wages: The Hidden Price We All Pay for Wal-Mart," February 16, 2004; AFL-CIO, "Wal-Mart: An Example of Why Workers Remain Uninsured and Underinsured," October 2003; Philip Mattera and Anna Purinton, "Shopping for Subsidies: How Wal-Mart Uses Taxpayer Money to Finance Its Never-Ending Growth," (Good Jobs First, May 2004); Labor Research Association, "Low Wage Nation," 2004.

SLICING UP AT THE LONG BARBEQUE:
Who Gorges, Who Serves, and Who Gets Roasted

JAMES M. CYPHER
January/February 2007

Economic inequality has been on the rise in the United States for 30-odd years. Not since the Gilded Age of the late 19th century—during what Mark Twain referred to as "the Great Barbeque"—has the country witnessed such a rapid shift in the distribution of economic resources.

Still, most mainstream economists do not pay too much attention to the distribution of income and wealth—that is, how the value of current production (income) and past accumulated assets (wealth) is divided up among U.S. households.

Some economists focus their attention on theory for theory's sake and do not work much with empirical data of any kind. Others who are interested in these on-the-ground data simply assume that each individual or group gets what it deserves from a capitalist economy. In their view, if the share of income going to wage earners goes up, that must mean that wage earners are more productive and thus deserve a larger slice of the nation's total income—and vice versa if that share goes down.

Heterodox economists, however, frequently look upon the distribution of income and wealth as among the most important shorthand guides to the overall state of a society and its economy. Some are interested in economic justice; others may or may not be, but nonetheless are convinced that changes in income distribution signal underlying societal trends and perhaps important points of political tension. And the general public appears to be paying increasing attention to income and wealth inequality. Consider the strong support voters have given to recent ballot questions raising state minimum wages and the extensive coverage of economic inequality that has suddenly begun to appear in mainstream news outlets like the *New York Times*, the *Los Angeles Times*, and the *Wall Street Journal*, all of which published lengthy article series on the topic in the past few years. Just last month, news outlets around the country spotlighted the extravagant bonuses paid out by investment firm Goldman Sachs, including a $53.4 million bonus to the firm's CEO.

By now, economists and others who do pay attention to the issue are aware that income and wealth inequality in the United States rose steadily during the last three decades of the 20th century. But now that we are several years into the 21st, what do we know about income and wealth distribution today? Has the trend toward inequality continued, or are there signs of a reversal? And what can an understanding of the entire post-World War II era tell us about how to move again toward greater economic equality?

The short answers are: (1) Income distribution is even more unequal that we thought; (2) The newest data suggest the trend toward greater inequality continues, with no signs of a reversal; (3) We all do better when we all do better. During the 30 or so years after World War II the economy boomed and every stratum of society did better—pretty much at the same rate. When the era of shared growth ended, so too did much of the growth: the U.S. economy slowed down and recessions were deeper, more frequent, and harder to overcome. Growth spurts that did occur left most people out: the bottom 60% of U.S. households earned only 95 cents in 2004 for every dollar they made in 1979. A quarter century of falling incomes for the vast majority, even though average household income rose by 27% in real terms. Whew!

The Classless Society?

Throughout the 1950s, 1960s, and 1970s, sociologists preached that the United States was an essentially "classless" society in which everyone belonged to the middle class. A new "mass market" society with an essentially affluent, economically homogeneous population, they claimed, had emerged. Exaggerated as these claims were in the 1950s, there was some reason for their popular acceptance. Union membership reached its peak share of the private-sector labor force in the early 1950s;

unions were able to force corporations of the day to share the benefits of strong economic growth. The union wage created a target for non-union workers as well, pulling up all but the lowest of wages as workers sought to match the union wage and employers often granted it as a tactic for keeping unions out. Under these circumstances, millions of families entered the lower middle class and saw their standard of living rise markedly. All of this made the distribution of income more equal for decades until the late 1970s. Of course there were outliers—some millions of poor, disproportionately blacks, and the rich family here and there.

Something serious must have happened in the 1970s as the trend toward greater economic equality rapidly reversed. Here are the numbers. The share of income received by the bottom 90% of the population was a modest 67% in 1970, but by 2000 this had shrunk to a mere 52%, according to a detailed study of U.S. income distribution conducted by Thomas Piketty and Emmanuel Saez, published by the prestigious National Bureau of Economic Research in 2002. Put another way, the top 10% increased their overall share of the nation's total income by 15 percentage points from 1970 to 2000. This is a rather astonishing jump—the gain of the top 10% in these years was equivalent to more than the total income received annually by the bottom 40% of households.

To get on the bottom rung of the top 10% of households in 2000, it would have been necessary to have an adjusted gross income of $104,000 a year. The real money, though, starts on the 99th rung of the income ladder—the top 1% received an unbelievable 21.7% of all income in 2000. To get a handhold on the very bottom of this top rung took more than $384,000.

The Piketty-Saez study (and subsequent updates), which included in its measure of annual household income some data, such as income from capital gains, that generally are not factored in, verified a rising trend in income inequality which had been widely noted by others, and a degree of inequality which was far beyond most current estimates.

The Internal Revenue Service has essentially duplicated the Piketty-Saez study. They find that in 2003, the share of total income going to the "bottom" four-fifths of households (that's 80% of the population!) was only slightly above 40%. (See Figure 1.) Both of these studies show much higher levels of inequality than were previously thought to exist based on widely referenced Census Bureau studies. The Census studies still attribute 50% of total income to the top fifth for 2003, but this number appears to understate what the top fifth now receives—nearly 60%, according to the IRS.

A Brave New (Globalized) World for Workers

Why the big change from 1970 to 2000? That is too long a story to tell here in full. But briefly, we can say that beginning in the early 1970s, U.S. corporations and the wealthy individuals who largely own them had the means, the motive, and the opportunity to garner a larger share of the nation's income—and they did so.

Let's start with the motive. The 1970s saw a significant slowdown in U.S. economic growth, which made corporations and stockholders anxious to stop sharing the benefits of growth to the degree they had in the immediate postwar era.

Opportunity appeared in the form of an accelerating globalization of economic activity. Beginning in the 1970s, more and more U.S.-based corporations began to set up production operations overseas. The trend has only accelerated since, in part because international communication and transportation costs have fallen dramatically. Until the 1970s, it was very difficult—essentially unprofitable—for giants like General Electric or General Motors to operate plants offshore and then import their foreign-made products into the United States. So from the 1940s to the 1970s, U.S. workers had a geographic lever, one they have now almost entirely lost. This erosion in workers' bargaining power has undermined the middle class and decimated the unions that once managed to assure the working class a generally comfortable economic existence. And today, of course, the tendency to send jobs offshore is affecting many highly trained professionals such as engineers. So this process of gutting the middle class has not run its course.

Given the opportunity presented by globalization, companies took a two-pronged approach to strengthening their hand vis-à-vis workers: (1) a frontal assault on unions, with decertification elections and get-tough tactics during unionization attempts, and (2) a debilitating war of nerves whereby corporations threatened to move offshore unless workers scaled back their demands or agreed to givebacks of prior gains in wage and benefit levels or working conditions.

A succession of U.S. governments that pursued conservative—or pro-corporate—economic policies provided the means. Since the 1970s, both Republican and Democratic administrations have tailored their economic policies to benefit corporations and shareholders over workers. The laundry list of such policies includes

- new trade agreements, such as NAFTA, that allow companies to cement favorable deals to move offshore to host nations such as Mexico;
- tax cuts for corporations and for the wealthiest households, along with hikes in the payroll taxes that represent the largest share of the tax burden on the working and middle classes;
- lax enforcement of labor laws that are supposed to protect the right to organize unions and bargain collectively.

Exploding Millionairism

Given these shifts in the political economy of the United States, it is not surprising that economic inequality in 2000 was higher than in 1970. But at this point, careful readers may well ask whether it is misleading to use data for the year 2000, as the studies reported above do, to demonstrate rising inequality. After all, wasn't 2000 the year the NASDAQ peaked, the year the dot-com bubble reached its maximum volume? So if the wealthiest households received an especially large slice of the nation's total income that year, doesn't that just reflect a bubble about to burst rather than an underlying trend?

To begin to answer this question, we need to look at the trends in income and wealth distribution since 2000. And it turns out that after a slight pause in 2000-2001, inequality has continued to rise. Look at household income, for example. According to the standard indicators, the U.S. economy saw a brief recession in 2000-2001 and has been in a recovery ever since. But the median household in-

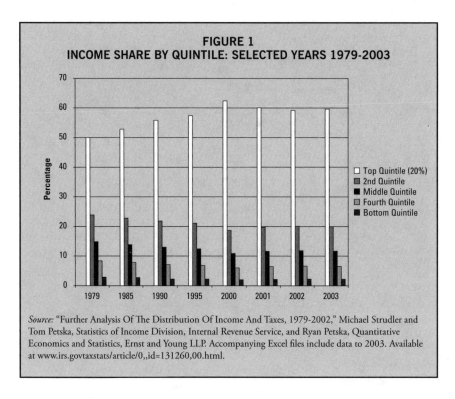

FIGURE 1
INCOME SHARE BY QUINTILE: SELECTED YEARS 1979-2003

Source: "Further Analysis Of The Distribution Of Income And Taxes, 1979-2002," Michael Strudler and Tom Petska, Statistics of Income Division, Internal Revenue Service, and Ryan Petska, Quantitative Economics and Statistics, Ernst and Young LLP. Accompanying Excel files include data to 2003. Available at www.irs.govtaxstats/article/0,,id=131260,00.html.

come has failed to recover.* In 2000 the median household had an annual income of $49,133; by 2005, after adjusting for inflation, the figure stood at $46,242. This 6% drop in median household income occurred while the inflation-adjusted Gross Domestic Product expanded by 14.4%.

When the Census Bureau released these data, it noted that median household income had gone up slightly between 2004 and 2005. This point was seized upon by Bush administration officials to bolster their claim that times are good for American workers. A closer look at the data, however, revealed a rather astounding fact: Only 23 million households moved ahead in 2005, most headed by someone aged 65 or above. In other words, subtracting out the cost-of-living increase in Social Security benefits and increases in investment income (such as profits, dividends, interest, capital gains, and rents) to the over-65 group, workers again suffered a decline in income in 2005.

Another bit of evidence is the number of millionaire households—those with net worth of $1 million or more excluding the value of a primary residence and any IRAs. In 1999, just before the bubbles burst, there were 7.1 million millionaire households in the United States. In 2005, there were 8.9 million, a record number. Ordinary workers may not have recovered from the 2000-2001 rough patch yet, but evidently the wealthiest households have!

Many economists pay scant attention to income distribution patterns on the assumption that those shifts merely reflect trends in the productivity of labor or the return to risk-taking. But worker productivity rose in the 2000-2005 period, by

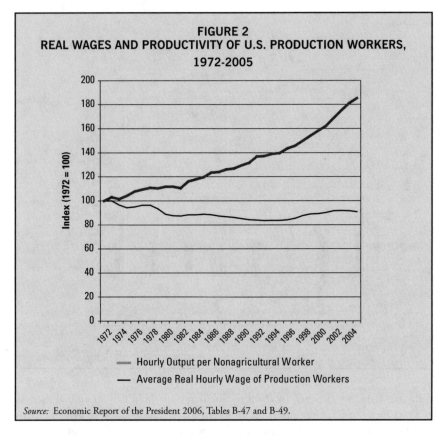

FIGURE 2
REAL WAGES AND PRODUCTIVITY OF U.S. PRODUCTION WORKERS,
1972-2005

—— Hourly Output per Nonagricultural Worker
—— Average Real Hourly Wage of Production Workers

Source: Economic Report of the President 2006, Tables B-47 and B-49.

27.1% (see Figure 2). At the same time, from 2003 to 2005 average hourly pay fell by 1.2%. (Total compensation, including all forms of benefits, rose by 7.2% between 2000 and 2005. Most of the higher compensation spending merely reflects rapid increases in the health insurance premiums that employers have to pay just to maintain the same levels of coverage. But even if benefits are counted as part of workers' pay—a common and questionable practice—productivity growth outpaced this elastic definition of "pay" by 50% between 1972 and 2005.)

And at the macro level, recent data released by the Commerce Department demonstrate that the share of the country's GDP going to wages and salaries sank to its lowest postwar level, 45.4%, in the third quarter of 2006 (see Figure 3). And this figure actually overstates how well ordinary workers are doing. The "Wage & Salary" share includes all income of this type, not just production workers' pay. Corporate executives' increasingly munificent salaries are included as well. Workers got roughly 65% of total wage and salary income in 2005, according to survey data from the U.S. Department of Labor; the other 35% went to salaried professionals—medical doctors and technicians, managers, and lawyers—who comprised only 15.6% of the sample.

Moreover, the "Wage & Salary" share shown in the National Income and Product Accounts includes bonuses, overtime, and other forms of payment not included in the Labor Department survey. If this income were factored in, the share going to nonprofessional, nonmanagerial workers would be even smaller. Bonuses and other forms of income to top employees can be many times base pay in important areas such as law and banking. Goldman Sachs's notorious 2006 bonuses are a case in point; the typical managing director on Wall Street garnered a bonus ranging between $1 and $3 million.

So, labor's share of the nation's income is falling, as Figure 3 shows, but it is actually falling much faster than these data suggest. Profits, meanwhile, are at their highest level as a share of GDP since the booming 1960s.

These numbers should come as no surprise to anyone who reads the paper: story after story illustrates how corporations are continuing to squeeze workers. For instance, workers at the giant auto parts manufacturer Delphi have been told to prepare for a drop in wages from $27.50 an hour in 2006 to $16.50 an hour in 2007. In order to keep some of Caterpillar's manufacturing work in the United States, the union was cornered into accepting a contract in 2006 that limits new workers to a maximum salary of $27,000 a year—no matter how long they work there—compared to the $38,000 or more that long-time Caterpillar workers make today. More generally, for young women with a high school diploma, average entry-level pay fell to only $9.08 an hour in 2005, down by 4.9% just since 2001. For male college graduates, starter-job pay fell by 7.3% over the same period.

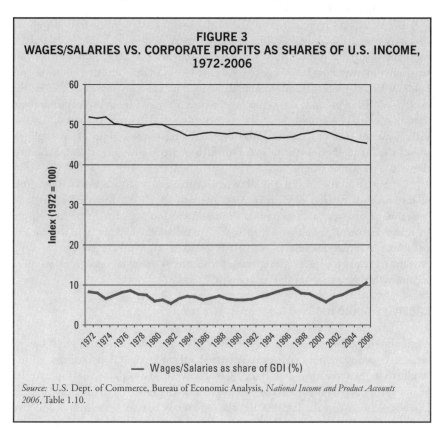

FIGURE 3
WAGES/SALARIES VS. CORPORATE PROFITS AS SHARES OF U.S. INCOME, 1972-2006

— Wages/Salaries as share of GDI (%)

Source: U.S. Dept. of Commerce, Bureau of Economic Analysis, *National Income and Product Accounts 2006*, Table 1.10.

Aiding and Abetting

And the federal government is continuing to play its part, facilitating the transfer of an ever-larger share of the nation's income to its wealthiest households. George W. Bush once joked that his constituency was "the haves and the have-mores"—this may have been one of the few instances in which he was actually leveling with his audience. Consider aspects of the four tax cuts for individuals that Bush has implemented since taking office. The first two cut the top nominal tax rate from 39.6% to 35%. Then, in 2003, the third cut benefited solely those who hold wealth, reducing taxes on dividends from 39.6% to 15% and on capital gains from 20% to 15%. (Bush's fourth tax cut—in 2006—is expected to drop taxes by 4.8% percent for the top one tenth of one percent of all households, while the median household will luxuriate with an extra nickel per day.)

So, if you make your money by the sweat of your brow and you earned $200,000 in 2003, you paid an effective tax rate of 21%. If you earned a bit more, say another $60,500, you paid an effective tax rate of 35% on the additional income. But if, with a flick of the wrist on your laptop, you flipped some stock you had held for six months and cleared $60,500 on the transaction, you paid the IRS an effective tax rate of only 15%. What difference does it make? Well, in 2003 the 6,126 households with incomes over $10 million saw their taxes go down by an average of $521,905 from this one tax cut alone.

These tax cuts represent only one of the many Bush administration policies that have abetted the ongoing shift of income away from most households and toward the wealthiest ones. And what do these top-tier households do with all this newfound money? For one thing, they save. This is in sharp contrast to most households. While the top fifth of households by income has a savings rate of 23%, the bottom 80% as a group dissave—in other words, they go into debt, spending more than they earn. Households headed by a person under 35 currently show a negative savings rate of 16% of income. Today overall savings—the savings of the top fifth minus the dis-savings of the bottom four-fifths—are slightly negative, for the first time since the Great Depression.

Here we find the crucial link between income and wealth accumulation. Able to save nearly a quarter of their income, the rich search out financial assets (and sometimes real assets such as houses and businesses) to pour their vast funds into. In many instances, sometimes with inside information, they are able to generate considerable future income from their invested savings. Like a snowball rolling downhill, savings for the rich can have a turbo effect—more savings generates more income, which then accumulates as wealth.

Lifestyles of the Rich

Make the rich even richer and the creative forces of market capitalism will be unleashed, resulting in more savings and consequently more capital investment, raising productivity and creating abundance for all. At any rate, that's the supply-side/neoliberal theory. However—and reminiscent of the false boom that defined the Japanese economy in the late 1980s—the big money has not gone into productive investments in the United States. Stripping out the money pumped into the residential real estate bubble, inflation-adjusted investment in machinery, equipment, technology, and structures increased only 1.4% from 1999 through 2005—an average of 0.23% per year. Essentially, productive investment has stagnated since the close of the dot-com boom.

Instead, the money has poured into high-risk hedge funds. These are vast pools of unregulated funds that are now generating 40% to 50% of the trades in the New York Stock Exchange and account for very large portions of trading in many U.S. and foreign credit and debt markets.

And where is the income from these investments going? Last fall media mogul David Geffen sold two paintings at record prices, a Jasper Johns ($80 million) and a Willem de Kooning ($63.5 million), to two of "today's crop of hedge-fund billionaires" whose cash is making the art market "red-hot," according to the *New York Times*.

Other forms of conspicuous consumption have their allure as well. Boeing and Lufthansa are expecting brisk business for the newly introduced 787 airplane. The commercial version of the new Boeing jet will seat 330, but the VIP version offered by Lufthansa Technik (for a mere $240 million) will have seating for 35 or fewer, leaving room for master bedrooms, a bar, and the transport of racehorses or Rolls Royces. And if you lose your auto assembly job? It should be easy to find work as a dog walker: High-end pet care services are booming, with sales more than doubling between 2000 and 2004. Opened in 2001, Just Dogs Gourmet expects to have 45 franchises in place by the end of 2006 selling hand-decorated doggie treats. And then there is Camp Bow Wow, which offers piped-in classical music for the dogs (oops, "guests") and a live Camper Cam for their owners. Started only three years ago, the company already has 140 franchises up and running.

According to David Butler, the manager of a premiere auto dealership outside of Detroit, sales of Bentleys, at $180,000 a pop, are brisk. But not many $300,000 Rolls Royces are selling. "It's not that they can't afford it," Butler told the *New York Times*, "it's because of the image it would give." Just what is the image problem in Detroit? Well, maybe it has something to do with those Delphi workers facing a 40% pay cut. Michigan's economy is one of the hardest-hit in the nation. GM, long a symbol of U.S. manufacturing prowess, is staggering, with rumors of possible bankruptcy rife. The best union in terms of delivering the goods for the U.S. working class, the United Auto Workers, is facing an implosion. Thousands of Michigan workers at Delphi, GM, and Ford will be out on the streets very soon. (The top three domestic car makers are determined to permanently lay off three-quarters of their U.S. assembly-line workers—nearly 200,000 hourly employees. If they do, then the number of autoworkers employed by the Big Three—Ford, Chrysler, and GM—will have shrunk by a staggering 900,000 since 1978.) So, this might not be the time to buy a Rolls. But a mere $180,000 Bentley—why not?

Had Enough of the "Haves"?

In the era Twain decried as the "great barbeque," the outrageous concentration of income and wealth eventually sparked a reaction and a vast reform movement. But it was not until the onset of the Great Depression, decades later, that massive labor/ social unrest and economic collapse forced the country's political elite to check the growing concentration of income and wealth.

Today, it does not appear that there are, as yet, any viable forces at work to put the brakes on the current runaway process of rising inequality. Nor does it appear that this era's power elite is ready to accept any new social compact. In a recent report on the "new king of Wall Street" (a co-founder of the hedge fund/private-equity buyout corporation Blackstone Group) that seemed to typify elite perspectives on today's inequality, the *New York Times* gushed that "a crashing wave of capital is minting new billionaires each year." Naturally, the *Times* was too discreet to mention is that those same "crashing waves" have flattened the middle class. And their backwash has turned the working class every-which-way while pulling it down, down, down.

But perhaps those who decry the trend can find at least symbolic hope in the new boom in yet another luxury good. Private mausoleums, in vogue during that earlier Gilded Age, are back. For $650,000, one was recently constructed at Daytona Memorial Park in Florida—with matching $4,000 Medjool date palms for shade. Another, complete with granite patio, meditation room, and doors of hand cast bronze, went up in the same cemetery. Business is booming, apparently, with 2,000 private mausoleums sold in 2005, up from a single-year peak of 65 in the 1980s. Some cost "well into the millions," according to one the nation's largest makers of cemetery monuments. Who knows: maybe the mausoleum boom portends the ultimate (dead) end for the neo-Gilded Age.

Sources: Jenny Anderson, "As Lenders, Hedge Funds Draw Insider Scrutiny," *New York Times* 10/16/06; Steven Greenhouse, "Many Entry-Level Workers Feel Pinch of Rough Market," *New York Times* 9/4/06; Greenhouse and David Leonhardt, "Real Wages Fail to Match a Rise in Productivity," *New York Times* 8/28/06; Paul Krugman, "Feeling No Pain," *New York Times*3/6/06; Krugman, "Graduates vs. Oligarchs," *New York Times* 2/27/06; David Cay Johnston, *Perfectly Legal: The Covert Campaign to Rig our Tax System to Benefit the Super-Rich—and Cheat Everybody Else,*(Penguin Books, 2003); Johnston, "Big Gain for Rich Seen in Tax Cuts for Investments," *New York Times* 4/5/06; Johnston, "New Rise in Number of Millionaire Families," *New York Times* 3/28/06; Johnston, "'04 Income in US was Below 2000 Level," *New York Times* 11/28/06; Leonhardt, "The Economics of Henry Ford May Be Passé," *New York Times* 4/5/06; Rick Lyman, "Census Reports Slight Increase in '05 Incomes," *New York Times* 8/30/06; Micheline Maynard and Nick Bunkley, "Ford is Offering 75,000 Employees Buyout Packages," *New York Times* 9/15/06; Jeremy W. Peters, "Delphi Is Said to Offer Union a One-Time Sweetener," *New York Times* 3/28/06; Joe Sharky, "For the Super-Rich, It's Time to Upgrade the Old Jumbo Jet," *New York Times* 10/17/06; Guy Trebay, "For a Price, Final Resting Place that Tut Would Find Pleasant" *New York Times* 4/17/06.

MIND-BOGGLING INEQUALITY
Enough to Make Even Adam Smith Worry

JOHN MILLER
January/February 2007

D o soaring corporate profits (higher as a share of national income than at any time since 1950) and a green Christmas on Wall Street (green as in record-setting multimillion dollar bonuses for investment bankers) have you worried about economic inequality? How about real wages that are lower and poverty rates higher than when the current economic expansion began five years ago? If that is not enough to make you worry, try this. The editors of the *Wall Street Journal* are spilling a whole lot of ink these days to convince their readers that today's inequality is just not a problem. Besides that, there is not much to be done about inequality, say the editors, since taxes are already soaking the rich.

Not even Ben Bernanke, the new head of the Fed, is prepared to swallow the editors' line this time. Inequality in the U.S. economy "is increasing beyond what is healthy," Bernanke told Congress, although like the editors he finds it a "big challenge to think about what to do about it."

There is real reason to worry. By nearly every measure, inequality today is at a level not seen since the Great Depression. And by historical standards, the rich have hardly overpaid in taxes for their decades-long economic banquet.

Once you remove the Journal editors' spin, the "actual evidence" from the Congressional Budget Office (CBO) makes clear that the charge of worsening inequality and a declining tax burden on the rich is anything but "trumped up." The CBO's latest numbers document a lopsided economic growth that has done little to improve the lot of most households while it has paid off handsomely for those at the top. From 1979 to 2004, the poorest quintile saw their average real (i.e., inflation-adjusted) income barely budge, increasing just 2.0% over the entire period. The middle-income quintile enjoyed a larger but still modest real-income gain of 14.6% over the 25-year span, while the best-off fifth enjoyed a 63.0% gain. But the 153.9% jump in the real income of the richest 1% far outdistanced even the gains of the near rich. (See figure page 130.)

The *Journal*'s editors are right about one thing: a widening income gap is a long-term trend that has persisted regardless of the party in power. The well-to-do made out like bandits during the Clinton years as well as the Bush years. In fact, postwar inequality, after peaking in 2000, did retreat somewhat in the first four Bush years as the stock market bubble burst, cutting into the income share of the most well-off, who hold the vast majority of corporate stock. (In 2004, the wealthiest 1% of U.S. households held 36.9% of common stock by value; the wealthiest 10% held 78.7%.)

The increase in the gulf between the haves and the have-nots during the Bush years, however, has hardly been modest. In 2004, as in 1999 and in 2000, the share of pre-tax income going to the richest 1% is greater than the share they received in any year since 1929, according to the ground-breaking historical study of inequality by economists Thomas Piketty and Emmanuel Saez. Barron's magazine, the Dow

Jones business and financial weekly, put it succinctly in their recent cover story, "Rich America, Poor America": "never in history have the haves had so much."

Feast and Famine

The editors' banquet scenario is unconvincing, to say the least. First off, before we examine the bill for the banquet, we ought to look at what the 100 guests were served. Not everyone got the same meal; in fact, the economic banquet of the last two and a half decades was a feast for some and a famine for others. Most people got modest portions indeed. The income, or serving size if you will, of the average guest was just one sixteenth of the economic feast lavished on the richest 1%. Surely even *Wall Street Journal* editors wouldn't expect the average taxpayer to subsidize the culinary indulgences of the rich.

Second, the well-to-do picked up much less of the tab for their banquet than the *Journal*'s editorials suggest. True enough, the richest 1% of taxpayers now pay more than one-third of all income taxes. But the federal tax bill is not confined to income taxes alone. It also includes payroll taxes (like FICA, the Social Security tax) and excise taxes (for example, on cars) that fall more heavily on low-income households than the income tax does, making up much of their tax bill. Taking those taxes into account does make a substantial difference in the share of the total federal tax bill shouldered by the rich. In 2004, the richest 1% paid just over one-quarter

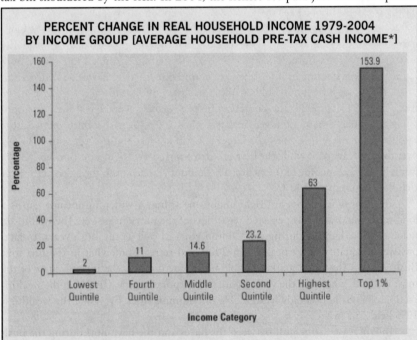

PERCENT CHANGE IN REAL HOUSEHOLD INCOME 1979-2004 BY INCOME GROUP [AVERAGE HOUSEHOLD PRE-TAX CASH INCOME*]

Source: Congressional Budget Office, Historical Effective Tax Rates: 1979 to 2004, Appendix Table 1C.

* Pre-tax cash income is the sum of wages, salaries, self-employment income, rents, taxable and nontaxable interest, dividends, realized capital gains, cash transfer payments, and retirement benefits plus employers' share of payroll taxes and employee contributions to 401(k) retirement plans.

(25.3%), not one-third, of all federal taxes. (See table.) No working American ate for free.

Beyond federal tax liabilities, the banquet tab also includes state and local taxes. Those taxes, especially state sales taxes, fall most heavily on those who were served the smallest portions: low-income earners. Once state and local taxes are included, the tax share of the richest 1% falls to just over one-fifth, not much more than their share of national income as calculated by the IRS. According to these estimates, provided by the Washington-based think tank Citizens for Tax Justice, the U.S. tax code taken in its entirety does little to redistribute income. By any definition, our tax system is at best mildly progressive, and surely not "highly progressive" as the *Journal* claims.

On top of all that, when the bill for today's economic banquet came due, the Bush administration somehow decided that the guests as a group had overpaid. The purported excess over the amount of the bill should, at least according to the Bush administration's reasoning, go back to each member of the group in tax cuts, in proportion with what they contributed toward paying the bill. Those who contributed the most should get the most back; those who contributed less should get less back. And those whom the rest are treating to dinner, of course, should get nothing back.

But the Bush tax cuts don't manage to conform to even this version of fairness, at least not when it comes to the share of the cuts going to the super-rich. The richest 1% of taxpayers, with average household income well over $1 million, get a whopping 35.9% of the benefits of the Bush tax cuts, or an annual tax cut of $48,311

SHARE OF TOTAL TAX LIABILITIES AND EFFECTIVE TAX RATES PAID BY DIFFERENT INCOME GROUPS, 2004

Income Category	Share of Total Tax Liabilities		Effective Tax Rate	
	Federal	Federal, State, and Local	Federal	Federal, State, and Local
Lowest Quintile	0.9%	2.2%	7.9%	19.7%
Second Quintile	4.5%	5.5%	11.4%	23.3%
Middle Quintile	9.7%	10.5%	15.8%	27.0%
Fourth Quintile	17.6%	19.0%	18.7%	29.8%
Highest Quintile	67.1%	62.6%	21.6%	31.8%
TOP 1%	25.3%	20.8%	24.6%	32.8%

Sources: Congressional Budget Office, *Historical Effective Tax Rates: 1979 to 2004*, Appendix Tables 1b. Citizens for Tax Justice, "Overall Tax Rates Have Flattened Sharply Under Bush," 4/13/04.

during this decade, well in excess of their one-quarter (or 25.3% to be exact) share of the federal tax burden.

All told, the U.S. tax system does not soak the rich, especially after the Bush tax cuts. In 2004, the effective federal tax rate—that is, the share of total income anyone hands over to the government in federal taxes—for the richest 1% was 24.6%, according to Citizens for Tax Justice, far lower than it was in the 1970s. By historical standards, or by any reasonable definition, taxes on the rich have not reached the saturation point.

On top of that, the effective tax rate for all federal, state, and local taxes combined for the poorest fifth of households is 19.7%—well over half the effective tax rate of 32.8% that the richest 1% pay—and that's after taking into account the Earned Income Tax Credit that some low-income households receive. With an average income of $1,259,700, as opposed to $15,400, that rate falls far short of exhausting the ability of the superrich to pay. It hardly represents a contribution to the bill for the economic banquet of the last two and a half decades that is in proportion to the large and lavish meal they've enjoyed.

What Would Adam Smith Say?

There is no reason to be flummoxed about how to address worsening inequality, even in the short run. *Wall Street Journal* columnist David Wessel, in a November 2006 article on how Democrats might tackle the wealth gap, had no problem enumerating several measures that would lessen inequality. Those included raising the minimum wage, restraining CEO pay, expanding the earned-income tax credit, and rolling back President Bush's upper-income tax cuts.

Just the thought that Congress might actually pass some of these measures was enough for the *Journal*'s editors to minimize the reality of rising inequality and to extol the supposed tax generosity of the rich.

Too bad. Unlike the *Wall Street Journal*'s editors, even Adam Smith, the patron saint of capitalism, recognized the corrupting effect of inequality in a market economy. As Smith put it in *The Theory of Moral Sentiments*, his often overlooked lectures on ethics, the "disposition to admire, and almost to worship, the rich and the powerful, and to despise, or, at least, to neglect persons of poor and mean condition is the great and most universal cause of the corruption of our moral sentiments."

A fitting description of the attitude the *Wall Street Journal*'s editors seem to have toward the rich and the poor. Business executives and policymakers would do well to skip the *Journal* and go back to Smith.

Sources: Congressional Budget Office, "Historical Effective Federal Tax Rates: 1979 to 2004," 12/04; Citizens for Tax Justice, "Overall Tax Rates Have Flattened Sharply Under Bush," 4/13/04; David Wessel, "Fed Chief Warns of Widening Inequality," *Wall Street Journal*, 2/7/07; David Wessel, "Democrats target wealth gap and hope not to hit economy," *Wall Street Journal*, 11/21/06; Adam Smith, *Theory of Moral Sentiments*, Sec. III, Chap. III, in The Essential Adam Smith ed. Robert Heilbroner (Norton, 1986), p. 86; "Incomes and Politics," *Wall Street Journal* editorial, 9/2/06; "The Top 1% Pay 35%," *Wall Street Journal* editorial, 12/20/06.

THE "DOUBLE-TAXATION" OF CORPORATIONS

RAMAA VASUDEVAN

January/February 2007

Dear Dr. Dollar:

My congressman, John Mica (R-Fla.), sent me a letter claiming that "the high income tax rate of 40% for U.S. corporations, unlike most competitors, does not provide relief for the double taxation of corporate income." Like the double talk? He wants to reduce the incentives for companies to move offshore by lowering corporate income taxes. But what's the best response to this claim about "double-taxation"? I don't know much about economics, but I do know enough to know that this position is a con job.   —Sandra Holt, Casselberry, Fla

When corporations and their friends in Washington go on about "double taxa-tion," what they're referring to is the notion that if corporations are taxed on their income and shareholders on their dividends, then the same income is getting taxed twice, with the implication that this is unfair or unduly burdensome. You're right to view this idea as a con job. Here's why:

First, the corporation as an entity is legally distinct from its shareholders. This distinction lies at the core of the notion of limited liability and protects individual shareholders from liability for damages caused by the corporation's pursuit of prof-its. The claim of "double-taxation" is bogus because the two taxes apply to different taxpayers—corporations versus individual shareholders.

Second, the double taxation claim is a bit of a red herring since many kinds of income are in effect double taxed. For instance, along with the income tax, workers also have to pay Medicare and Social Security taxes on their earnings.

In fact, investment income is currently treated more favorably by the tax code than wage income. Investment income is taxed at an average rate of 9.6%, com-pared to 23.4 % for wages. One reason for this disparity is that investment income is exempt from Medicare and Social Security taxes. But a second key reason is the reduced special tax rate for investment income approved by Congress during Bush's first term. This includes cutting the top tax rate on dividends from around 35% to 15%. As David Cay Johnston of The *New York Times* has observed, "the wealthi-est Americans now pay much higher direct taxes on money they work for than on money that works for them."

Who benefits when the tax code rewards investment rather than wage earning? The wealthy, who garner most investment income: about 43% of total investment income goes to the top 1% of taxpayers.

Repealing the dividend tax would only exacerbate that disparity. According to Federal Reserve Board data, fewer than 20% of families hold stocks outside of retirement accounts. Individual stockholdings are concentrated among the richest families, who would be the real beneficiaries of a dividend tax break. Some 42% of benefits from repealing the dividend tax would go to the richest 1% of taxpayers, and about 75% would go to the richest 10% of taxpayers.

In contrast, the vast majority of those who own any stock at all hold their stocks in retirement accounts. They neither receive dividends on these shares directly nor pay a dividend tax—but they'll find themselves paying the normal income tax as soon as they begin drawing on their retirement accounts.

Do taxes impose a disproportionately heavy burden on U.S. corporations? The oft-quoted 40% tax rate applies only to a tiny proportion of corporate income. The official tax rate for most corporate profits is 35%; the very smallest corporations (those with income under $50,000 per year) are subject to a rate of only 15%. More-over, the official tax rates are higher than the effective tax rates that corporations ac-tually end up paying. A variety of tax breaks allow corporations to reap tremendous tax savings, estimated at $87 billion to $170 billion in 2002-2003 alone, according to a study by Citizens for Tax Justice. The double-taxation argument would have meaning only if the actual burden of corporate taxes were excessive. But it is not. In 2002-03, U.S. corporations paid an effective tax rate of only about 23%. Forty-six large corporations, including Pfizer, Boeing, and AT&T, actually received tax rebates (negative taxes)! Far from being a crushing burden, corporate income tax in the United States has fallen from an average of nearly 5% of GDP in the fifties to 2% in the nineties and about 1.5% (projected) in 2005-2009.

Is the U.S. corporate tax burden higher that that of its competitors? Compari-sons of 29 developed countries reveal that only three—Iceland, Germany, and Po-land—collected less corporate income tax as a share of GDP than the United States. This represents a reversal from the 1960s, when corporate income tax as a share of GDP in the United States was nearly double that of other developed countries.

The demand for cutting dividend taxes needs to be exposed for what it is: an attempt to create yet another windfall for upper income families who earn the bulk of their income from financial investments. It would not stimulate business invest-ment. And it would exacerbate, rather than redress, the many *real* inequities in the tax code.

Sources: John Miller, "Double Taxation Double Speak: Why repealing the dividend tax is unfair," *Dollars & Sense*, March-April 2003; Dean Baker "The Dividend Taxbreak; Taxing Logic," Center for Economic and Policy Research, 2003; Joel Friedman, "The Decline of Corporate income tax revenues," Center on Budget and Policy Priorities, 2003; David Cay Johnston, *Perfectly Legal: The Covert Campaign to Rig our Tax System to Benefit the Super-Rich—and Cheat Everybody Else,* Penguin Books, 2003.

Chapter 7

THE GLOBAL ECONOMY
Inequalities of Wealth and Power

DOLLAR ANXIETY: REAL REASONS TO WORRY

The advantages of imperial finance have propped up the U.S. economy—but they may not last.

JOHN MILLER
January/February 2005

T he value of the dollar is falling. Does that mean that our economic sky is falling as well? Not to sound like Chicken Little, but the answer may well be yes. If an economic collapse is not in our future, then at least economic storm clouds are gathering on the horizon.

It's what lies behind the slide of the dollar that has even many mainstream economists spooked: an unprecedented current account deficit—the difference between the country's income and its consumption and investment spending. The current account deficit, which primarily reflects the huge gap between the amount the United States imports and the amount it exports, is the best indicator of where the country stands in its financial relationship with the rest of the world.

At an estimated $670 billion, or 5.7% of gross domestic product (GDP), the 2004 current account deficit is the largest ever. An already huge trade deficit (the amount exports fall short of imports) made worse by high oil prices, along with rock bottom private savings and a gaping federal budget deficit, have helped push the U.S. current account deficit into uncharted territory. The last time it was above 4% of GDP was in 1816, and no other country has ever run a current account deficit that equals nearly 1% of the world's GDP. If current trends continue, the gap could reach 7.8% of U.S. GDP by 2008, according to Nouriel Roubini of New York University and Brad Setser of University College, Oxford, two well-known finance economists.

Most of the current account deficit stems from the U.S. trade deficit (about $610 billion). The rest reflects the remittances immigrants send home to their families plus U.S. foreign aid (together another $80 billion) less net investment income (a positive $20 billion because the United States still earns more from investments abroad than it pays out in interest on its borrowing from abroad).

The current account deficit represents the amount of money the United States must attract from abroad each year. Money comes from overseas in two ways: foreign investors can buy stock in U.S. corporations, or they can lend money to corporations or to the government by buying bonds. Currently, almost all of the money must come from loans because European and Japanese investors are no longer buying U.S. stocks. U.S. equity returns have been trivial since 2000 in dollar terms and actually negative in euro terms since the dollar has lost ground against the euro.

In essence, the U.S. economy racks up record current account deficits by spending more than its national income to feed its appetite for imports that are now half again exports. That increases the supply of dollars in foreign hands.

At the same time, the demand for dollars has diminished. Foreign investors are less interested in purchasing dollar-dominated assets as they hold more of them (and as the self-fulfilling expectation that the value of the dollar is likely to fall sets in). In October 2004 (the most recent data available), net foreign purchases of U.S. securities—stocks and bonds—dipped to their lowest level in a year and below what was necessary to offset the current account deficit. In addition, global investors' stock and bond portfolios are now overloaded with dollar-denominated assets, up to 50% from 30% in the early '90s.

Under the weight of the massive current account deficit, the dollar has already begun to give way. Since January 2002, the value of the dollar has fallen more than 20%, with much of that dropoff happening since August 2004. The greenback now stands at multiyear lows against the euro, the yen, and an index of major currencies.

Should foreign investors stop buying U.S. securities, then the dollar will crash, stock values plummet, and an economic downturn surely follow. But even if foreigners continue to purchase U.S. bonds—and they already hold 47% of U.S Treasury bonds—a current account deficit of this magnitude will be a costly drag on the economy. The Fed will have to boost interest rates, which determine the rate of return on U.S. bonds, to compensate for their lost value as the dollar slips in value and to keep foreigners coming back for more. In addition, a falling dollar makes imports cost more, pushing up U.S inflation rates. The Fed will either tolerate the uptick in inflation or attempt to counteract it by raising interest rates yet higher. Even in this more orderly scenario of decline, the current expansion will slow or perhaps come to a halt.

Imperial Finance

You can still find those who claim none of this is a problem. Recently, for example, the editors of the *Wall Street Journal* offered worried readers the following relaxation technique—a version of what former Treasury Secretary Larry Summers says is the sharpest argument you typically hear from a finance minister whose country is saddled with a large current account deficit.

First, recall that a large trade deficit requires a large surplus of capital flowing into your country to cover it. Then ask yourself, would you rather live in a country that continues to attract investment, or one that capital is trying to get out of? Finally, remind yourself that the monetary authorities control the value of currencies and are fully capable of halting the decline.

Feel better? You shouldn't. Arguments like these are unconvincing, a bravado borne not of postmodern cool so much as the old-fashioned, unilateral financial imperialism that underlies the muscular U.S. foreign policy we see today.

True, so far foreigners have been happy to purchase the gobs of debt issued by the U.S. Treasury and corporate America to cover the current account deficit. And that has kept U.S. interest rates low. If not for the flood of foreign money, Morgan Stanley economist Stephen Roach figures, U.S. long-term interest rates would be between one and 1.5 percentage points higher today.

The ability to borrow without pushing up interest rates has paid off handsomely for the Bush administration. Now when the government spends more than it takes in to prosecute the war in Iraq and bestow tax cuts on the rich, savers from foreign shores finance those deficits at reduced rates. And cash-strapped U.S. consumers are more ready to swallow an upside-down economic recovery that has pushed up profit but neither created jobs nor lifted wages when they can borrow at low interest rates.

How can the United States get away with running up debt at low rates? Are other countries' central banks and private savers really the co-dependent "global enablers" Roach and others call them, who happily hold loads of low-yielding U.S. assets? The truth is, the United States has taken advantage of the status of the dollar as the currency of the global economy to make others adjust to its spending patterns. Foreign central banks hold their reserves in dollars, and countries are billed in dollars for their oil imports, which requires them to buy dollars. That sustains the demand for the dollar and protects its value even as the current account imbalance widens.

If the United States were an Emerging Market

If the United States were a small or less-developed country, financial alarm bells would already be ringing. The U.S. current account deficit is well above the 5%-of-GDP standard the IMF and others use to pronounce economies in the developing world vulnerable to financial crisis.

Just how crisis-prone depends on how the current account deficit affects the economy's spending. If the foreign funds flowing into the country are being invested in export-producing sectors of the economy, or the tradable goods sectors, such as manufacturing and some services, they are likely over time to generate revenues necessary to pay back the rest of the world. In that case, the shortfall is less of a problem. If those monies go to consumption or speculative investment in non-tradable (i.e., non-export producing) sectors such as a real estate, then they surely will be a problem.

By that standard, the U.S. current account deficit is highly problematic. Economists assess the impact of a current account deficit by comparing it to the difference between net national investment and net national savings. (Net here means less the money set aside to cover depreciation.) In the U.S. case, that difference has widened because saving has plummeted, not because investment has picked up. Last year, the United States registered its lowest net national savings rate ever, 1.5%, due to the return of large federal budget deficits and anemic personal savings. In addition, U.S. investment has shifted substantially away from tradable goods as manufacturing has come under heavy foreign competition toward the non-traded goods sector, such as residential real estate whose prices have soared in and around most major American cities.

Capital inflows that cover a decline in savings instead of a surge in investment are not a sign of economic health nor cause to stop worrying about the current account deficit.

The U.S. strong dollar policy in the face of its yawning current account deficit imposes a "shadow tax" on the rest of the world, at least in part to pay for its cost of empire. "But payment," as Robert Skidelsky, the British biographer of Keynes, reminds us, "is voluntary and depends at minimum on acquiescence in U.S. foreign policy." The geopolitical reason for the rest of the capitalist world to accept the "seignorage of the dollar"—in other words, the advantage the United States enjoys by virtue of minting the reserve currency of the international economy—became less compelling when the United States substituted a "puny war on terrorism" for the Cold War, Skidelsky adds.

The tax does not fall only on other industrialized countries. The U.S. economy has not just become a giant vacuum cleaner that sucks up "all the world's spare investible cash," in the words of University of California, Berkeley economist Brad DeLong, but about one-third of that money comes from the developing world. To put this contribution in perspective: DeLong calculates that $90 billion a year, or one-third of the average U.S. current account deficit over the last two decades, is equal to the income of the poorest 500 million people in India.

The rest of the world ought not to complain about these global imbalances, insist the strong dollar types. That the United States racks up debt while other countries rack up savings is not profligacy but a virtue. The United States, they argue, is the global economy's "consumer of last resort." Others, especially in Europe, according to U.S. policymakers, are guilty of "insufficient consumption": they hold back their economies and dampen the demand for U.S. exports, exacerbating the U.S. current account deficit. Last year U.S. consumers increased their spending three times as quickly as European consumers (excluding Britain), and the U.S. economy grew about two and half times as quickly.

Global Uprising

Not surprisingly, old Europe and newly industrializing Asia don't see it that way. They have grown weary from all their heavy lifting of U.S. securities. And while they have yet to throw them overboard, a revolt is brewing.

Those cranky French are especially indignant about the unfairness of it all. The editors of Le Monde, the French daily, complain that "The United States considers itself innocent: it refuses to admit that it lives beyond its means through weak savings and excessive consumption." On top of that, the drop of the dollar has led to a brutal rise in the value of the euro that is wiping out the demand for euro-zone exports and slowing their already sluggish economic recoveries.

Even in Blair's Britain the Economist, the newsweekly, ran an unusually tough-minded editorial warning: "The dollar's role as the leading international currency can no longer be taken for granted. ... Imagine if you could write checks that were accepted as payment but never cashed. That is what [the privileged position of the dollar] amounts to. If you had been granted that ability, you might take care to hang to it. America is taking no such care. And may come to regret it."

But the real threat comes from Asia, especially Japan and China, the two largest holders of U.S. Treasury bonds. Asian central banks already hold most of their reserves in dollar-denominated assets, an enormous financial risk given that the value of the dollar will likely continue to fall at current low interest rates.

In late November, just the rumor that China's Central Bank threatened to reduce its purchases of U.S. Treasury bonds was enough to send the dollar tumbling.

No less than Alan Greenspan, chair of the Fed, seems to have come down with a case of dollar anxiety. In his November remarks to the European Banking Community, Greenspan warned of a "diminished appetite for adding to dollar balances" even if the current account deficit stops increasing. Greenspan believes that foreign investors are likely to realize they have put too many of their eggs in the dollar basket and will either unload their dollar-denominated investments or demand higher interest rates. After Greenspan spoke, the dollar fell to its lowest level against the Japanese yen in more than four years.

A Rough Ride From Here

The question that divides economists at this point is not whether the dollar will decline more, but whether the descent will be slow and orderly or quick and panicky. Either way, there is real reason to believe it will be a rough ride.

First, a controlled devaluation of the dollar won't be easy to accomplish. Several major Asian currencies are formally or informally pegged to the dollar, including the Chinese yuan. The United States faces a $160 billion trade deficit with China alone. U.S. financial authorities have exerted tremendous pressure on the Chinese to raise the value of their currency, in the hope of slowing the tide of Chinese imports into the United States and making U.S. exports more competitive. But the Chinese have yet to budge.

Beyond that, a fall in the dollar sufficient to close the current account deficit will slaughter large amounts of capital. The *Economist* warns that "[i]f the dollar falls by another 30%, as some predict, it would amount to the biggest default in history: not a conventional default on debt service, but default by stealth, wiping trillions off the value of foreigners' dollar assets."

Even a gradual decline in the value of dollar will bring tough economic consequences. Inflation will pick up, as imports cost more in this bid to make U.S. exports cheaper. The Fed will surely raise interest rates to counteract that inflationary pressure, slowing consumer borrowing and investment. Also, closing the current account deficit would require smaller government deficits. (Although not politically likely, repealing Bush's pro-rich tax cuts would help.)

What will happen is anyone's guess given the unprecedented size of the U.S. current account deficit. But there is a real possibility that the dollar's slide will be anything but slow or orderly. Should Asian central banks stop intervening on the scale needed to finance the U.S. deficit, then a crisis surely would follow. The dollar would drop through the floor; U.S. interest rates would skyrocket (on everything from Treasury bonds to mortgages to credit cards); the stock market and home values would collapse; consumer and investment spending would plunge; and a sharp recession would take hold here and abroad.

The Bush administration seems determined to make things worse. Should the Bush crew push through their plan to privatize Social Security and pay the trillion-dollar transition cost with massive borrowing, the consequences could be disastrous. The example of Argentina is instructive. Privatizing the country's retirement program, as economist Paul Krugman has pointed out, was a major source of the debt that brought on Argentina's crisis in 2001. Dismantling the U.S. welfare state's most successful program just might push the dollar-based financial system over the edge.

The U.S. economy is in a precarious situation held together so far by imperial privilege. Its prospects appear to fall into one of three categories: a dollar crisis; a long, slow, excruciating decline in value of the dollar; or a dollar propped up through repeated interest rates hikes. That's real reason to worry.

Sources: "Dollar Anxiety," editorial, *Wall Street Journal*, 11/11/04; D. Wessel, "Behind Big Drop in Currency: U.S. Soaks Up Asia's Output," *WSJ*, 12/2/04; J. B. DeLong, "Should We Still Support Untrammeled International Capital Mobility? Or are Capital Controls Less Evil than We Once Believed," *Economists' Voice*, 2004; R. Skidelsky, "U.S. Current Account Deficit and Future of the World Monetary System" and N. Roubini and B. Setser "The U.S. as A Net Debtor: The Sustainability of the U.S. External Imbalances," 11/04, Nouriel Roubini's Global Macroeconomic and Financial Policy site <www.stern.nyu.edu/globalmacro>; Rich Miller, "Why the Dollar is Giving Way," *Business Week*, 12/6/04; Robert Barro, "Mysteries of the Gaping Current-Account Gap," *Business Week*, 12/13/04; D. Streitford and J. Fleishman, "Greenspan Issues Warning on Dollar," *L.A. Times*, 11/20/04; S. Roach, "Global: What Happens If the Dollar Does Not Fall?" Global Economic Forum, Morgan Stanley, 11/22/04; L. Summers, "The U.S. Current Account Deficit and the Global Economy," The 2004 Per Jacobsson Lecture, 10/3/04; "The Dollar," editorial, *The Economist*, 12/3/04; "Mr. Gaymard and the Dollar," editorial, *Le Monde*, 11/30/04.

CHINA AND THE GLOBAL ECONOMY

THOMAS I. PALLEY
November/December 2005

Over the last twenty years China has undergone a massive economic transformation. A generation ago, China's economy was largely agricultural; today, the country is an industrial powerhouse experiencing rapid economic growth. Now, however, many economists question the sustainability of China's development model. Ironically, this debate has been triggered by recent acceleration in China's growth, which exceeded 9% in both 2003 and 2004. Some analysts claim this acceleration is being driven by a private investment bubble and by misdirected state investment, posing the risks of inflation and a hard landing when the bubble pops.

China's development model is indeed unsustainable—but not for the reasons most economists suggest. It is not overinvestment or excessive growth that is the problem. Instead, it is China's impact on the global economy. China's export-led development model threatens to trigger a global recession that will rebound and hit China itself. In short, in the same kind of scenario that Keynes addressed in the 1930s, China has failed to develop the demand side of its economy, and so its massive production growth threatens to swamp a weakening demand picture worldwide, with potentially severe consequences for both China and its customers.

A Brief Review of China's Development Model

Broadly speaking, China's development model aims to reduce the size of the centrally planned economy and increase the size of market-based private sector activity. The first step in this transition was taken with the historic 1979 reforms of the agricultural sector, which allowed small farmers to produce for the market. Since then, the government has allowed private sector activity to spread more widely by removing controls on economic activity; at the same time, it is privatizing state owned enterprises (SOEs) on a limited basis.

This spread of market-centered activity has been accompanied by both external and internal capital accumulation strategies. The external strategy rests on foreign direct investment (FDI) and export-led growth. The internal strategy uses credit creation by state-controlled banks to fund SOEs and infrastructure investment.

Though FDI is small relative to total Chinese fixed asset accumulation, it serves a number of important functions. Construction and operation of foreign-owned plants has created employment. FDI has also brought capital goods and high technology into the country, and the inflow has been financed by foreign multinational companies (MNCs). Industrialization inevitably requires importing capital goods from developed economies. Most poor countries have borrowed to pay for these capital goods, which has constrained their growth and made them vulnerable to ever-fluctuating global currency markets. In China, FDI has been a form of self-financing development that short-circuits these foreign financing problems.

Significantly, FDI has provided a key source of export earnings, since a significant portion of MNC output in China is exported. In 2004, MNCs provided 57% of total exports. These exports earnings have bolstered China's balance of payments and ensured external investor confidence.

Low-wage labor plus the advanced technology and capital that FDI has brought into the country have made China the world's low-cost manufacturing leader. With exports booming, foreign MNCs have been willing to continue building new plants in China. This has given rise to an anomalous situation in which low-income China has been a lender (in the form of its trade surplus) to the high-income United States. Normally, it is expected that high-income households save and lend to low-income households. However, there is a logic to this situation. Exports and a trade surplus (i.e., Chinese savings) are the price that China pays for getting foreign MNCs to invest there. For the Chinese government this is a deal worth striking, since China gains productive capacity, high technology, and jobs. It also gains foreign exchange from the trade surplus, which provides protection against the vagaries of the international economy.

This external capital accumulation strategy has been complemented by an internal strategy predicated on state-directed bank credit expansion. The state-owned banking system has been used to fund large industrial and infrastructure investment projects, as well as to maintain employment in unprofitable SOEs. This has helped support aggregate demand and avoid a precipitous collapse of employment in the SOE sector. With no alternative places to invest their money, Chinese savers have effectively been forced to finance these state investments; the government keeps interest rates low by fiat and thus controls the interest cost of these public investments.

External Contradictions: Limits to Export-Led Growth

Though highly successful to date, China's development strategy is ultimately fundamentally flawed. China has become such a global manufacturing powerhouse that it is now driving the massive U.S. trade deficit and undermining the U.S. manufacturing sector. This threatens the economic health of its major customer. China is putting pressure on the European Union's manufacturing sector, slowing economic growth there as well. The contradiction in China's model, then, is that China's success threatens to undermine the U.S. economy, which has provided the demand that has fueled that success.

China's trade surpluses with the United States have been growing rapidly for several years. In 2004, the United States' bilateral trade deficit with China was $162.0 billion, representing 38.8% of the U.S. trade deficit with all non-OPEC countries. The bilateral China deficit is growing fastest, too: by 30.5% from 2003 to 2004, compared to 16.8% growth in the non-China, non-OPEC trade deficit.

The U.S. trade deficit threatens to become a source of financial instability. More important, the deficit is contributing to the problems in manufacturing that are hindering a robust, investment-led recovery in the United States. There are two ways in which the trade deficit has hindered recovery. First, the deficit drains spending out of the U.S. economy, so that jobs are lost or are created offshore instead of at home. Using a methodology that estimates the labor content embodied in the deficit, economist Robert Scott of the Economic Policy Institute estimates that the U.S. trade deficit with China in 2003 represented 1,339,300 lost job opportunities. Using Scott's job calculations and assuming the composition of trade remained unchanged in 2004, the 2004 trade deficit with China of $162 billion represents 1,808,055 lost job opportunities.

Second, China's policies hurt U.S. investment spending through a range of channels. The draining of demand via the trade deficit creates excess capacity, which reduces demand for new capital. The undervaluation of China's currency makes production in China cheaper, and this encourages firms to both shift existing facilities to China and build new facilities there. Undervaluation also reduces the profitability of U.S. manufacturing and this reduces investment spending.

The U.S. economy is of course a huge economy and these China effects are small in terms of total investment. However, China is likely exerting a chilling effect at the margin of manufacturing investment, and it is at this margin where the recessionary impacts of investment decline have been and continue to be felt.

Together, these employment and investment effects risk tipping the U.S. economy back into recession after what has already been a weak expansion. If this happens, there will be significant adverse consequences for the Chinese economy, and for the global economy as a whole, since the U.S. economy is the main engine of demand growth that has been keeping the world economy flying. (Much is made of

China as itself an engine of demand growth, particularly benefiting Japan. China *is* buying capital goods and production inputs from Japan. However, China's internal demand growth depends on the prosperity generated by exporting to the U.S. economy. In this sense, the U.S. economy is the ultimate source of demand growth; this demand growth is then multiplied in the global economy, where China plays an important role in the multiplier process.)

That's why China must replace its export-led growth strategy with one based on expanding domestic demand. China's people need to have the incomes and the institutions that will enable them to consume a far larger share of what they produce.

For the moment, thanks to continued debt-financed spending by U.S. households, China's adverse impact has not derailed the U.S. economy. China has therefore continued to grow despite the weak U.S. recovery from recession. But there are reasons to believe the U.S. economy is increasingly fragile—a Wily Coyote economy running on thinner and thinner air. The recovery has been financed by asset price appreciation, especially in real estate, which has provided collateral for the home-equity loans and other borrowing consumers have used to keep spending. This means the U.S. economy is increasingly burdened by debt which could soon drive the economy into recession. Once in recession, with private sector balance sheets clogged with debt taken on at current low interest rates and not open to refinancing, the U.S. would not have recourse to another recovery based on consumer borrowing and housing price inflation.

Policymakers, including those in China, tend to have a hard time grasping complex scenarios such as this one, where the damage to China is indirect, operating via recession in the United States. Now that it has become a global manufacturing powerhouse, China's export-led manufacturing growth model is exerting huge strains on the global economy. Until now, China has been able to free-ride on global aggregate demand. The strategy worked when Chinese manufacturing was small, but it cannot continue working now that it is so large. The difficulty is to persuade China's policymakers of the need for change now, when the model still seems to be working and the crash has not come.

Developing the Demand Side of the Chinese Economy

In place of export-led growth, China must adopt a model of domestic demand-led growth. Such a model requires developing structures, institutions, and economic relations that generate sustained, stable internal demand growth. This is an enormous task and one that is key to achieving developed-country status, yet it is a task that has received little attention.

Economic theory and policy have traditionally focused on expansion of the supply side in developing countries. This is the core of the export-led growth paradigm, which emphasizes becoming internationally competitive and relying on export markets to provide demand and absorb increases in production. The demand side is generally ignored in the main body of development economics because economists assume that supply generates its own demand, a proposition known as Say's Law.

Nor are traditional Keynesian policies the right answer. Though Keynesian economics does emphasize demand considerations, it operates in the context of mature market economies in which the institutions that generate stable, broad-based demand are well established. For Keynesians, demand shortages can be remedied by policies that stimulate private sector demand (e.g., lowering interest rates or cutting taxes) or by direct government spending. These policies address temporary failures in an established demand generation process.

Developing countries, however, face a different problem: they need to build the demand generation process in the first place. Application of standard Keynesian policies in developing countries tends to create excessive government deficits and promote an oversized government sector. Increased government spending adds to demand but it increases deficits, and it also does little to generate "market" incomes that are the basis of sustainable growth in demand. What is needed is a new analytic approach, one focused on establishing an economic order that ensures income gets into the hands of those who will spend it and encourages production of needed goods that have high domestic employment and expenditure multipliers. This can be termed "structural Keynesianism," in contrast with conventional "demand-side Keynesianism."

In China, then, the challenge is to develop sustainable, growing sources of non-inflationary domestic purchasing power. This means attending to both the investment allocation process and the income allocation process. The former is critical to ensure that resources are efficiently allocated, earn an adequate rate of return, and add to needed productive capacity. The latter is critical to ensure that domestic demand grows to absorb increased output. Income must be placed in the hands of Chinese consumers if robust consumer markets are to develop. But this income must be delivered in an efficient, equitable manner that maintains economic incentives.

While banking reform is critical to improving China's capital allocation process, the greater challenge is to develop an appropriate system of household income distribution that supports domestic consumer markets. Investment spending is an important source of demand, but the output generated by investments must find buyers or investment will cease. Likewise, public sector investment can be an important source of demand, but private sector income must grow over time or else the government sector will come to dominate, with negative consequences.

With a population of 1.3 billion people, China has an enormous potential domestic market. The challenge is to distribute its rapidly growing income in a decentralized, equitable fashion that leaves work and production incentives intact. The conventional view is that markets automatically take care of the problem by paying workers what they are worth and that all income is spent, thereby generating the demand for output produced. In effect, the problem is assumed away. Indeed, to intervene and raise wages to increase demand would be to cause unemployment by making labor too expensive.

This conventional logic contrasts with Keynesian economics, which identifies the core economic problem as one of ensuring a level of aggregate demand consistent with full utilization of a nation's production capacity. Moreover, the level of aggregate demand is affected by the distribution of income, with worsened income distribution lowering aggregate demand because of the higher propensity to save among higher-income households. From a Keynesian perspective, market forces do not automatically generate an appropriate level of aggregate demand. Demand can be too low because of lack of confidence among economic agents that lowers investment and consumption spending. It can also be too low because the distribution of income is skewed excessively toward upper income groups.

In sum, for neoclassical economists, labor markets set wages such that there is full employment, and income distribution is a by-product that in itself has no effect on employment. For Keynesians, full employment requires an appropriate level of aggregate demand, which is strongly affected by the distribution of income.

The importance of income distribution for demand means that labor markets are of critical significance. Labor markets determine wages, and wages affect income distribution. The problem is that bargaining power can be highly skewed in favor of owners, leading to wages that are too low. This problem is particularly acute in developing countries. Trade unions are a vital mechanism for rectifying imbalances of bargaining power and achieving an appropriate distribution of income. Evidence shows that improved freedom of association in labor markets is associated with improved income distribution and higher wages.

Rather than representing a market distortion, as described in conventional economics, trade unions may correct market failure associated with imbalanced bargaining power. Viewed in this light, trade unions are the market-friendly approach to correcting labor market failure

CHINA: RAPID ECONOMIC GROWTH, RAPID EXPORT GROWTH	
Average annual GDP growth 1980-2002:	9.5%
Average annual export growth 1980-2002:	15.5%
Trade as a share of GDP in 1980:	13%
Trade as a share of GDP in 2002:	50%
Market share in the United States in 1980:	0.5%
Market share in the United States in 2002:	11.1%

Source: Internal Monetary Fund, www. imf.org/external/np/apd/seminars/2003/newdelhi/wang.pdf. Box prepared by *Dollars & Sense.*

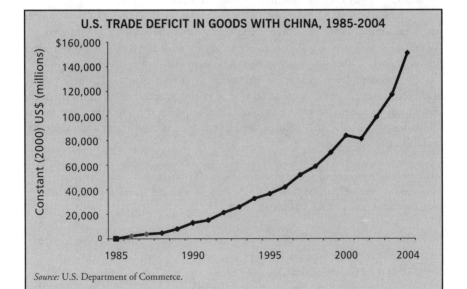

U.S. TRADE DEFICIT IN GOODS WITH CHINA, 1985-2004

Constant (2000) US$ (millions)

Source: U.S. Department of Commerce.

because unions set wages in a decentralized fashion. Though set by collective bargaining, wages can differ across firms with unions in more efficient firms bargaining higher wages than those at less efficient firms. This contrasts with a government-edict approach to wage setting.

This suggests that a key priority for China is to develop democratic trade unions that freely bargain wages. Just as China is reforming its corporate governance and financial system, so too it must embrace labor market reform and allow free democratic trade unions. This is the market-centered way of establishing an income distribution that can support a consumer society. Outside of Western Europe, only the United States, Canada, Japan, South Korea, Australia and New Zealand have successfully made the transformation to mature developed market economies. In all cases this transformation coincided with the development of effective domestic trade unions.

Free trade unions should also be supported by effectively enforced minimum wage legislation that can also promote demand-led growth. China is a continental economy in which regions differ dramatically by level of development. This suggests the need for a system in which minimum wages are set on a regional basis and take account of regional differences in living costs. Over time, as development spreads and backward regions catch up, these settings can be adjusted with the ultimate goal being a uniform national minimum wage.

Lastly, these wage-targeted labor market reforms should be paired with the development of a social safety net that provides insurance to households. This will increase households' sense of confidence and security; with less need for precautionary saving, households can spend more on consumption.

These reforms raise the issue of wage costs. As long as China follows an export-led growth strategy, production costs will be paramount. This is because export-led growth forces countries to try to ever lower costs to gain international competitive advantage, thereby creating systemic downward pressure on wages.

A domestic demand-led growth paradigm reverses this dynamic. Now, higher wages become a source of demand that strengthens the viability of employment. Capital must still earn an adequate return to pay for itself and entice new investment, but moderately higher wages strengthen the system rather than undercutting it.

Independent democratic trade unions are key to a demand-led growth model, as they are the efficient decentralized way of raising wages. However, independent unions are unacceptable to the current Chinese political leadership. That means China must also solve this political problem as part of moving to a domestic demand-led growth regime.

This paper is a shortened and revised version of "External Contradictions of the Chinese Development Model: Export-led Growth and the Dangers of Global Economic Contraction," *Journal of Contemporary China*, 15:46 (2006).

Sources: Blecker, R.A. (2000) "The Diminishing Returns to Export-Led Growth," paper prepared for the Council of Foreign Relations Working Group on Development, New York; Palley, T.I. (2003) "Export-led Growth: Is There Any Evidence of Crowding-Out?" in Arestis et al. (eds.), *Globalization, Regionalism, and Economic Activity*, Cheltenham: Edward Elgar; Palley, T.I. (2002)

"A New Development Paradigm: Domestic Demand-Led Growth," *Foreign Policy in Focus*, www. fpif.org; Jacobs, Weaver and Baker (eds.), *New Rules for Global Finance*, Washington, DC, 2002; Palley, T.I. (2005) "Labor Standards, Democracy and Wages: Some Cross-country Evidence," *Journal of International Development* 17:1–16; Hong Kong Trade & Development Council, www. tdctrade.com/main/china.htm.

THE GLOBALIZATION CLOCK
Why corporations are winning and workers are losing

THOMAS I. PALLEY
May/June 2006

Political economy has historically been constructed around the divide between capital and labor, with firms and workers at odds over the division of the economic pie. Within this construct, labor is usually represented as a monolithic interest, yet the reality is that labor has always suffered from internal divisions—by race, by occupational status, and along many other fault lines. Neoliberal globalization has in many ways sharpened these divisions, which helps to explain why corporations have been winning and workers losing.

One of these fault lines divides workers from themselves: since workers are also consumers, they face a divide between the desire for higher wages and the desire for lower prices. Historically, this identity split has been exploited to divide union from nonunion workers, with anti-labor advocates accusing union workers of causing higher prices. Today, globalization is amplifying the divide between people's interests as workers and their interests as consumers through its promise of ever-lower prices.

Consider the debate over Wal-Mart's low-road labor policies. While Wal-Mart's low wages and skimpy benefits have recently faced scrutiny, even some liberal commentators argue that Wal-Mart is actually good for low-wage workers because they gain more as consumers from its "low, low prices" than they lose as workers from its low wages. But this static, snapshot analysis fails to capture the full impact of globalization, past and future.

Globalization affects the economy unevenly, hitting some sectors first and others later. The process can be understood in terms of the hands of a clock. At one o'clock is the apparel sector; at two o'clock the textile sector; at three the steel sector; at six the auto sector. Workers in the apparel sector are the first to have their jobs shifted to lower-wage venues; at the same time, though, all other workers get price reductions. Next, the process picks off textile sector workers at two o'clock. Meanwhile, workers from three o'clock onward get price cuts, as do the apparel workers at one o'clock. Each time the hands of the clock move, the workers taking the hit are isolated. In this fashion globalization moves around the clock, with labor perennially divided.

Manufacturing was first to experience this process, but technological innovations associated with the Internet are putting service and knowledge workers in the firing line as well. Online business models are making even retail workers vulnerable—consider Amazon.com, for example, which has opened a customer support center and two technology development centers in India. Public sector wages are also in play, at least indirectly, since falling wages mean falling tax revenues. The problem is that each time the hands on the globalization clock move forward, workers are divided: the majority is made slightly better off while the few are made much worse off.

Globalization also alters the historical divisions within capital, creating a new split between bigger internationalized firms and smaller firms that remain nationally centered. This division has been brought into sharp focus with the debate over the trade deficit and the overvalued dollar. In previous decades, manufacturing as a whole opposed running trade deficits and maintaining an overvalued dollar because of the adverse impact of increased imports. The one major business sector with a different view was retailing, which benefited from cheap imports.

However, the spread of multinational production and outsourcing has divided manufacturing in wealthy countries into two camps. In one camp are larger multinational corporations that have gone global and benefit from cheap imports; in the other are smaller businesses that remain nationally centered in terms of sales, production and input sourcing. Multinational corporations tend to support an overvalued dollar since this makes imports produced in their foreign factories cheaper. Conversely, domestic manufacturers are hurt by an overvalued dollar, which advantages import competition.

This division opens the possibility of a new alliance between labor and those manufacturers and businesses that remain nationally based—potentially a potent one, since there are approximately 7 million enterprises with sales of less than $10 million in the United States, versus only 200,000 with sales greater than $10 million. However, such an alliance will always be unstable as the inherent labor-capital conflict over income distribution can always reassert itself. Indeed, this pattern is already evident in the internal politics of the National Association of Manufacturers, whose members have been significantly divided regarding the overvalued dollar. As one way to address this division, the group is promoting a domestic "comp etitiveness" agenda aimed at weakening regulation, reducing corporate legal liability, and lowering employee benefit costs—an agenda designed to appeal to both camps, but at the expense of workers.

Solidarity has always been key to political and economic advance by working families, and it is key to mastering the politics of globalization. Developing a coherent story about the economics of neoliberal globalization around which working families can coalesce is a key ingredient for solidarity. So too is understanding how globalization divides labor. These narratives and analyses can help counter deep cultural proclivities to individualism, as well as other historic divides such as racism. However, as if this were not difficult enough, globalization creates additional challenges. National political solutions that worked in the past are not adequate to the task of controlling international competition. That means the solidarity bar is further raised, calling for international solidarity that supports new forms of international economic regulation.

GLOBALIZATION: GOOD FOR WHAT AILS YOU?

JOHN MILLER
July/August 2006

"Open-Door Policy"

Now would seem a good time [for politicians tempted by protectionism] to re-call how well their countries and others have done by flinging doors open to trade, capital, services and people.

The emergence of China and India as global giants in the making dates directly to their decisions to liberalize. The current U.S. expansion is powered in part by capital from abroad. The Asian Tigers grew off trade. The singular achievement of the European Union was to create the biggest zone on the planet for the free trade of goods, capital and people.

In the past four decades, open economies (mostly from Europe, East Asia, North America) have fared far better than closed ones (Africa, Latin America, parts of Eastern Europe). Economists Jeffrey Sachs and Andrew Warner found that from 1970-1989 average annual growth in open developed economies was 2.3%, compared with 0.7% in the closed. In developing countries, those numbers were 4.5% and 0.7%. That trend hasn't changed much as trade and foreign invest-ment have powered global growth.

As befits the dismal science, not to mention the dismal profession of politics, this evidence hasn't settled the intellectual argument.

—*Wall Street Journal* editorial (3/30/06)

"Globalizing Good Government"

The Federal Reserve Bank of Dallas set out to document the connection be-tween globalization and public policy. We found that the more globalized na-tions tend to pursue policies that achieve faster economic growth, lower inflation, higher incomes and greater economic freedom. The least globalized countries are prone to policies that interfere with markets and lead to stagnation, inflation and diminished competitiveness.

The gist is clear: as nations become more integrated into the world economy, they tend to maintain fewer barriers to trade and the movement of money. They are less likely to impose punishing corporate taxes and onerous regulations. Their technology policies are more favorable to innovation. Nations more open to the world economy score above the less globalized countries in respect for the rule of law and protection of property rights. More globalized countries also offer greater political stability.

Globalization's critics argue that a more open world economy sets off a race to the bottom by encouraging countries to jettison protections for consumers, work-ers and the environment. In reality, the opposite is true. If our data demonstrate anything, it is that globalization prompts a race to the top by pushing countries to abandon policies that burden their economies in favor of those that fuel growth and economic opportunity.

—Op-ed by Richard W. Fisher and W. Michael Cox, *New York Times* (4/10/06)

Got a problem with a corrupt, inefficient government? Does economic growth in your country just limp along? Try globalization, neoliberal globalization that is. Rapid growth and good government are sure to follow.

That is not some online advertisement, but comes straight from the opinion pages of the *Wall Street Journal* and the *New York Times*.

In March, the *Journal* editors published their umpteenth editorial praising globalization. And the *Times*, home of Thomas Friedman, elite journalism's best known apologist for globalization, devoted most of an April op-ed page to "Globalizing Good Government," complete with tables and elaborate illustrations, penned by Richard W. Fisher and W. Michael Cox, president and chief economist at the Federal Reserve Bank of Dallas.

There is just one problem with this latest round of pro-globalization hype: it is simply not true. Debunking the hype is particularly easy this time, since the evidence presented in each of the two editorials exposes the distortions in the other.

Globalization and Growth

We have been over this ground before. Study after study has failed to link more open trade and investment policy to more rapid economic growth. Most of these studies rely on a sleight of hand: they substitute "trade," a performance variable that reflects multiple factors (usually measured as the sum of exports and imports over Gross Domestic Product), for the policy variable "trade openness" (typically measured by tariff and non-tariff barriers to trade). There is indeed a tight correlation between trade and economic growth. But that correlation tells us only that countries that trade a lot grow a lot. It says nothing about whether free trade or managed trade policies best promote trade and economic growth.

None of that stopped the *Journal* editors from once again asserting that globalization leads to faster economic growth. But give them credit for this much. In an attempt to avoid those earlier mistakes, the editors reached all the way back to an influential 1995 paper by Harvard economists Jeffrey Sachs and Andrew Warner that does address the right question: how the policy variable "openness to international trade" relates to how fast a country grows. For them, the evidence from Sachs and Warner's paper, "Economic Reform and the Process of Global Integration," settles the intellectual argument that an "open-door policy" is the key to fast economic growth in today's global economy.

The Sachs and Warner paper constructs a complex aggregate measure of openness to international trade out of average tariff rates, non-tariff barriers, state control of exports, and the premium in black-market prices. And, as the editors report, the Sachs and Warner study finds that from 1970 to 1989, "open" developed countries grew more quickly than those closed to international trade according to their composite measure. The same was true for "open" developing economies: they grew more quickly than developing economies closed to international trade by their measure.

A closer look at the Sachs and Warner measure of openness, however, reveals some serious flaws in their study, as mainstream economists Francisco Rodriguez and Dani Rodrik point out in their exhaustive 2000 survey of the major studies of trade policy and economic growth. First, most of the correlation between growth and the measure of openness in their study comes from the premium in black-market prices and the state monopoly of exports and not the more standard measures of trade openness, tariff and non-tariff barriers to trade. (Sachs and Warner argue that a black-market exchange rate for a country's currency that is 20% lower than the official rate suggests that non-market forces are interfering with trade. Similarly, a state monopoly almost by definition indicates that trade is not governed by market forces.) In addition, Sachs and Warner's measure biases the result by leaving out two of the fastest growing economies with state monopolies on exports, Indonesia and Mauritius.

Finally, the robust connection between high black-market premiums and state monopoly of exports on the one hand, and slower economic growth on the other, can be explained by other institutional variables. Countries with a state monopoly of exports (especially after Indonesia and Mauritius are excluded) are concentrated in Sub-Saharan Africa, one of the slowest growing regions of the world economy. But the slow growth in that region might equally well be explained by the fact that it is saddled with massive foreign debt that consumes 40% of its export revenues, and by the fact that it lacks infrastructure, skills, and political stability.

Likewise, large and sustained black market premiums are usually due to serious macroeconomic policy problems, such as a massive current account deficit and large levels of external debt, that are likely to have depressed economic growth (as opposed to a lack of openness to trade).

For all these reasons, Rodriguez and Rodrik are skeptical that the Sachs-Warner measure is "a meaningful indicator of trade policy." Likewise, it pays to be skeptical when the *Journal* editors parrot their claim that trade openness promotes rapid economic growth.

Beyond the technical problems with the study their editorial relies on, the rest of what the editors write casts doubt on their claims. For instance, India and China might be more open to international trade than in the past, but they hardly make good poster children for neoliberal globalization. For instance, China remains a country that does not have a convertible currency, maintains state control of its banking system, and allows little foreign ownership in equity markets.

Nor does the rapid growth of the Asian Tigers make the case for openness. South Korea and Taiwan, whose most formative growth period was during the 1960s and 1970s, faced a world economy with far less capital mobility and engaged that world with policies antithetical to free trade—export subsidies, domestic-content requirements, import-export linkages, and restrictions on capital flows, including on foreign direct investment.

Overall, Rodriguez and Rodrik find "little evidence that open trade policies—in the sense of lower tariff and non-tariff barriers to trade—are significantly associated with economic growth."

Globalization and Good Government

The *Wall Street Journal* editors have done us a service by focusing our attention on the effects of globalization on economic growth. That alone should inoculate readers against the misleading arguments in "Globalizing Good Government." Despite claiming that "globalization prompts a race to the top ... that fuels growth and economic opportunity," authors Fisher and Cox never provide data to show that globalization is associated with faster economic growth. And that is the Achilles' heel of their editorial, and of the Dallas Fed study, "Racing to the Top: How Global Competition Disciplines Public Policy," on which it is based.

"Racing to the Top" divides 60 countries into four groups—least globalized, less globalized, more globalized, and most globalized—using the A.T. Kearney/Foreign Policy Magazine Globalization Index. The index has its problems, for it indiscriminately mixes together performance variables (such as the level of trade or direct foreign investment) with policy variables (such as tariff levels).

The index does, however, suggest the slipshod way the *Wall Street Journal* editors use countries as examples to justify free-market globalization. Ireland, the editors' favorite, is appropriately enough number two, in the top "most globalized" tier, while France and Germany, whose labor policies the editors rail against, only make it into the second tier. But Asian Tigers South Korea and Taiwan, two of the editors' exemplars of openness, are in the second and third tier of the globalization index. And India and China, the other *Journal* examples of successful globalization, are among the least globalized economies in the world.

Back to Fisher and Cox, who use the Kearney index to show that the more globalized economies have many of the characteristics of what they consider good government and sound economic policy. For instance, more globalized economies have more open trade and investment policies (although their measure of openness has all the flaws of the Sachs and Warner measure), lower corporate taxes, lower inflation rates, less regulation of business, more political stability, more rule of law, more strictly enforced property rights, and less corruption (at least as the Dallas Fed and the Frazier Institute, the Canadian free-market think tank, measure these things). That is enough for Fisher and Cox to conclude, "the more globalized nations tend to pursue policies that achieve faster economic growth, lower inflation, higher incomes, and greater economic freedom."

But nowhere in their study or in their op-ed piece do Fisher and Cox show that economic growth rates pick up with globalization. That is because they can't. Journalist David Shipley emphasizes this point nicely in Extra!, the publication of the left media group Fairness & Accuracy in Reporting. He finds that in 2003-2004, the most globalized countries according to the Kearney index grew the most slowly and the more globalized countries the next most slowly, while the less globalized grew second most quickly and the least globalized fastest of all—just the opposite of the Fisher and Cox claim that more globalized nations tend to pursue policies that achieve faster economic growth!

That inverse relationship between globalization and economic growth holds up over longer periods as well. For the period from 1988 to 2005, the less and least globalized economies with the poorer measures of government performance in the Dallas Fed study grew on average 4.1% and 4.0% a year respectively, while the most and more globalized economies with the supposedly better government performance grew just 3.1% and 3.2% a year respectively.

Only their pro-globalization predilections could explain why the *Times* editors never asked to see growth statistics to back up Fisher's and Cox's assertion. But blaming their editors lets Fisher and Cox off far too easily. The authors were no doubt aware that the data are inconsistent with the contention that globalization leads to faster growth. Consider how gingerly they treat China, whose rapid growth rates, along with those of India, helped to push up the average growth of the least globalized nations. They make a feeble attempt to finesse the obvious contradiction, claiming that China's growth is the result of its abundant cheap labor and foreign investment, and cannot be sustained if China maintains the vestiges of its state-dominated past and its lack of labor flexibility.

So the evidence is clear: freer trade, greater capital market openness, fewer regulations, and lower corporate taxes, all correspond to slower growth. Each of those measures increases as the Kearney index moves from the least globalized to the most globalized category and growth rates slow. That should be enough to give the *Times* editors, and even the *Journal* editors, pause.

Beyond that contradiction, what Fisher and Cox say constitutes good government and economic freedom needs to be held up to closer scrutiny. For instance, since when did lower taxes become desirable in and of themselves? Aren't lower taxes desirable only if they lead to faster economic growth? It is not clear that they do. Economists Joel Slemrod and Jon Bakija, in their respected primer on tax policy, Taxing Ourselves, report that "sophisticated statistical analyses of the relationship between economic growth and the level of taxation, which attempt to hold constant the impact of the other determinants of growth to isolate the tax effect, have come to no consensus."

Neoliberal policies stand in the way of most people gaining control over their economic lives and obtaining genuine economic freedom in today's global economy. True, the Economic Freedom Index put out by the Heritage Foundation and the *Wall Street Journal* correlates nicely with the Kearney globalization index. But it does nothing other than measure corporate and entrepreneurial freedom from accountability, including "burdensome" taxes on corporate profits and "meddlesome" legislation requiring honest corporate accounting or environmental safeguards.

Even if neoliberal globalization did promote economic freedom, political freedom is another matter. Take the city-state Singapore, which tops the Kearney index of the most globalized nations. Singapore is only "partially free" according to Freedom House, which the *Journal* editors have called "the Michelin Guide to democracy's development." In Singapore, freedom of the press and rights to demonstrate are limited, films and TV are censored, preventive detention is legal, and you can do jail time for littering.

Other measures in the Dallas Fed study are just as problematic. For example, Fisher and Cox see globalization as a force for better labor policies. They rightly lament that the international mobility of most workers remains limited, despite countries becoming more globalized. At the same time, they complain that many nations maintain laws that hinder the hiring and firing of workers. They add, "job protection may sound appealing at first, but such policies impede workers' ability to compete." The nations that impose "huge burdens" on employers that lay off workers—including the equivalent of 90 weeks of pay in China—are relatively poor countries. Countries that impose fewer burdens on employers are usually richer. But, hiring labor in China has not been a problem. Fisher and Cox suggest as much when they attribute China's rapid growth to an abundance of cheap labor. The abuse of Chinese factory workers, however, is a problem regularly acknowledged even in the business press, and one that the deregulation of Chinese labor markets would only worsen.

Globalization and the Elite Media

Nowadays studies that endorse neoliberal, free-market globalization, no matter how flawed, make good copy in the liberal and conservative elite media. That crowd is prepared to believe that the world is flat—the title of Thomas Friedman's latest paean to globalization—if it fits their worldview.

SOURCES: "Open-Door Policy," *Wall Street Journal*, 3/30/06; March 30, 2006; "Globalizing Good Government," by Richard W. Fisher and W. Michael Cox, *The New York Times*, April 10, 2006; Richard W. Fisher and W. Michael Cox, "Racing To The Top: How Global Competition Disciplines Public Policy," 2005 Annual Report of the Federal Reserve Bank of Dallas; A.T. Kearney, Inc., "Measuring Globalization: The Global Top 20," *Foreign Policy*, May/June 2005; Joel Slemrod and Jon Bakija, *Taxing Ourselves: A Citizen's Guide to the Debate Over Taxes*; Francisco Rodriguez and Dani Rodrik, "Trade Policy and Economic Growth: A Skeptic's Guide To The Cross-National Evidence," May 2000; Jeffrey Sachs and Andrew Warner, "Economic Reform and the Process of Global Integration," Brookings Papers on Economic Activity, 1995: 1.

WORLD TRADE TALKS COLLAPSE
Why the world's poor countries are breathing a sigh of relief.

TIMOTHY A. WISE
September/October 2006

This summer, the globalization bandwagon came to a screeching halt—although you wouldn't know it from the headlines. In July, the current round of World Trade Organization talks collapsed for good. This was only the latest breakdown in multilateral negotiations to liberalize and regulate global trade. The WTO's initial effort to launch this most recent round of global trade negotiations failed during the 1999 "Battle in Seattle," and talks fell apart again in 2003 in Cancún.

Most news reports pinned the blame on the United States and the European Union for their intransigence over trade-distorting farm supports. Lost in the blame game was a simpler but more profound explanation. This round of talks, launched in

2001 in Doha, Qatar, with the promise of delivering the benefits of trade to developing countries, had lost any hint of pro-poor development impacts. To resounding cheers from popular organizations in many parts of the world—organizations that view the WTO as a Trojan horse for extending the reach of multinational corporations—these talks collapsed partly because developing countries had almost nothing to gain, and a lot to lose.

In 2003, as trade negotiators approached the Cancún meetings, World Bank projections promised $832 billion in estimated gains in economic growth from this round of global trade liberalization, with the bulk—$539 billion—going to the developing world.

What a difference two years made! By 2005, free-trade advocates themselves were projecting far smaller gains for developing countries. New projections from the same World Bank sources now promised global gains of $287 billion, with just $90 billion going to developing countries—an 80% drop from the 2003 projections. Moreover, the newer projections pegged developing countries' share of global gains at just 31%, down from 60% in the 2003 projections—hardly a good advertisement for a so-called "development round" of global trade talks.

And even these figures, based on the unrealistic assumption that tariffs and trade-related subsidies would be completely eliminated, overstated the case. The same World Bank report gives projections for a "likely Doha scenario" of partial liberalization: global gains of just $96 billion, with only $16 billion going to the entire developing world. That's less than a penny a day per capita for those living in developing countries.

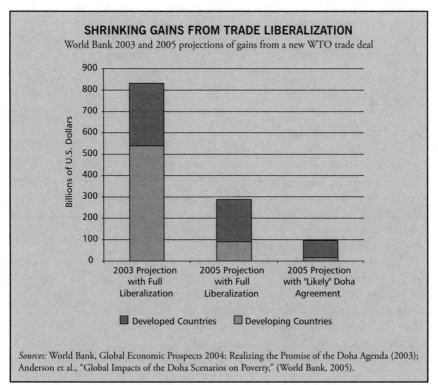

SHRINKING GAINS FROM TRADE LIBERALIZATION

World Bank 2003 and 2005 projections of gains from a new WTO trade deal

Sources: World Bank, Global Economic Prospects 2004: Realizing the Promise of the Doha Agenda (2003); Anderson et al., "Global Impacts of the Doha Scenarios on Poverty," (World Bank, 2005).

Not surprisingly, the poverty impacts vanished along with the income gains. The Cancún promise of bringing 144 million people out of poverty had been cut by 2005 to 66 million in the full-liberalization scenario. Under the "likely Doha scenario," projections suggested just 2.5 million people (out of 622 million worldwide) would be lifted above the dollar-a-day extreme poverty line.

And the gains appear even more minuscule if we look at the numbers in their proper context:

- Trade liberalization brings a one-time increase in GDP, not a sustained increase in growth rates.
- The World Bank's projections are for 2015. Spread the gains over 10 years, and the numbers shrink to complete insignificance—barely one-hundredth of a percent of GDP. For someone making $100 a month, that would amount to a 16¢ raise in monthly salary after 10 years.
- Half of the developing-country benefits would go to just eight countries: Brazil, Argentina, China, India, Thailand, Vietnam, Mexico, and Turkey, with per capita GDPs ranging from $3,000 to over $14,000. Meantime, some of the world's poorest countries stood to gain nearly nothing, or even experience losses in important sectors; for instance, the World Bank's "likely" scenario showed sub-Saharan Africa outside of South Africa losing $0.3 billion dollars in agricultural output following a Doha trade deal.

Why did projections of the benefits of trade liberalization drop so dramatically between 2003 and 2005? In short, the World Bank researchers found ways to bring their abstract models a few steps closer to—if still many simplifying assumptions away from—the real world. For instance, they updated their "base year" from 1997 to 2001, recognizing China's liberalization and its entry into the WTO as already achieved. In the 2003 projections China's gains had accounted for a significant proportion of overall developing-country gains—although the results were frequently reported as if all developing countries stood to gain equally from an "ambitious" WTO agreement.

High Costs of a Doha Deal

A Doha Round agreement promised few gains to the world's poor countries; at the same time, it would have imposed substantial costs, including a sharp drop in tariff revenues, likely deindustrialization, and the loss of autonomy in crafting development policies. Juxtapose these costs with the relatively small projected gains from the draft deal, and we can see why many developing-country governments are shedding few tears over the demise of the Doha Round.

Reducing or eliminating tariffs is at the core of trade liberalization agreements. But many developing-country governments rely on tariffs for more than a quarter, and in some cases closer to a half, of their revenue. Using the same model as the World Bank, the U.N. Conference on Trade and Development (UNCTAD) projected that tariff revenue losses under the draft Doha agreement could amount to $63.4 billion. Even India, one of the supposed winners from a Doha deal, stood to lose $7.9 billion in tariff revenues while gaining only $2.2 billion in income.

PROJECTED DOHA TRADE DEAL BENEFITS VS. TARIFF LOSSES (BILLIONS OF 2001 U.S.DOLLARS)		
	Benefits under "Likely Doha Scenario"	Tariff Lossesunder NAMA*
Developed countries	79.9	38.8
Developing countries	16.1	63.4
Selected developing regions		
Middle East & North Africa	-0.6	7.0
Sub-Saharan Africa	0.4	1.7
Latin American & the Caribbean	7.9	10.7
Selected countries		
Brazil	3.6	3.1
India	2.2	7.9
Mexico	-0.9	0.4
Bangladesh	-0.1	0.04

*NAMA, or Non-Agricultural Market Access, is the segment of WTO negotiations dealing with trade in all goods other than agricultural products.

Sources: Anderson and Martin, Agricultural Trade Reform and the Doha Development Agenda (World Bank, 2005), Table 12.14; DeCordoba and Vanzetti, Coping with Trade Reforms (UNCTAD, 2005), Table 11.

Recently, prominent globalization advocate Jagdish Bhagwati commented in Foreign Affairs that more attention needed to be paid to this issue: "If poor countries that are dependent on tariff revenues for social spending risk losing those revenues by cutting tariffs, international agencies such as the World Bank should stand ready to make up the difference until their tax systems can be fixed to raise revenues in other, more appropriate, ways." This is the sort of promise poor countries have learned to take with a grain of salt, to say the least; even the most ambitious "aid for trade" plans come nowhere near filling the gap in lost tariff revenue predicted by UNCTAD.

Another cost is the threat of deindustralization. Economic development means investing in human, physical, and natural capital in a diversifying range of manufacturing and services industries while moving away from extractive industries and low-productivity agriculture. Projections showed, however, that a likely Doha agreement would have pushed developing-country economies in precisely the opposite direction. For instance, India was predicted to experience significant output and employment losses in sectors such as chemicals, leather, and food processing while gaining in industries further down the technological ladder such as textiles and apparel. Brazil was predicted to lose in the metals, machinery, motor vehicle, and chemical industries in exchange for modest gains in its soy and meat sectors. In both cases, these large and dynamic developing countries were projected to see their levels of industrial development decline with a Doha agreement. And countries that have yet to develop their industrial sectors would have found themselves even more locked into primary production.

The greatest cost to developing countries from a likely Doha agreement is the hardest to quantify: the loss of policy space. In exchange for limited gains in agriculture and low-technology manufacturing, Doha-style agreements force developing countries to surrender the right to use many of the policy instruments—for instance, selective tariffs and export and credit subsidies—that have proven successful in moving countries toward higher levels of development and improved incomes for their people.

Under the proposed agreement on manufactured goods, for example, nations would no longer have been allowed to keep their average tariffs low while using high tariffs in strategic industries. Like the United States and European countries before them, nations such as Taiwan and South Korea have relied on such tariff strategies to industrialize their economies, and China and India now make heavy use of such measures.

In the end, the losers from the proposed Doha agreement outnumbered the winners, and perhaps for the first time the losers saw the deal for what it was and said no. Now the possible winners, rich countries and the multinational companies based in them that benefit the most from globalization, are scrambling to revive global trade talks. The losers, meanwhile, have a chance to reassess—and to come back to the table demanding policies that truly favor development for the countries that need it most.

This article is adapted from two RIS Policy Briefs by Timothy A. Wise and Kevin Gallagher, "Doha Round's Development Impacts: Shrinking Gains and Real Costs" (11/05) and "Doha Round and Developing Countries: Will the Doha deal do more harm than good?" (4/06).

Chapter 8

ENVIRONMENTS
Global and Local

AFTER KYOTO
A better way to ensure climate stabilization and fair development.

PAUL CUMMINGS AND **ADRIA SCHARF**
July/August 2005

If a council of wise elders were to recommend a design for the basic business organization of this age, the current form of corporation would not likely be their choice.

Today's version of the corporation evolved about 150 years ago, at a time when space seemed vast and earth's resources even vaster. The economic task was simple: cover the continent, exploit its resources, build a muscular industrial machine equal to those of Europe. It was simply to grow. Today the task is more complex. The habitat can no longer absorb all the effluents of our striving—nor, for that matter, can we. The noxious side effects of production often loom larger than the supposed benefits; the factory that employs hundreds may befoul the water that is used by millions.

The corporation is not responsible for all this harm, of course. But it is the central engine of the economy for better or worse. It wields the most resources, cuts the widest swath. If the economy is to meet not just its age-old obligations to workers but its newer challenge of treading more lightly upon the earth, a remade corporation will have to play a central role.

As it stands, the corporation is not designed to deal with the negative dimensions of its activities, the way a person can. Like the 19th-century economic assumptions it embodies, it has little capacity to think beyond the boundaries of its own balance sheet. The large "publicly traded" corporation—one with shares of ownership traded on the stock exchanges—is especially captive to its form. A CEO fails to maximize monetary return and Wall Street analysts breathe fire. Shareholders can even sue if the company doesn't fulfill its legally enshrined duty to gain for them the greatest possible return.

Markets and corporations are whatever we choose to make them. The corporation does not exist in nature; unlike real persons it has no existence independent of the government that creates it. And it is past time for the corporation to grow up.

It is a little like seeing the appetite of a 13-year-old in a body pushing forty—19th-century assumptions bumping up against a crowded world on the threshold of the 21st. The corporation needs a broader concept of the bottom line, and more ability to think about things besides itself.

The strange part is that's pretty much where the corporation started—a broader bottom line. The early corporations of Europe were not businesses but literally embodiments of social stability and cohesion—monasteries and universities, boroughs and guilds. They reconciled individual behavior with larger social ends. Even the early business corporations were defined largely by a public purpose (by the lights of the era). Only in the last century did this connection unravel.

To piece it together again, we need to understand that the original business corporations in the United States grew out of a bargain. Individual responsibility is a bedrock principle of common law. Owners were once personally responsible for the activities of the business, including the employees who toiled on their behalf. Your employee fouled a neighbor's well, the neighbor could sue you. That principle endured for centuries, but it broke down as business ventures grew in scale. When the British Crown sought to explore the New World, for example, few would put up capital if they could be personally on the line if something went wrong—a shipwreck, say. In today's terms, it would be like getting sued for the Valdez oil spill because you owned a hundred shares of Exxon stock.

To resolve this impasse, the Crown established the principle of limited liability for investor-owners. This new privilege could not be dispensed willy-nilly. It went only to companies chartered specifically to carry out a mission of state, such as the trading companies which returned large revenues to the Crown. This was the concept of the corporation which took root in the New Land.

The trading companies had come to embody all that American colonists detested about British rule, and their suspicions regarding legal agglomerations of all kinds. So the colonists kept the corporation on a very tight leash. The colonial (and later state) legislatures granted corporate charters one by one, to enterprises that served a clearly public purpose, such as operating a toll road or a ferry service. They loaded the charters with provisions to ensure that the public interest was served. There were restrictions on how large the corporation could become and even how long it could exist.

During the nineteenth century this bargain unraveled. The burgeoning enterprise of the era, the rise of factories and railroads, and the national market the latter made possible, were simply too much for the old restraints. First the states enacted "free incorporation laws" which enabled anyone to form a corporation to do just about anything they wanted. Historians have hailed this as part of "Jacksonian Democracy," a blow for the common folk against special privilege. There was that element; the bestowal of charters had become a bastion of cronyism and political deals. But the free incorporation laws led directly to the huge industrial monopolies of the end of the century, and scrapped the premise of the corporate arrangement. The corporation kept its exemption from common law principles of responsibility, but shed the inconvenient obligation to serve the public in return.

Even so, there were lingering echoes of the old bargain. For example, many states still imposed size limits; as late as 1890, New York State permitted corporations to be no larger than $5 million in capital. (It was to evade such restrictions that John D. Rockefeller put together the web of secret agreements that became known as the Standard Oil Trust.)

But then a governor of New Jersey had a supply-side inspiration: Lure enough corporations with weak, permissive laws and you could collect enough revenue in incorporation fees to cut taxes substantially for individuals. That set off a race to the bottom, in which the states competed to enact the most permissive laws and thus attract the most corporations. The eventual champ was Delaware, where many of the nation's largest corporations exist today as files in a lawyer's office in the state capital of Wilmington. The relationship between the corporation and the states had turned upside down. Once the creature of the states, the corporation was now the demanding taskmaster which played them off against one another.

The Supreme Court contributed to this shift when in 1886 it declared, with no explanation, that the Fourteenth Amendment applied to corporations. These legal "persons" now had all the Constitutional protections that real people had; an amendment intended to guarantee the rights of the most vulnerable in the land was turned into a bill of rights for the most powerful. This decision would shape permanently the legal context for regulation and the nature of politics itself. One of the Constitutional rights now extended to corporations was freedom of speech. As things now stand, business lobbies can buy all the time and space they want to tell the public that global warming is not a problem. Real people who lack that kind of money don't get any time or space at all.

Eventually, the corporation could do whatever it wanted, grow as big as it wanted; it could even live forever. In the case of railroads, the first mega-corporations, they could take the vast portions of the public (originally native American) do-

The Charter Challenge

Some environmentalists are starting to confront corporations by challenging the privileges granted to them by state charters. "Battles with regulatory agencies are very limited," says Richard Grossman, whose Cambridge, Mass.-based Program on Corporations, Law, and Democracy has led the intellectual charge to rethink corporate charters. "It is challenging corporate behavior one item at a time"—and tacitly upholds corporate political rights Grossman believes are illegitimate.

After regulators failed to rein in Waste Management, the huge garbage conglomerate, Pennsylvania environmentalists asked their attorney general to revoke its charter and thus its ability to operate in the state. When the attorney general refused, the Community Environment Legal Defense Fund took him to court in 1996. The Fund lost its case, but Tom Linzey of the Legal Defense Fund explains the principle at stake: A charter is "a contract between the people of the state, who charter corporations to create wealth... and the corporation agrees to abide by the state's laws. Somebody has to police these contracts."

If state officials do not bow to grassroots pressure, the activists plan to lobby for local ordinances to hold corporations accountable. The idea, according to Grossman, is to "provoke a crisis of jurisdiction" by creating more stringent laws than that of the states or feds, igniting a debate on state officials who shirk their duty to challenge corporate misdeeds.

—Loren McArthur

main—bestowed on them by legislatures to help support rail service—and use these gifts for their own gain instead. At the same time the corporation shed most of the corresponding obligations that were built into its organic structure. Instead of a creature of society, it became the dominant institution in it besides the government (and some would say including the government).

The result today is that the corporation is an anomaly. It developed in a way that the seminal thinkers about democracy and the economy could not have foreseen. When Adam Smith wrote *The Wealth of Nations* (1776), for example, the modern corporation did not exist. The corporation of his experience was a government franchise along the lines of the East India Company, a form of business he did not consider promising. In one of his less prescient passages, Smith wrote that the corporation would never amount to much in the international marketplace; it was too cumbersome and bureaucratic, too lacking in the "dexterity and judgement" of individual entrepreneurs who assuredly would run circles around it.

Thus it was possible for Smith to envision an economy of individual shopkeepers and entrepreneurs whose atomistic strivings would keep one another in check—and whose social affinities as members of a community would tend to keep their enterprises on a tether of community norms. Similarly with the Founding Fathers: The home-grown corporations within their ken were local franchises that ran bridges and the like. They were a state and local issue. Matters seemed well in hand and it did not occur to most of the authors of the Constitution to include the corporation within the scheme of checks and balances by which they sought to restrain agglomerations of power in the body politic.

This helps explain why the corporation has come to so dominate the nation's politics and market. With the original bargain broken, there is nothing in our institutional genetic coding to reconcile the corporation with the larger whole. The odd part is that pollution occupies a similar place in our economics. At the end of the 18th century, when Adam Smith wrote, the earth still seemed immense. It took six weeks to get a wagon from Smith's Edinburgh to London and back. That there might be limits to the ability of the habitat to absorb the effluents of human activity could seem remote. Remote too was the possibility that commercial transactions might one day have a greater effect upon the millions who aren't party to them than upon those who are, thus upsetting the central calculus of market economics.

Today economists try to deal with these environmental ripple effects under the rubric of "externalities," a revealing term. The toxic emissions from a smelter are not "external" to the lives of the neighbors who must suffer them; they are so only to the preconceptions of economists who regard the smelter and its customers as the core reality, and everything besides that as "external." The large literature on "externalities" suggests that a central fact of modern economic life—degradation of the habitat—fits awkwardly with a central assumption of the discipline: that the center of the economic universe is still an isolated transaction between a buyer and a seller.

There's a need for a new economics that integrates the toxic impacts of economic activity into the core reality, and which seeks to promote human well-being instead of just money-making transactions. At the same time, there's a need to integrate the most important part of the economy—the corporation—into economic and political reality. In environmental terms, the corporation is going to have to take more responsibility for its impacts upon others, just as we expect real people to do.

The most prominent corner in the environmental debate today is called "market based" environmentalism. The basic idea is to establish financial carrots and sticks instead of ordinary regulation. Instead of mandating a smokestack scrubber, say, charge the company heavily for what it emits and let it find the most efficient way to clean up its discharges. There's a tendentious quality to a lot of market-based environmentalism, especially when its advocates dismiss ordinary regulation as "command and control," with the Stalinist overtones of that phrase. The fact is, there will always be a need for plain old regulation; you can't let some people poison others just because they pay a market price to do so.

Still, the market-basers have a point. If you can build environmental and other concerns into a company's ordinary financial metabolism—make them the warp and woof of the market calculus—then the need for external regulation will be less. Very likely you will achieve your goals in a more elegant and efficient way. The discussion usually starts with taxes, which is where public policy affects prices most directly. Tax petroleum and other fuels more heavily, and you set up a dynamic in which companies strive to conserve in order to save money. Less pollution should be the result. The revenues could be used to cut the payroll tax on work. It is insane to tax work heavily but the use of natural resources hardly at all.

But the tax system is just one way to use the infrastructure of the market to prod corporations towards a broader bottom line. The information system is another. Even in orthodox market theory, buyers are supposed to have complete information about the implications of their buying so they can make choices that express their values. Today such information is in short supply. We have little idea where the stuff we buy comes from, the conditions under which it is made, or the effluents and other impacts created in the process.

Sixty years ago, in the midst of the Depression, Congress established the Securities and Exchange Commission to require rigorous financial reporting by corporations. The idea was that informed investors would help avert another financial crash. Today we need more environmental-impact reporting so that informed buyers can help avert an environmental crash. The so-called Toxics Release Inventory, enacted in the 1980s, requires plants to disclose to their neighbors the toxic substances they use and emit. It has been an environmental success story and a model for the way disclosure can affect corporate behavior.

More broadly, there's a need for more and better indicators of environmental well-being that establish a context of concern about these matters. Today, readers of the daily papers find out about the stock and bond markets and baseball standings in great detail. About environmental conditions they learn very little. If people seem indifferent to such matters as the emissions from their sport utility vehicles, it is partly because there is little in our daily cognitive environments to impress such a concern upon us, and much advertising to make us want to buy the SUVs. The nation's current index of economic progress, the Gross Domestic Product or GDP, is perverse in this regard. It merely adds up all economic activity—constructive or destructive. The more gas we guzzle, the worse the air gets and the more medical problems that result, the more the GDP goes up. Walk or ride a bike and the GDP goes down because you are spending less money.

This is idiotic. The nation needs an index of economic well-being, not just of money spent. Starting close to home, over 200 states and localities around the country are developing their own indicators of well-being.

Such steps could affect the context in which the corporation operates. Eventually the corporation must change internally, through new forms of ownership which embody environmental concerns so they don't have to be injected from without. One example is local ownership along the lines of the Green Bay Packers football team, owned entirely by residents of Green Bay, Wisconsin. Local owners are likely to think a little longer about fouling their own nest (and about such things as moving their own or their neighbors' jobs abroad). There is no guarantee, but at least the decision takes on a personal dimension that is lacking now in the abstracted Wall Street calculus.

Employee ownership can work in similar fashion, especially regarding workplace environmental issues. There also should be new corporate structures offering tax breaks and other advantages in exchange for high levels of environmental performance. The law offers special privileges for people who want to assemble a real estate investment empire. Why not for people who want to do environmental good?

There's also a need to revive the corporate charter as a genuine agreement between the institution and society. Today it is little more than a permissive carte blanche for management, and that won't change as long as states must grovel to attract corporate charter business. Early in the century, President Taft proposed federal chartering for very large corporations. This is a good Republican idea whose time has come. Global corporations should operate under ground rules in proportion to their impact and scale, and that means more than a file drawer in a law office in permissive Delaware. The growing movement to reopen the corporate charter debate at the state level could lead eventually in this direction (see box); at the very least there needs to be a floor that limits the ability of corporations to play states off against one another.

At the same time, the political impact of the corporation needs to be brought back into scale with the rest of society. If, as Congressional Republicans argue, labor unions should have to get the consent of their members to make political contributions, shouldn't corporations have to get the consent of their customers who are the source of the corporation's political funds? At the very least, shouldn't they have to inform their customers about which politicians get a cut of the money shoppers spend at the store?

Ultimately the nation is going to have to revisit the question of corporate personhood, which the Supreme Court declared but never really justified. As long as corporations have the same speech rights as individuals, they will have more such rights, because they have so much more by way of money and resources to make use of them. The next strict-constructionist Supreme Court nominee should be asked to explain where precisely the Constitution says that artificial persons should have the same rights and protections that real people do.

Techno-futurists say the new information-based economy will make most environmental concerns moot. But paper use has burgeoned along with computers. Pressures on forests, offshore oil, and mineral deposits have not abated. If some forms of physical pollution have diminished in the United States, it is often because those dirty industries do their business now in developing countries instead. The frantic competitive pressures and centrifugal pulls of the global market make the need to rework the corporation into the larger social weave all the more important.

There is nothing strange or radical about the task. It is a traditionalist agenda that would restore the corporation to what it was supposed to be—a way to mobilize economic resources to meet current human needs. It would correct an omission that the framers of our guiding economic and political concepts could not have foreseen. Unless one believes that history has basically stopped, and all that remains is an expansion from an institutional status quo—that is, unless one thinks like an economist—then the kinds of government agencies and programs, corporations and the rest are going to have to change, along with changing needs.

TOWARD A GLOBAL ENERGY TRANSITION
What would it take to reverse climate change?

ROSS GELBSPAN
March/April 2004

In 1998, Hurricane Mitch killed 10,000 people in Central America. Last May, the worst flooding in memory in Sri Lanka killed about 300 people, left another 500 missing, and left 350,000 homeless. The president of Tuvalu, an island nation in the Pacific threatened by rising sea levels, calls climate change "a form of slow death." These are just a few recent natural disasters that scientists fear may be linked to global warming.

To avert climate catastrophe, humanity needs to cut its use of fossil fuels by at least 70% in a very short time. That is the consensus of more than 2,000 scientists from 100 countries reporting to the U.N.-sponsored Intergovernmental Panel on Climate Change in the largest and most rigorously peer-reviewed scientific collaboration in history.

The urgency of the threat is spelled out in two other recent peer-reviewed studies corroborating the U.N. panel's findings. The first, written in 2001 by researchers at the Hadley Center, Britain's principle climate research institute, estimated that the climate will change 50% more quickly than scientists had previously believed. Earlier computer models had assumed a relatively static biosphere. But when researchers factored in the warming that has already taken place, they found that the rate of change is compounding. They project that most of the world's forests will begin to die off and emit, rather than absorb, CO_2 by around 2040.

The other study is equally troubling. Several years ago, a team of 11 researchers published a study in Nature suggesting that unless the world gets half its energy from non-carbon (that is, non-fossil fuel) sources by 2018, a doubling—and possible tripling—of pre-industrial carbon dioxide (CO_2) levels later in this century will be inevitable. A follow-up study, published in Science in November 2002, calls for a crash program to develop a carbon-free energy economy. Using conservative projections of future energy use, the researchers concluded that within 50 years, the world will need to generate at least three times more energy from alternative sources than it currently produces from fossil fuels in order to avoid a catastrophic build-up of atmospheric CO_2.

The science is taken very seriously outside the United States. In other countries, hardly anyone debates whether human activities are affecting the climate. Policymakers in Europe are in agreement about the urgency of the climate threat. Holland has completed a plan to cut emissions by 80% in the next 40 years. The United Kingdom has committed itself to 60% reductions in 50 years. Germany is planning for 50% cuts in 50 years.

By contrast, the White House has become the East Coast branch office of ExxonMobil and Peabody Coal, and climate and energy policy has become the pre-eminent case study in the contamination of the U.S. political system by money.

Two years ago, U.S. President George W. Bush reneged on a campaign promise to cap carbon emissions from coal-burning power plants. He then unveiled his administration's energy plan, which is basically a shortcut to climate hell. In a truly Orwellian stroke, the White House excised all references to the dangers of climate change on the Environmental Protection Agency's website in mid-2003. Finally, Bush withdrew the United States from the Kyoto climate negotiations, and the administration's chief climate negotiator declared that the United States would not engage in the Kyoto process for at least 10 years.

A Strategy to Reverse CO_2 Emissions

A plan that could actually stabilize the climate does exist. Provisionally called the World Energy Modernization Plan, it was developed by an ad hoc group of about 15 economists, energy policy experts, and others who met at the Center for Health and the Global Environment at Harvard Medical School three years ago.

The plan addresses a stark reality: The deep oceans are warming, the tundra is thawing, the glaciers are melting, infectious diseases are migrating, and the timing of the seasons has changed. All this has resulted from only one degree of warming. The U.N.-sponsored Intergovernmental Panel on Climate Change (IPCC) expects the earth to warm another three to 10 degrees later in this century.

To date, no other policy proposals have adequately addressed either the scope or the urgency of the problem. While some of its particulars may require revamping, the World Energy Modernization Plan reflects an appropriate scale of action, given the magnitude of the crisis.

The plan calls for three interacting strategies. One is a subsidy switch: industrial countries would eliminate government subsidies for fossil fuels and establish equivalent subsidies for renewable, non-carbon energy technologies. Another is a clean-energy transfer fund—a pool of money on the order of $300 billion a year to provide renewable energy technologies to developing countries. The last element is a progressively more stringent fossil-fuel efficiency standard that would rise by 5% per year.

While each of these strategies can be viewed as a stand-alone reform, they are better understood as a set of interactive policies that could speed the energy transition far more rapidly together than if they were implemented piecemeal.

Subsidy Switch

The United States now spends more than $20 billion a year to subsidize fossil fuels through corporate tax write-offs and direct payments to oil, gas, and coal companies (for research and development, and oil purchases for the Strategic Petroleum Reserve, for example). Subsidies for fossil fuels in industrial countries total an estimated $200 billion a year.

Under this proposal, industrial countries would withdraw those subsidies from fossil fuels and establish equivalent subsidies for renewable energy sources. A small portion of U.S. subsidies must be used to retrain or buy out the nation's approximately 50,000 coal miners. But the lion's share of the subsidies would go to aggressive development of fuel cells, wind farms, and solar systems. The major oil companies would be forced to re-tool and retrain their workers to stay afloat in the renewable energy economy.

Fund to Help Poor Countries Go Green

The second element of the plan involves the creation of a new $300-billion-a-year fund to help transfer renewable energy technologies to the global South. Developing countries such as China, Mexico, Thailand, and Chile contain some of the world's smoggiest cities. Many would love to go solar, but virtually none can afford to.

One attractive source of revenue to fund the transfer lies in a so-called "Tobin tax," named after its developer, Nobel prize-winning economist James Tobin. This tax would be levied on banks and other agents that conduct international currency transactions. Tobin conceived his tax as a way of damping volatility in capital markets by discouraging short-term trading and encouraging longer-term capital investments. But it would also generate enormous revenues. Today currency swaps by banks and speculators total $1.5 trillion per day. A tax of a quarter-penny on a dollar would net $300 billion a year, which could go for wind farms in India, fuel-cell factories in South Africa, solar equipment assemblies in El Salvador, and vast, solar-powered hydrogen-producing farms in the Middle East.

If a Tobin tax proves unacceptable, a fund of the same magnitude could be raised from a tax on airline travel or a carbon tax in industrial countries, although both these sources are more regressive.

Regardless of its revenue source, the fund would be allocated according to a United Nations formula. Climate, energy use, population, economic growth rates, and other factors would determine each developing country's allocation.

Recipient countries would negotiate contracts with renewable energy vendors to ensure domestic ownership of new energy facilities and substantial employment of local labor in their construction and operation. Although not explicitly mentioned in the initial version of the plan, it would be important for governments to be required to include representatives of ethnic and indigenous minorities, universities, nongovernmental organizations (NGOs), and labor unions in making decisions about the procurement and deployment of new energy resources.

An international auditing agency would monitor transactions to ensure equal access for all energy vendors and to review contracting procedures between banks, vendors, and recipient governments.

Individual countries would decide how to use their share. For example, if India received $5 billion in the first year, it could pick its own mix of wind farms, small-scale solar installations, fuel cell generators, and biogas facilities.

In this hypothetical example, the Indian government would entertain bids for these clean energy projects. Vendors might include large or small private companies, state-owned entities, and even nonprofit organizations. As these contractors met specified development and construction goals, they would be paid directly by the banks. And the banks would receive fees for administering the fund.

As developing countries acquired technology, the fund could simply be phased out, or the money in it could be diverted to other global needs.

If funded by a Tobin tax, it would transfer resources from speculative, nonproductive finance-sector transactions to the industrial sectors of developing nations for productive, job-creating, wealth-generating projects. A clean-energy transfer fund of this sort could have a massive impact on developing and transitional economies, similar to the Marshall Plan's effect on Europe after World War II.

Strict International Efficiency Standards

Third, the plan calls on the parties to the Kyoto talks to adopt a simple and equitable fossil-fuel efficiency standard that becomes 5% more stringent each year.

This mechanism, if incorporated into the Kyoto Protocol, would harmonize and guide the global energy transition in a way that the current ineffectual and inequitable system of international emissions trading cannot.

The system of international emissions trading at the heart of the Kyoto Protocol is based on the concept that a country that exceeds its allowed quantity of carbon emissions can buy emission credits from a country that emits less than its allowed quantity. The United States, for instance, can pay Costa Rica to plant more trees to absorb carbon dioxide, and subtract the resulting reduction from its own allowance.

This system of international "cap and trade," as it is called in the jargon of the Kyoto negotiators, has significant failings: It's not enforceable and is plagued by irreconcilable equity disputes between the countries of the North and South. (See box "Cap and Trade: Environmental Colonialism?")

International carbon trading cannot be the primary vehicle to propel a worldwide energy transition. Alone, it simply will not succeed in reversing—or even slowing—global CO_2 emissions at anywhere near an adequate rate. Even if all the problems with monitoring, enforcement, and equity could be resolved, emissions trading would at best be a fine-tuning instrument to help countries meet the final 10 to 15% of their obligation to reduce CO_2 emissions. We simply can't finesse nature with accounting tricks.

Instead, the parties to the Kyoto talks should increase their fossil-fuel energy efficiency by 5% every year until the global 70% reduction is attained. That means a country would either produce the same amount of goods as in the previous year with 5% less carbon fuel, or produce 5% more goods with the same amount of carbon fuel use as the previous year. During the first few years under the proposed ef-

Cap and Trade: Environmental Colonialism?

The global South has long contended that the Kyoto cap and trade system is unjust. Under Kyoto, each country's emissions cap is based on its 1990 emission levels—but developing countries argue that only a per-capita allocation of emission rights is fair. What's more, they argue, provisions in the Kyoto Protocol allow industrial nations to buy limitless amounts of cheap emission reductions in developing countries and to bank them indefinitely into the future. As the late Anil Agarwal, founder of the Centre for Science and Environment in New Delhi, has pointed out, when developing nations eventually become obligated to cut their own emissions (under a subsequent round of the Kyoto Protocol), they will be left with only the most expensive options. Agarwal considered this a form of environmental colonialism.

ficiency standard, most countries would likely meet their goals by implementing low-cost improvements to their existing energy systems. After a few years, however, more expensive technology would be required to meet the progressively higher standard, making renewable energy sources more cost effective in comparison to fossil-fuel efficiency measures. The growing demand would create mass markets and economies of scale for renewables.

Given both fossil-fuel efficiency improvements and the growing use of alternatives, emissions reductions would outpace long-term economic growth, benefiting the environment.

Every country would begin at its current baseline for emission levels, which would reduce the inequities inherent in the cap-and-trade system.

This approach would be far simpler to negotiate than the current protocol, with its morass of emissions trading details, reviews of the adequacy of commitments, and differentiated emission targets for each country. It would also be easier to monitor and enforce. A nation's compliance would be measured simply by calculating the annual change in the ratio of its carbon fuel use to its gross domestic product. That ratio would have to change by 5% a year. Although this plan does not include an enforcement mechanism, one would be devised.

The approach has a precedent in the Montreal Protocol, under which companies phased out ozone-destroying chemicals. That protocol was successful because the companies that made the destructive chemicals were able to produce their substitutes with no loss of competitive standing within the industry. The energy industry must be restructured in the same way. Several oil executives have said in private conversations that they could, in an orderly fashion, decarbonize their energy supplies—but only if the governments of the world regulate the process to require all companies to make the transition in lockstep. A progressive fossil-fuel efficiency standard would provide that type of regulation.

A Regulated Transition

Even from the perspective of capitalist financial institutions, this plan should make perfect sense. Recently, Swiss Re-Insurance said it anticipates losses from climate impacts to reach $150 billion a year within this decade. Munich Re, the world's largest reinsurer, estimates that within several decades, losses from climate impacts will reach $300 billion a year. Climate change will destroy property; raise health care costs; ruin crops; and damage energy, communications and transportation infrastructures. It will likely wound the insurance and banking sectors in the process. Last year, the largest re-insurer in Britain said that unchecked climate change could bankrupt the global economy by 2065. And its effects hit poor countries hardest—not because nature discriminates against the poor, but because poor countries can't afford the kinds of infrastructure needed to buffer its impacts.

By contrast, a worldwide energy transition would create a dramatic expansion of the overall wealth in the global economy. It would raise living standards in the South without compromising those in the North. Rewiring the planet with clean energy in time to meet nature's deadline will generate a staggering number of new jobs for the global labor force. By blocking a transition to clean energy, the coal and oil industries are hindering a huge surge in new jobs all over the world.

This transition cannot be accomplished by unregulated free markets. A global energy conversion will require the world's governments to put in place a strong regime of mandatory regulation to control the economic activity of some of the world's largest and most powerful corporations. Without a binding structure of regulation to level the corporate playing field, competing energy companies will undercut today's voluntary initiatives by selling artificially cheaper oil and coal products. This would turn any investment in solar, wind, and hydrogen into money losers. On the other hand, energy firms that submit to the strong new regulations would gain a new $300-billion-a-year market.

A meaningful solution to the climate crisis could potentially be the beginning of a much larger transformation of our social and economic dynamics. This proposal is ambitious. But the alternative—given the escalating instability of the climate system and the increasing desperation caused by global economic inequities—is truly too horrible to contemplate.

Adapted with permission from Foreign Policy In Focus (FPIF) <www.fpif.org>, a joint project of the Interhemispheric Resource Center and the Institute for Policy Studies. A longer version of this article was prepared for the PetroPolitics conference co-sponsored by FPIP and the Sustainable Energy and Economy Network (SEEN), a project of the Institute for Policy Studies. For more information, and to read the web version of the article online, see <www.PetroPolitics.org>.

CORPORATE RIGHTS FIGHT
Townships in rural Pennsylvania take on factory farms—and corporate rights.

- **ADAM D. SACKS**
July/August 2005

> They hang the man and flog the woman,
> Who steals the goose from off the common,
> Yet let the greater villain loose,
> That steals the common from the goose.
>
> *—17th-century English protest rhyme*

In the late 1990s, life was getting tough for agribusiness in North Carolina. Over the previous decade or so, the state had risen from the number 15 hog producer in the country to number two. With more hogs than people, North Carolina's largely African-American Duplin and Sampson counties were the two largest pork-producing counties in the nation. By 1997, pollution, public health, and environmental justice problems were causing such widespread outcry that the state imposed a moratorium on all new pig farms that would last for almost six years. Soon factory farm corporations went on the prowl for greener pastures, so to speak.

Central Pennsylvania looked like an attractive target. It has an excellent system of roadways and accessible distribution centers. Land is relatively cheap. Many small farmers were, as usual, struggling. The Pennsylvania Farm Bureau, nominally a farmer advocacy organization, is firmly in the pocket of big agribusiness and highly influential in the state legislature. The central part of the state is rural, with township populations ranging from several hundred to a few thousand. This means there were no zoning regulations—the townships didn't think they needed them—to get in the way of large-scale hog farming. Rural township governments had no idea how to deal with powerful businesses. In short, the townships between Philadelphia in the east and Pittsburgh in the west were sitting ducks. Or so the ag boys thought.

Onslaught

The phone was ringing off the hook in the office of Thomas Linzey, a young attorney at the nonprofit organization he founded, the Community Environmental Legal Defense Fund (CELDF). Three years out of law school, Linzey was one of a rare breed of lawyer dedicated full time to public interest law. Idealistic and determined, he had set up a regulatory practice to help communities appeal permits issued to businesses they didn't want in their backyards. And he was good at it. In hearing after hearing, he pointed out defects in permit applications and convinced regulators and judges that these irresponsible corporate entities shouldn't be allowed to ply their noxious trades. Permits were rescinded, communities celebrated victories, Linzey and CELDF won prizes and kudos and were invited to Environment Day at the White House as guests of Vice President Al Gore. But there was a problem.

A few months after a community victory, the heretofore unpermitted corporation would return, permit in hand, ready to do business. What had happened? The only relevant issue in the regulatory appeal, whether all the bureaucratic dotted i's and crossed t's were in place, was resolved: the community had unearthed the problems with the permit, and the corporation proceeded to fix them. By challenging the permit and exposing the defects, the community had unwittingly done the corporation's work for free. Since townships of a few thousand people generally don't stand much of a chance against corporate legal budgets, practically speaking there was no further recourse.

Linzey had been puzzling over the battles won and wars lost in his first three years when the factory farm onslaught began. Local township officials, farmers, and concerned citizens were calling him, desperate, saying, "They're telling us that all we can do is regulate manure odor—but we don't want these toxic and destructive factory farms in our community at all! Please help us figure this out."

Factory pig farm operations produce tons of manure a day, which ends up in lakes, rivers, and drinking water. They not only seriously damage the environment—they also wreak havoc on the local economy and put independent family farmers out of business. Struggling farmers enter into one-sided output contracts with agribusiness corporations, agreeing to sell only to them. On their face, these contracts appear to be a way of guaranteeing a small farmer a market. But farmers soon find themselves trapped. The contracts hook them into expensive capital improvements that can cost hundreds of thousands of dollars, often paid for with loans issued by the corporations themselves. The contracts give the corporation ownership over all of the farm's animals—unless some die, in which case responsibility for the carcasses reverts to the farmers for disposal. And they allow the corporations to evade responsibility for environmental damage, since the giant firms don't technically own the property.

The result is an unequal arrangement in which the farmers own their land, but are so in hock to their corporate buyers, and utterly dependent on them, that they effectively lose control of their operations. The corporate party can unilaterally terminate the contract at any time, leaving the farmers to bail themselves out if they can. Most lose everything.

Like the township officials, Linzey was at a loss at first, but figured it was worth looking around to see what the possibilities were. He discovered that nine states, from Oklahoma in 1907 to South Dakota in 1998, had passed laws or constitutional amendments against corporate ownership or control of farms. Some of these laws contained exceptions for incorporated farms that were family owned and operated on a daily basis by one or more family members. That is, they didn't affect real farmers—people who wake up before sunrise, mingle with cows and pigs, and get their hands and boots dirty—but did cover the farms owned by corporate executives. Linzey converted text from these existing laws into a "Farm Ownership Ordinance" that many townships considered, and some passed. The ordinance template stated: "No corporation or syndicate may acquire, or otherwise obtain an interest, whether legal, beneficial, or otherwise, in any real estate used for farming in this Township, or engage in farming."

Taking the Constitution Away from Corporations

In 2002, Licking and Porter Townships in Clarion County, Pa., passed ordinances that strip corporations of their constitutional rights. The ordinances arose from residents' concern about a corporation suing them over their right to regulate sewage sludge. By abolishing corporate constitutional rights, the township eliminated the corporation's right to go to court against it, in effect returning the corporation to its status in the late 18th and early 19th centuries, before the courts began granting corporations the constitutional rights of people.

The ordinance reads, in part:

- An Ordinance by the Second Class Township of _____, _____ County, Pennsylvania, Eliminating Legal Personhood Privileges from Corporations Doing Business Within _____ Township to Vindicate Democratic Rights

- Section 5. Statement of Law. Corporations shall not be considered to be "persons" protected by the Constitution of the United States or the Constitution of the Commonwealth of Pennsylvania within the Second Class Township of _____, _____ County, Pennsylvania.

- Section 6. Statement of Law. Corporations shall not be afforded the protections of the Commerce Clause (Article I, §8) of the United States Constitution; or the Contracts Clause of the United States Constitution (Article I, §10) and the Constitution of the Commonwealth of Pennsylvania (Article I, §17), as interpreted by the Courts, within the Second Class Township of _____, _____ County, Pennsylvania.

The full text is available at <www.celdf.org/scm/ord/ord7.asp>.

What Happened to Our Local Democracy?

Although the citizens of rural Pennsylvania townships would be the last to call themselves activists or revolutionaries, their battles to preserve the health and integrity of their lives and homes against corporate assault have the makings of a sociopolitical earthquake. These mostly conservative Republican communities found themselves asking what had happened to their democracy.

How did it come to pass that a small handful of corporate directors a thousand miles away got to decide what takes place in their backyards? Why does the democratic decision of hundreds or thousands of citizens to keep out dangerous and destructive activity get trumped by distant interests whose only concern is how much of the community's wealth they can run away with, regardless of the collateral damage to the environment, economy, and social fabric of the community? As one town supervisor put it, "What the hell are rights of corporations?"

In short, the townspeople began having conversations about what it means to be a sovereign people, with inalienable rights, whose government operates only with their consent—conversations that hadn't been heard in the town commons or around kitchen tables for a long, long time. Organized by community leaders among friends and neighbors who had never before been active in civic affairs, their meetings took various forms. There were formal county-wide gatherings of hundreds of people, small conclaves in living rooms, and backyard barbecue chats. Armed with copies of the Constitution and Declaration of Independence, they asked and tried to answer basic questions, such as: What is a democracy? What are the people's rights, responsibilities, and privileges? What is the law? Who makes it and who enforces it? What are the courts? Whose side are they on?

Citizens realized that the issue was not really the factory farm or the sludged field. The issue was who has the right to decide what happens in our communities: we the people, or the corporations that have taken over our economy and our government for the benefit of the very few to the detriment of the rest of us. Farms are just one of a thousand different fronts to fight harms from pollution to corruption to war. But after all, in a democracy—and perhaps in human society in general—there's only one fundamental issue, from which all governing process derives: the right to decide.

People in many central Pennsylvania townships had these conversations. They began shunning the regulatory system and instead passed ordinances to control both factory farms and another threat that appeared at around the same time: land-applied sewage sludge (which had caused the tragic deaths of two teenagers in 1995). Seventy townships passed antisludge ordinances, which imposed a fee to render land application of sewage sludge unprofitable. They remain sludge-free. Eleven townships passed factory farm ordinances, which outlawed nonfamily corporate ownership and control of farming operations. None has a factory farm to date. Two townships, Licking and Porter, even passed ordinances stripping corporations of their constitutional rights outright. Within their towns, corporations would no longer have the status of "persons" (see "Taking the Constitution Away from Corporations").

All of this exercise of local control began to cause some serious discomfort among agribusiness interests. Of course, corporations could go ahead and sue the townships, which they did, claiming that their constitutional rights as legal persons had been abrogated. Such outrageous but judicially and legislatively supported claims infuriated the people in targeted communities: citizen response to the corporate claim of personhood became a crucial component in the subsequent organizing. But soon corporations were pursuing a more efficient tactic than lawsuits. It involved having elected officials do their heavy lifting.

Political Blowback

On May 2, 2001, Pennsylvania Senate Bill 826 was filed with the Agriculture and Rural Affairs Committee. Couched as an amendment to a 1982 act protecting agricultural operations from nuisance suits and ordinances under certain circumstances, the bill aimed to crack down on township efforts. The amendment further limited the ability of localities to pass ordinances, and it wasn't the least bit subtle, reading: "No municipality shall adopt or enact a frivolous ordinance that would prohibit, restrict, or regulate an agricultural operation." What counts as "frivolous"? Any attempt to "regulate the type of business that may own or conduct an agricultural operation." Just to drive home the point and punish any township that tried to protect itself, the bill entitles the aggrieved party to recover costs and attorney fees from lawsuits they file to challenge the ordinances.

When Linzey heard about 826, he set out to rally the people. An unprecedented coalition formed to oppose this assault on local democracy. The Sierra Club, the United Mine Workers of America, Common Cause, the Pennsylvania Farmers Union, the Pennsylvania Association for Sustainable Agriculture, and 400 rural township governments all joined to defeat 826. Groups that ordinarily wouldn't be talking to each other found common ground not because they were fighting sewage sludge or factory farms or some other single issue, but because they could all agree that the state was out of bounds in usurping basic democratic rights. Senate Bill 826 never made it out of committee.

But it wasn't over yet.

In one of those dark backrooms of the statehouse where corporate politics thrive, the bill was renumbered, and on May 2, 2002, it was slipped back into the Senate, where it passed 48 to 2. A leaked Pennsylvania Farm Bureau memorandum said that the renumbering was necessary to avoid any bad publicity. People told Linzey, "Nice try—but you'll never win against a vote like that." Undaunted, the coalition stormed into action, and threatened enough legislators with loss of a job that the bill never came to a vote in the House.

And it still wasn't over—illustrating the Jeffersonian wisdom that the price of liberty is constant vigilance.

This time, in 2003, the agribusiness forces attached the substance of the bill to an anti-sexual predator law on the last day of the legislative session. They figured that in an election year no legislator would want to be vulnerable to charges of favoring molesting children (although the freshman sponsor of that bill withdrew her sponsorship, saying that the bill was intended to protect children, not corporations). As soon as the bill landed on the desk of Democratic Governor Ed Rendell, the local democracy forces barraged him. He backed down and didn't sign the bill, but explained that this was only because better top-down regulatory protection was in order. With better state rules, he implied, it would be okay to strip municipalities of their rights.

In 2004, Rendell unveiled his ACRE initiative (Agriculture, Communities, and Rural Environment), under which an appointed political board would have the authority to overturn local laws. In other words, laws passed democratically by a majority of citizens in a community could be struck down by an unelected collection of corporate appointees. The coalition has beat that one back too for now—it will likely come up again in the next legislative session.

So the vigilance continues. Each time the state government attempts such pro-business shenanigans, it increasingly reveals on whose behalf it is working. And each time, more people see with growing clarity how relentlessly their lives and rights are sold and legislated away, and begin to understand how the failure of democracy leads to very real harms in their communities.

There is broader significance to such fights to save the sustainable family farm. It's about the underlying political power structure and its links to economic power. It's about who decides the fate of communities, and in whose interest those decisions are made. Just as past empires established colonies—including those that rebelled to form our nation—for the purposes of expropriating resources to feed and entertain the nobility and the rising merchant class, so today do corporate-driven governments sustain a culture of expropriation of the commons, with a blindness and ferocity that threatens to render the earth unlivable.

Saving the sustainable family farm is also about uniting all of us who are fighting important single-issue battles. As long as we are divided and scattering our energies in a thousand different directions, we will continue to lose. When we finally unite on the common terra firma of local control over sustainability, health, well-being, and democracy, we will be in a position to create an irresistible force.

Learn more about strategies for challenging corporate constitutional rights by attending Democracy School, a two-day course developed by Thomas Linzey and Richard Grossman. For more information see <www.constitution411.org/dem_schl.php>.

For more on community efforts to oppose corporate rights, see: the Program on Corporations, Law and Democracy <www.poclad.org> and the Community Environmental Legal Defense Fund <www.celdf.org> (whose website includes numerous sample ordinances, a "Model Legal Brief to Eliminate Corporate Rights," and more on the Pennsylvania story). The Center for Democracy and the Constitution <www.constitution411.org> is building on the Pennsylvania work in Massachusetts and New England.

A version of this article was published by Food First/Institute for Food and Development Policy < www.foodfirst.org> in April, 2005.

KATRINA HITS CANCER ALLEY
An Interview with Environmental Justice Activist Monique Harden.

BEN GREENBERG
March/April 2006

The environmental, economic justice, and anti-racism movements have not always been on the same page. A growing number of activists in all three, however, have begun to recognize that comprehensive analyses and strategies that address ecological devastation and economic and racial injustice together are indispensable. No one better embodies that crucial advance than Monique Harden. Harden is co-director of Advocates for Environmental Human Rights, a nonprofit, public interest law firm in New Orleans that she co-founded with attorney Nathalie Walker in 2002. Harden also coordinates international coalitions of community organizations advocating for human rights and environmental justice. Here are excerpts from D&S collective member Ben Greenberg's interview with Harden in New Orleans this January.—Eds.

BEN GREENBERG: Let's start with the immediate environmental impacts of Katrina. What kinds of hazardous substances did the storm release?

MONIQUE HARDEN: It's important to understand the significant number of industrial facilities operating in Louisiana and the massive amount of toxic pollution that these industries release into our air, water, and land. Between New Orleans and Baton Rouge, an area known as "Cancer Alley," there are approximately 130 oil refineries and petrochemical facilities. When you are aware of the industrial pollution all around us, you can understand the toxic impact of forceful hurricane winds pushing onto communities the water and sediment that have received industrial discharges for many decades.

Our organization, Advocates for Environmental Human Rights, has been working with several groups to take samples of the sediment left behind after the flood waters were drained. We didn't want a replay of what EPA did in New York after 9/11—claiming that air quality was good when in fact it was very unhealthy. So, early on, Wilma Subra, a chemist in Louisiana, began taking sediment samples and analyzing them for our organizations. Both her sampling analysis and the tests that EPA conducted revealed high levels of contaminants in the sediment covering yards, streets, and sidewalks in flooded communities. Arsenic and diesel fuel substances are the most prevalent but not the only contaminants. However, EPA concluded that only more retesting and analysis was needed. We saw it very differently and have been demanding that the agency take action to immediately clean up the sediment.

The problem here is that EPA has not established a standard for cleaning up toxic sediment or soil; instead the agency has only established standards for further assessment. But we have looked at various Superfund sites and found that EPA has set, on a case-by-case basis, requirements for cleaning up these sites that should, at the very least, apply to our Gulf Coast communities. For example, in the PAB Oil & Chemical Services site in Louisiana, EPA required that arsenic in the soil be cleaned up so that no more than 10 milligrams per kilogram of arsenic remains in the soil on this site. In neighborhoods that were flooded in New Orleans, there are sediment-arsenic concentrations that are over 70 milligrams per kilogram. EPA's inaction threatens the health of residents who have returned to communities with contaminated sediment. Children, the elderly, and other people with poor health are particularly vulnerable to the toxins that EPA refuses to clean up.

After Hurricane Katrina, federal and state health agencies posted notices advising people to wear protective gear, such as Tyvek suits, respirator masks, gloves, and shoe covers, but not one government agency provides this protective gear to people returning to the area. Instead, a few nonprofit organizations have raised funds to deliver protective gear and health information to people. But these efforts are a drop in the bucket. For example, on December 1st, when a section of the Lower Ninth Ward was opened to residents, our organizations ran out of Tyvek suits—we had 1,000—and all the other protective gear in the first two and a half hours. Many more people needed this protective gear, but we couldn't help them. I felt terrible that our help was not enough and that our government could care less about protecting our health. In response to our requests, the city of New Orleans submitted an application to FEMA for protective gear, but there has been no response.

BG: Tell me about the work that Advocates for Environmental Human Rights was doing before Katrina.

MH: Our mission is to advance and defend the human right to a healthy environment. We provide litigation, public advocacy, and community organizing support—all with the aim of reforming severe flaws in the U.S. environmental regulatory system that allow fundamental human rights to life, health, and racial equality to be violated. The failure of EPA to clean up contaminated sediment in Gulf Coast communities is part of a systemic problem; it underscores just how irrelevant human health protection is to the environmental regulatory system, notwithstanding the volumes of environmental laws and regulations established by our government.

BG: So your approach is to work on local issues but affect national policy?

MH: That's correct. In March 2005, AEHR filed the first-ever human rights legal challenge against the United States for its failed environmental regulatory system. We prepared that litigation on behalf of Mossville, a historic African-American community in the southwest corner of Louisiana. In this petition, we sought specific health and environmental remedies for Mossville residents, as well as reform of the U.S. environmental regulatory system. We filed the petition with the Inter-American Commission on Human Rights of the Organization of American States.

BG: What company or companies were in violation of those residents' human rights and what were the specific environmental problems?

MH: First of all, let me clarify: we are not charging the companies; we are charging the U.S. government for violating the human rights of Mossville residents. The government has authorized corporations that own fourteen toxic facilities in and around Mossville to endanger the lives of Mossville residents, harm their health, and burden this African-American community with millions of pounds of toxic chemicals that have made the air unhealthy, poisoned fish in local waters, and contaminated the soil.

What's more, a federal agency, the Agency for Toxic Substances and Disease Registry, has conducted dioxin testing of Mossville residents' blood, showing average dioxin concentrations that are three times higher than the national average. Dioxin can cause cancer and other serious health problems. However, this agency has resisted assisting the community in its demands for medical monitoring and health care.

Notwithstanding years of work by Mossville Environmental Action Now, our federal and state environmental and health agencies have not taken any meaningful action that protects the health of people living in Mossville. Instead these agencies issue more and more permits that allow the industrial facilities to increase pollution.

Demanding human rights protection is critical to ending this injustice, which is why Mossville Environmental Action Now and AEHR filed the legal petition with the Inter-American Commission on Human Rights. This commission, like so many other human rights judicial bodies, has determined that a government's failure to adequately protect the environment can violate human rights. In Mossville, and many other people of color and poor communities, fundamental human rights to life, health, and racial equality are trampled on by the U.S. system of so-called "environmental protection."

BG: Can you give a little background on Mossville?

MH: Mossville was founded in the 1790s by emancipated Blacks. It was a place where people could go and raise their families in a safe haven from the racial hostility that was all around them. There's some history written on Mossville—elder Mossville residents will tell you that in the past the community was able to thrive because of its rich natural resources. Folks were able to farm, hunt, and fish; businesses were able to develop from those natural resources.

However, Mossville was never incorporated and did not have governance authority. Zoning and other decisions were made by the parish [county], state, and federal governments. Remember, when industrial facilities were getting their foothold in Mossville and other parts of Louisiana, the 1930s through the 1950s, African Americans in the South did not have the right to vote and were oppressed and discriminated against by Jim Crow laws. So when industrial facilities began popping up in Louisiana, Mossville residents had no say in where they would locate, and this became an area that was targeted for industrial development. People in Mossville were not able to challenge, much less resist, the industrialization of their community.

Today, in and around Mossville, there are an oil refinery complex owned by Conoco Phillips, a coal-fired power plant owned by Entergy, five vinyl production facilities—the largest of which are PPG Industries and Georgia Gulf—and six other petrochemical facilities. All of these facilities are operating and spewing pollution within a quarter-mile of the community. Several have reported that Mossville residents would be killed if there was a catastrophic leak of chlorine gas or an explosion of petroleum-based products. You would think that with such hazards these facilities would operate safely, but they have frequent industrial accidents.

BG: How large a community is Mossville?

MH: It's a community of approximately 1,000 residents.

BG: Listening to you speak about Mossville, it's staggering to understand just how directly the situation there is the outgrowth of U.S. racism. It's a very direct relationship.

MH: Absolutely, and Mossville shares many commonalities with other communities—whether the residents are African American, Latino, Asian American, Native American, or poor whites. When you're dealing with environmental justice there are very strong historical ties to political and economic systems that have marginalized and exploited people of color and the poor.

BG: Can you talk about how economic policies have contributed to environmental racism in Louisiana?

MH: Sure. You have to understand that Louisiana has only known two forms of economic development: slave plantations and heavy industry. In fact, many of the industrial facilities are located on former slave plantations, and a few companies have applied the names of these plantations to their facilities. It's no accident that many of these facilities are located in close proximity to communities with mostly African-American residents.

Seventy years or so after the Civil War, investment in industrial manufacturing began to pick up in the state because of its natural resources, especially oil and navigable waters. The state government lured companies by enacting a statewide tax exemption in 1936. Under the Industrial Property Tax Exemption, as it's called, new facilities are exempt from paying property taxes on their facilities for up to 10 years. Then, if a company puts new capital investment into an existing facility, its exemption is renewed; this can go on into perpetuity.

The problem with the industrial tax exemption, of course, is that it has become a form of corporate welfare for companies like Exxon and Shell that are now wealthier than many countries. The largesse that these companies have acquired has also made them politically powerful in the legislature and allowed them to run roughshod over environmental and worker-safety laws. So, we now have aging and accident-prone industrial facilities largely dumping pollution in African-American communities like Mossville. And a prevailing political and economic climate in Louisiana and the United States in which these industrial corporations set the agenda.

One result is poverty. Dr. Paul Templet, a professor at Louisiana State University, has correlated pollution and poverty. In a nutshell, his research shows that the more industrial pollution a state has, the more poverty that state has. In Louisiana, we have one of the highest rates both of poverty and of industrial pollution. His analysis shows that stricter environmental standards that reduce industrial pollution require more jobs, which means more economic investment in the state and in the people in the state. A thriving economy requires good environmental conditions.

BG: Can you talk about where Katrina fits in?

MH: Katrina hit a state that has encouraged oil companies to install a broad network of oil pipelines that have destroyed coastal wetlands. If they were still intact, these wetlands would have absorbed some of the hurricane's force and reduced its damage. At the same time, our state embraces industries whose increasing emissions contribute to the global warming effect of hurricanes becoming more intense. And our state has provided these companies with a man-made canal—the Mississippi River Gulf Outlet—that not only damaged wetlands, but actually served to funnel Katrina's storm surge into our communities in St. Bernard and Orleans parishes.

BG: New Orleans obviously faces a crisis now in terms of rebuilding a viable economy. What are the roles of these companies in creating the new economic life of the area?

MH: I want to be clear that before Hurricane Katrina, neither New Orleans nor the state of Louisiana had what could be called a viable economy. Basic things like public school education and health care have been underfunded for years. It's now a struggle for all of us just to get back to having poor and inadequate public school and health care systems.

Instead of figuring out how we can do it better, much of the focus has been on planning ways to keep poor and mostly African-American people out of the state. The people who suffered the most from the failed levee systems and outrageous governmental neglect in the days following Katrina are now being targeted with governmental plans and actions that block their return home. I guess the thinking is that if you lock out poor people, the economy will improve.

Millions of our taxpayer dollars have gone to restoring oil company pipelines and other infrastructure that has devastated our environment and made us more vulnerable to hurricanes. In contrast, hurricane-damaged communities have not been restored. Another glimpse into how oil companies and the economy may intersect after Katrina is the announcement that Shell will cosponsor, for the first time, the New Orleans Jazz Fest. The company has been lauded as a savior of this cultural event; this view completely ignores how Shell has contributed to the disastrous consequences of Hurricane Katrina.

BG: Could you give a breakdown of some of the specific communities in New Orleans and the environmental problems they face?

MH: Gert Town is an African-American neighborhood in New Orleans where the Thompson Hayward Company mixed pesticides, herbicides, and dry cleaning agents across the street from residents' homes and churches for approximately 40 years. This plant was shut down in the 1980s when it was discovered to be illegally dumping chemicals into the city's drainage system. That triggered enforcement that amounted to nothing more than a "cooperative agreement" between the state Department of Environmental Quality (DEQ) and the company owners for cleaning up waste contaminated with DDT and other banned chemicals. The agreement set out a series of cleanup steps and a schedule of 90 days or less for each step. However, nearly 20 years later, four million pounds of contaminated waste have yet to be removed.

Days before Hurricane Katrina struck, the community, organized as Gert Town Revival Initiative, and AEHR had compelled DEQ to allow the community to participate in the design of the cleanup plan. Then the hurricane came, causing four feet of flooding in Gert Town. Sediment sampling now shows the presence of DDT and other chemicals from Thompson Hayward, in addition to the arsenic and diesel fuel substances. This means that the storm moved pesticides and other chemicals from the site into the community.

BG: And there are other communities with similar problems?

MH: Yes. There's the Agriculture Street community. This subdivision was built in the 1960s and 1970s and marketed to African Americans. People who bought these houses or moved into the rental units had no idea their homes were built on top of a toxic landfill. It was only after residents began to realize that they and their neighbors suffered serious health problems, including cancer, that they learned about the toxic landfill underneath them. A study by a state agency showed that Agriculture Street residents had the highest incidence of breast cancer statewide for both women and men.

In 1994 the community was designated a Superfund site. EPA provided a ridiculous cleanup that involved removing one to two feet of contaminated soil from yards that have 17 feet of soil contaminated with over 150 toxic chemicals and heavy metals. And EPA refused to temporarily relocate residents who were exposed to toxins during over a year of excavation.

Residents have had to sue federal and state housing agencies and other responsible government agencies for building their subdivision on top a toxic landfill. A few weeks ago, residents won their lawsuit in a state court, but the government defendants are expected to appeal.

BG: How has the situation been compounded since Katrina?

MH: People have no homes! During Katrina, the failure of the levees flooded this neighborhood with water as high as nine feet. Homes are covered in toxic mold and many have extensive structural damage. Many of the hazardous contaminants that triggered EPA's Superfund site designation and were supposed to be trapped underground are now present in the sediment. Residents are wrestling with insurance companies and mortgage companies. Some have been able to secure homes elsewhere, but not others.

BG: What are some of the challenges facing New Orleans residents who want to return home to environmentally safe neighborhoods?

MH: Sediment contamination is a representative problem. EPA is not cleaning up the sediment because reconstruction money is being spent on everything *except for* enabling people to return and rebuild their communities. Federal spending on Hurricane Katrina is a boondoggle for contractors and government agencies. For example, $3 million of hurricane relief spending went to the Department of Defense for the purchase of ammunition. This is outrageous! Meanwhile, six months after Katrina, we still have communities that look like the hurricane passed yesterday.

In October 2004, the federal government instituted the so-called "Assistance to Internally Displaced Persons Policy," which states what our government is committed to do in order to protect the human rights of people displaced from their communities by natural disasters. This policy commits our government to providing comprehensive assistance, from immediate disaster response through long-term development support. Even though this policy was developed by the U.S. Agency for International Development and, presumably, directed to internally displaced persons in foreign countries, we believe that our government should, at a minimum, exercise the same care and commitment to protecting the human rights of people in our country who are still in need of the humanitarian assistance, the return and transition assistance, and the long-term development assistance that are articulated in this policy.

BG: A lot of the organizing in New Orleans now involves local groups allied with national ones. Can you talk about the role of people and nonprofits outside of New Orleans?

MH: Post-Hurricane Katrina, there are national and local organizations that are doing a great job of working together for justice. There are also groups that are exploiting Hurricane Katrina for their own benefit. People who couldn't find the Ninth Ward or Chalmette on a map are now working in the position of "Katrina Policy Chief"—I'm not making this up, it's an actual position—in organizations that have no relationship with local communities.

In my organizing experience, the formula for success is working in service of communities that are directly harmed by injustice. The formula for failure is creating coalitions that do not respect the need for communities to be organized and self-determined. Social transformation can only be achieved through community organizing. Without organized communities speaking for themselves and guiding the work of coalitions, you just have a bunch of groups trying to feel important.

BG: Last September you said on the radio show "Living On Earth" that you were optimistic, that "this is an opportunity for us to transform in a progressive and positive way the lives of people in New Orleans and along the Gulf Coast of the United States." Five months later, are you still feeling optimistic?

MH: I'll go to my grave feeling optimistic about achieving social justice. And I say that because I know that the seed for achieving a just world is community organizing, and I know from experience that when communities are organized there's nothing that they can't achieve.

PERMITTING POLLUTION IN TEXAS
Activists push back against TXU's proposed coal-fired power plants.

ESTHER CERVANTES
May/June 2007

In April 2006—two days after Dallas experienced rolling blackouts as residents cranked up their air conditioners to deal with an early heat wave—Dallas-based energy company TXU announced an ambitious plan to build 11 new coal-fired power plants in Texas by 2010. Claiming that "coal is the only viable near-term" way to meet "growing Texas electric demand without increasing our dependence on costly and volatile natural gas," the company promised to "voluntarily" reduce its overall emissions of sulfur dioxide, nitrogen oxide, and mercury by 20%.

Almost immediately, citizens groups, environmental organizations, natural gas companies, and others began to protest.

Environmental Defense pointed out that TXU's promised pollution reductions were hardly voluntary. Recent federal laws require the cuts—TXU's only other option would be to buy enough pollution credits to cover its overlimit emissions.

Nor were these cuts enough, according to the Rainforest Action Network. Other pollutants aside, the new plants would emit 78 million tons a year of the greenhouse gas carbon dioxide (CO_2)—more than Japan's entire pledged CO_2 reduction under the Kyoto Protocol. It would have been like putting 14 million new passenger cars (more than were registered in Texas in 2006) on the road each year.

National and local environmental and citizens groups opposed the plants because of the health costs their emissions would impose on the public and on local governments. Scott Lipsett of northeast Texas' Citizens Organized for Resources and the Environment, some of whose members are trying to break into the grass-fed beef and organic dairy markets, pointed out that not only does particulate matter hurt people's lungs, it also "ruins the forage for your cattle."

Dallas mayor Laura Miller and officials in other cities were unwilling to risk falling into nonattainment status under the federal Clean Air Act. Sanctions for nonattainment include cuts in federal highway funding and restrictions on automobile travel. This possibility turned many real estate developers and construction contractors, worried that travel restrictions could force their crews to work at night and on overtime pay, into activists.

But TXU's opponents were fighting the clock. In October 2005, Texas Gov. Rick Perry, citing the need for more electricity, issued an executive order reducing the duration of permit hearings for new plants from eighteen months to only six. The number of proposals for coal-fired plants went from five to nineteen within months of the order, and Perry's 2006 re-election campaign received more than $100,000 from entities associated with those proposals.

For nearly a year after TXU announced its expansion plans, opponents maintained loud and insistent public protest. They attended public hearings, published editorials and reports, rallied at the Texas capitol, lobbied Texas legislators and environmental regulators, convinced their neighbors to join in. The Rainforest Action Network, through private meetings and public protests, put pressure on the banks slated to finance the new plants—Citi, Morgan Stanley, and Merrill Lynch.

In all, at least five national environmental organizations, seven local or regional citizens groups, three major religious groups, 36 local governments, 400 business leaders, the state of Oklahoma and the Chickasaw Nation (both concerned about plants to be built near their borders), and a group of spelunkers joined the fight.

Their agitation helped delay the permitting process, giving the Texas legislature time to intervene. And many Texas legislators showed up for the 2007 session ready for a showdown. Although TXU had hired, according to Tom Smith of Public Citizen, "enough lobbyists to twist both arms, both legs, and the heads of all the members of the key committees at once," the legislative docket quickly filled with proposed moratoria on coal-plant permitting, clean air bills, and incentives for energy conservation and cleaner fuels.

In February, private finance gave the story an unexpected twist. Former EPA administrator (under Bush I) William K. Reilly, who now works for the private equity firm Texas Pacific Group, called Fred Krupp, head of Environmental Defense, with a deal. Texas Pacific and Kohlberg Kravis Roberts were negotiating to buy TXU, and if they succeeded, they wanted, according to the *New York Times*, "to negotiate a cease-fire" with TXU's opponents.

On February 26, the buyout went through, and TXU's new owners announced that they were withdrawing eight of the company's eleven permit applications. They also promised to end TXU's plan to expand in other states, endorse a federal cap on CO2 emissions, reduce TXU's CO2 emissions to 1990 levels by 2020, double the company's spending on energy efficiency measures, double its purchase of wind power, and establish a Sustainable Energy Advisory Board.

After the announcement, Krupp praised Environmental Defense's Texas office for its activism, saying that their work and that of the other opposition groups was of "enormous value" in this victory.

Ken Kramer, director of the Lone Star chapter of the Sierra Club, said that "what forced the negotiations was the unprecedented and vigorous opposition ... from a diverse coalition." However, says Kramer, "There is a danger that some people will ... think that [this] takes care of all of the concerns that have been raised about the use of coal as an energy source and that we can now continue with business as usual."

The Sierra Club points out that the three coal plants that TXU's new owners still intend to build are the dirtiest of the original eleven, and that eight coal plants proposed by other companies are still in permitting. Texas' new coalition of clean energy activists will have to keep up the pressure if they hope to see the state legislature pass proposed new air quality and CO2 regulations and to limit the number of new coal-fired power plants their state will host.

Resources: Rainforest Action Network, ran.org/new/dirty_money/home/no_new_coal/ ; Environmental Defense, www.environmentaldefense.org; Sierra Club, www.sierraclub.org/environmentallaw/coal/news.asp.

Chapter 9

DISEASE, DISASTER, AND WAR

ABCs OF AIDS PREVENTION

Uganda has been widely recognized for its successes in stemming the AIDS crisis, but its policies fail to address the inequalities that make women vulnerable to the disease.

JESSICA WEISBERG
January/February 2005

U ganda is one of a handful of countries to have dramatically reduced its overall HIV infection rate in the past 10 years. It's widely viewed as a global leader in AIDS policy and is seen as a model for other countries in Africa and the global South. Its approach, known as "ABC," stands for "Abstinence, Be faithful, and Condoms"—but critics refer to it as "A-B-and sometimes-C" because of policymakers' emphasis on the first two over the third.

Despite Uganda's notable successes in stemming the AIDS epidemic, ABC has serious limitations. The policy primarily targets male behavior and fails to protect a particularly vulnerable population: married women. It offers little to girls forced by poverty to exchange one of their only assets—their bodies—for basic necessities or school fees. And by focusing on prevention, the policy fails to expand affordable and available treatments to those who've already contracted the disease—or address the core economic and social inequalities that make women susceptible to infection.

Nevertheless, President Bush has routinely cited Uganda's emphasis on abstinence and fidelity in defending its own abstinence-oriented global initiatives. In fact, the United States has adopted the ABC model as the centerpiece of its international AIDS policy.

In his 2004 State of the Union address, Bush declared optimistically, "AIDS can be prevented." Prevented? AIDS can be *treated*; with anti-retroviral therapies, widely available since early 1996, the otherwise fatal illness takes on a chronic character. By prevention, the president was referring not to a vaccine but to abstinence. He's been known to say it "works every time."

A few months after the address, in May 2004, Congress passed the President's Emergency Plan for AIDS Relief (PEPFAR). It allocated $15 billion dollars for AIDS programs worldwide over five years, with a focus on 15 "target countries" which are home to more than 50% of all people with HIV: Botswana, Côte d'Ivoire, Ethiopia, Kenya, Mozambique, Namibia, Nigeria, Rwanda, South Africa, Tanzania, Uganda,

Zambia, Vietnam, Guyana, and Haiti.

Twenty percent of PEPFAR funding will go to prevention programs. (The balance goes to support services and treatment.) By law, at least one-third of those prevention funds must be used to promote abstinence. The first allocation of $100 million in PEPFAR grants for abstinence programs was announced in October. Nine of the 11 organizations that won the grants were faith-based organizations. Under PEPFAR, such groups are allowed to exclude information about contraception from their educational programs. Ambassador Randall Tobias, head of the State Department's Office of Global AIDS, has cited Uganda's accomplishments when PEPFAR's abstinence program has faced questions.

Uganda's Way

Since Ugandan President Yoweri Museveni initiated the ABC program in the mid-1990s, the country has undergone enormous reductions in HIV prevalence (the percentage of individuals living with HIV/AIDS). The percent of infected individuals in Uganda has declined from around 30% in the early 1990s to 6% in 2004, according to the United Nations and the Ugandan government. Although some scientists question the validity of those specific figures, arguing that survey methodology is flawed and that the reduction in prevalence rates may in part reflect the deaths of those who had HIV in the 1990s, most agree that Uganda has secured the most dramatic turnaround in AIDS of any country to date. Museveni brought this about by aggressively raising AIDS awareness, by using radio and other modes of mass communication, involving churches and nongovernmental organizations, and by crafting messages that resonated with Ugandan culture; for example, he introduced the slogan "zero grazing" to encourage monogamy in the cattle-oriented society.

The effectiveness of Uganda's AIDS prevention and treatment policies has varied, though, with respect to gender. Far more women than men have become infected with HIV since ABC was implemented. According to the Uganda AIDS Commission, there were 99,031 new HIV cases in the country in 2001. Of these, females were three to six times more likely to become infected by HIV than males in the 15 to 19 age bracket, according to the Uganda Women's Network. In the 20 to 24 age bracket, the HIV infection rate among women remains twice as high as that of men.

There are several reasons for this disparity. Most importantly, research indicates that marriage actually *increases* the chance of HIV infection. In fact, the most dramatic increase in prevalence rates in recent years has occurred among monogamous married women; even as the overall percentage of people with HIV has fallen, the percentage of married women with HIV has increased. One study found that in rural Uganda, 88% of HIV-infected women age 15 to 19 are married.

For the majority of married couples in Uganda, the woman is at least six years younger than her husband. Paul Zeitz of the advocacy group Global AIDS Alliance points out that abstinence programs could "in effect be encouraging women to marry earlier," placing them at risk of infection by older husbands. "What use is abstinence, what use is fidelity if he is already infected and brings it into the marriage?" Stephen Lewis asked the *Agence France Presse*. Zeitz goes so far as to argue:

"Abstinence [promotion] could be leading to a public health crisis."

Take Suzan, a 17-year-old mother from Ndeeba, a Kampala suburb, whose 62-year-old husband recently died of AIDS. She was infected by her late husband, and is unable to afford treatment.

With such large age differences between wives and husbands, Ugandan women like Suzan often outlive their husbands. When a man dies, his family typically repossesses his assets, robbing the woman of all her property and making her remaining years all the more difficult. In Suzan's case, her husband's family has taken away both their land and her child.

Another Ugandan woman, Juliet, is a 27-year-old widow with four children. Her in-laws also took away her home and land upon her husband's death. She is now hospitalized with an advanced case of AIDS, and her children are struggling to support themselves.

Women like Suzan and Juliet are overlooked by the ABC program's emphasis on abstinence and fidelity. Both women were abstinent before marriage and then faithful, but neither their own behavior nor the ABC program did anything to protect them from contracting the disease or to treat them once they were infected.

Condoms too are of little use to married women in a culture where extramarital polygamy is common but wives are unaware of their husbands' affairs. Even if women have suspicions, many adhere to patriarchal mores against vocally questioning their husbands' behavior. Those same mores also deter women from telling their husbands to wear condoms.

Harriet Abwoli, interviewed in 2003 for the Human Rights Watch report "Just Die Quietly," described her experience: "He used to force me to have sex with him. He would beat me and slap me when I refused. I never used a condom with him. ... When I got pregnant I went for a medical check-up. When I gave birth, and the child had passed away, they told me I was HIV-positive. I cried. The doctor told me, 'Wipe your tears, the whole world is sick.'"

"Women do not have negotiation power," says researcher Sarah Kalloch, who has done considerable fieldwork in Uganda. "Women do not have control over their own bodies." Kalloch describes instances of wife-swapping, wife inheritance, and widespread marital rape. Rape and domestic violence are "virtually impossible to prosecute" due to legal discrimination. "ABC is not enough for women in Uganda. They need legal rights that give them control over their bodies, their relationships, and who they marry," Kalloch says.

They also need basic economic security. Uganda's abstinence program has attempted to reach "high risk" populations such as soldiers and truck drivers, but has sent mixed messages by disparaging female HIV victims for indulgent or "promiscuous" behavior. So long as extreme economic deprivation continues to force young girls to barter for food and basic economic needs with sex, this sort of message will do little to save those who lack access to income and resources.

In the poverty-stricken northern region of Uganda, it's common for parents to force their teen and pre-teen daughters into sex work. "The mother will simply say to her daughters, 'come back with food,'" said Paul Zeitz of Global AIDS Alliance. Zeitz refers to this practice as "survival sex," since selling sex is not a profession for most of these girls, but a measure driven by dire economic necessity. Most customers are truck drivers and traveling soldiers, who prefer young girls, believing that they are free of HIV. Truck drivers synchronize their routes with school tuition deadlines (which vary by region), when girls are most likely to be waiting at truck stops for customers, according to a study conducted by the group.

When asked if abstinence programs fail women, Randall Tobias said, "One of the best ways to protect vulnerable women from HIV is to instill the 'ABC' message in men...." To Tobias, "the ABC model is a simple conceptualization of the major tenets of what happened in Uganda and can be implemented elsewhere with some local adaptation."

But as Lynn Amowitz, a Harvard medical school professor who has researched women's health and human rights in Afghanistan, observes: "The forms discrimination and stigma take differ from country to country. In some places, it's widow inheritance, in others it's that women are considered minors." Extending abstinence programs to these countries, with their distinct social dynamics, is unlikely to slow the feminization of HIV and AIDS. Without specific prevention programs that take such practices into account, the burden of HIV/AIDS will continue to disproportionately affect women.

Already, 58% of the 25 million people living with AIDS in sub-Saharan Africa are women. Adult women are up to 1.3 times more likely to be infected with HIV than their male counterparts, and women and girls now make up three-quarters of the 6.2 million young people (age 15 to 24) with AIDS. Because women serve as the primary caregivers for their own children and work in disproportionate numbers in schools, as nurses, and in social services, the feminization of AIDS ravages the socioeconomic fabric of their communities. Furthermore, the epidemic will be passed on to future generations, as the likelihood of mother-to-child transmission is estimated at 30%.

Treatment Possibilities

The situation is not hopeless. Life-extending drugs such as nevaripine and anti-retroviral therapies do exist. The World Health Organization (WHO) has engineered generic anti-retrovirals that will reduce the cost of therapy to $148 dollars a year, compared to an average $548 a year for name-brand drugs.

But the Bush administration has put the breaks on treatment. Under PEPFAR, all drugs sold abroad must be approved by the FDA. Even generic drugs that have already undergone the WHO's meticulous prequalification standards must be reexamined by the FDA before they are distributed abroad through the program. This rule will indefinitely delay the availability of affordable medication.

What's more, PEPFAR allocates no funds for distributing nevaripine, which at a cost of $4 per person can reduce the likelihood of mother-to-child transmission by almost 90%. Likewise, it does not fund the development of microbicides, topical products that women could use, undetected, to prevent sexual transmission of HIV. Protesters at the International AIDS Conference in Bangkok last July condemned Ambassador Tobias and President Bush for prioritizing pharmaceutical patent rights over public health needs and ideology over efficacy.

Women's economic marginalization is a global problem, and severe in the 15 countries that PEPFAR will target. President Bush's vague declaration that "AIDS can be prevented" is, in fact, correct. Prevention programs can provide a cost-effective means of gradually reducing HIV prevalence, but only if such programs address specific economic inequities that underlie patterns of transmission, dismantle barriers to economic independence for women, empower married women, and deliver messages in a culturally accessible manner. Just as important, they cannot ignore the necessity of investing in treatment for women and their daughters, who are already infected. Otherwise, women's social and economic powerlessness will continue to render them disproportionately vulnerable to the HIV epidemic. For women, the solution to the AIDS crisis is a lot more complicated than A-B-C.

Resources: "The ABC Debate Heats Up," *Africa News*, July 13, 2004; Lisa Garbus and Elliot Marseille, *Country AIDS Analysis Project: HIV/AIDS in Uganda,* San Francisco: AIDS Policy Research Center, University of California San Francisco, 2003; "Health: Women Demand Stepped-Up AIDS Treatment, Prevention," Inter Press Service, 2002; Richard Ingham, "U.N. Envoy Blasts U.S. for "Ideological Agenda" on Abstinence to Combat AIDS," Agence France Presse, Bangkok, July 15, 2004; "Just Die Quietly," Human Rights Watch, 2003; Alonso Luiza Klein, "Women's Social Representation of Sex, Sexuality, and AIDS in Brazil," *Women's Experiences with HIV/AIDS: An International Perspective.* New York: Columbia University Press, 1996; Catherine Ntabade, "Abolish Polygamy," The Uganda Women's Network; Sharon Otterman, "AIDS: The U.S. Anti-AIDS Program," Council of Foreign Relations, November 28, 2003; www.siecus.org/policy/PUpdates/pdate0073.html; "Uganda Puts Morality Before Condoms," Global News Wire, July 15, 2004.

FISHERFOLK OUT, TOURISTS IN
Sri Lanka's tsunami reconstruction plans displace devastated coastal residents to make way for tourism industry expansion.

VASUKI NESIAH
July/August 2005

Two days after the south Asian tsunami struck last December, as thousands around him were grappling with its devastating impact, former German chancellor Helmut Kohl was airlifted from the roof of his holiday resort in southern Sri Lanka by the country's air force. Kohl is, of course, among the most elite of tourists, and his privileges are not representative of all tourists. Nonetheless, that aerial exit is symptomatic of the tourist industry's alienation from the local community. His easy flight away from the devastation, at a time when official relief supplies were still to reach the majority of victims, was an early indicator of the interplay between tsunami relief and the tourism industry. Kohl was barely airborne, and the waves barely receding, when plans were already afoot to ensure that the beaches of Sri Lanka were cleared of fisherfolk and rendered pristine for a new wave of tourists.

"Natural" Disasters?

Right from the start, global attention to the tsunami was no doubt heightened by the fact that tourists were among the victims. Reporters conducted their share of riveting tsunami escape interviews in airport departure lounges: first-rate, first-person accounts with first-world tourists. This is not the first time viewers in the rich countries have been plied with images of "natives" being overwhelmed by natural disasters, passively awaiting international humanitarian relief and rescue. Some parts of the globe are just scripted into tragedy and chaos; first-world television screens are accustomed to their loss, their displacement, their overwhelming misery. Against this backdrop, the tales of tourists offered a more newsworthy break from stories that simply echo yesterday's news reports about locals caught up in floods in Bangladesh or mudslides in Haiti.

But while being located in the trajectory of tsunami waves or monsoons is a given, the acute vulnerability of countries like Sri Lanka, Haiti, or Bangladesh to natural disasters only appears spontaneous. It is the socio-political landscape that determines the extent of exposure to adverse impact from such natural disasters. The political economy of exposure to natural disaster is disastrous for those made vulnerable—but not natural. For example, coastal mangrove forests would have contained the fury of the tsunami waves, except that they've been rapidly destroyed in recent years to make way for resorts and industrial shrimp farms. (See sidebar, "The Tsunami and the Mangroves.")

Defining that vulnerability as natural is, however, important to the tourism industry, whose job it is to produce exotic destinations through comparison and contrast. The devastation of repeated natural disasters is simply the "native predicament" in places like Sri Lanka, and one of the principle drives behind western tourism to the global South hinges on that predicament. Tourism often is, after all, a quest for a departure from the everyday of western suburbia—but in a neatly packaged module that insulates the visitor from the actual risks of the locale. Trafficking in that balance of otherness and insulation is the task of the tour masters.

The tsunami penetrated that insulation to some degree. However, even through the bloodletting of the last two decades, tourists visiting Sri Lanka have been remarkably insulated from it all: both from the civil war and from the country's impoverished social and economic circumstances. In fact, on the tourism industry's map, Sri Lanka is an adventure zone whose attraction lies at least partly in those circumstances, which make it a cheap vacation spot, a low-cost listing in a travel catalog of exotic but consumer-friendly destinations.

What Does Tourism Do?

Does the tourist industry simply feed off a pre-existing socio-economic predicament and perhaps even mitigate it, or does the industry exacerbate that predicament and entrench a country like Sri Lanka in an itinerary of peripheral economies served up for tourist consumption?

The argument is not that tourism per se is bad for Sri Lanka. Clearly the broader tradition of tourism and international travel has had a mixed, complex history.

For the many who came, surfed, littered, took photographs, bought sex, batik shirts, or barefoot sarongs and left, there are others who ended up engaged by newly discovered solidarities. Even the interface with colonial exploration was double-edged. As political scientist Kumari Jayewardene and others have shown us, we have always had a line of itinerant travelers who washed onto our shore as tourists of one sort or another, only to develop more fundamental commitments to local communities— commitments that then fed into, or even helped catalyze, traditions of dissent and struggles for justice that have had enormous reach in our collective histories.

Such solidarity aside, tourism can be a significant source of revenue, employment, and infrastructure development. It also has a range of indirect effects since tourism generates demand in many sectors; every job created in the tourism industry is said to result in almost 10 jobs in other industries, with enhanced demand in areas like agriculture and small industries, a whole spectrum of service-sector employment, and so on—the kind of thing that excites Central Bank policymakers, not to mention the middlemen who profit from those batik shirts and barefoot sarongs, from the increased demand for sex work and other informal sector labor. At a micro level, the jobs generated by the industry have enabled some financial autonomy for some sections of the working poor. Even when pay and working conditions are exploitative, this is an autonomy that may have particular significance for women and other groups who yield less financial decisionmaking power in the "old" economy.

Yet this baby came with a lot of muddy bath water even before the tsunamis washed in. The growth it has generated has often been of an unbalanced kind that worsened the country's financial vulnerability with little accountability to local communities. As they discovered through the shifting fortunes of the ceasefire, the post-9/11 drop in international travel, and recessions in distant lands, communities that work in the tourism industry have a heightened dependence on a fickle, fluctuating transnational market. The majority of the jobs tourism creates in the formal sector are service-sector jobs that are exploitative, badly paid, seasonal, and insecure; these problems are replicated many times over in the industry's large informal sector, ranging from prostitution to handicrafts. Its untrammeled exploitation of the coast has created unsustainable demands on the local environment that have had particularly bad impacts on coastal ecology. Equally pernicious, it has transformed more and more public land such as beaches into private goods, fencing out local residents.

Reconstruction for Whom?

The tragedy is that many of tourism's downsides may be exacerbated by the tsunami reconstruction plans. From Thailand to Sri Lanka, the tourist industry saw the tsunami through dollar signs. The governments concerned were on board from the outset, quickly planning massive subsidies for the tourism industry in ways that suggest the most adverse distributive impact. Infrastructure development will be even further skewed to cater to the industry rather than to the needs of local communities. Within weeks of the tsunami, the Alliance for the Protection of National Resources and Human Rights, a Sri Lankan advocacy group, expressed concern that "the developing situation is disastrous, more disastrous than the tsunami itself, if it is possible for anything to be worse than that."

The tsunami arrived at a critical moment in the recent history of Sri Lanka's political economy. Beginning in the late 1970s, Sri Lankan governments of both major parties followed the neoliberal prescriptions to cut tariffs and quotas, privatize, and deregulate more slavishly than many other Asian states. In 2002, the then-ruling center-right UNP issued a major blueprint for continued liberalization, "Regaining Sri Lanka," under the rubric of the "Poverty Reduction Strategy Plans" (PRSPs) that the World Bank and the IMF now require. But public opposition to these policies has intensified over time. In 2004 a center-left coalition won election on an anti-liberalization platform. Once in office, however, the chief party in the coalition appeared unwilling to truly change direction, and the "Regaining Sri Lanka" plan is still very much on the table.

Now, activists are warning that many of the plan's liberalization proposals will be revived and pushed through with little public dialogue and debate, given the emergency powers the government has given itself under cover of tsunami relief and reconstruction. In January, for example, the government revived a plan for water privatization that had earlier been tabled after public opposition. Official recon-

The Tsunami and the Mangroves

Since the 1980s, Asia has been plundered by large industrialized shrimp farms that have brought environmentally unfriendly aquaculture to its shores. Nearly 72% of global shrimp farming takes place in Asia, where the World Bank has been its largest funder. Even before the tsunami struck last December, shrimp cultivation, once termed a "rape-and-run" industry by the U.N. Food and Agricultural Organization, had already caused havoc in the region. Shrimp farms are only productive for two to five years. The ponds are then abandoned, leaving behind toxic waste, destroyed ecosystems, and displaced communities that have lost their traditional livelihoods. The whole cycle is then repeated in another pristine coastal area.

Now the shrimp farms—along with rapid tourism development—are also responsible for a share of the death and destruction the tsunami brought. Shrimp farming was expanded at the cost of tropical mangrove forests, which are among the world's most important ecosystems. Mangrove swamps have long been nature's protection for coastal regions, holding back large waves, weathering the impact of cyclones, and serving as a nursery for the three-fourths of commercial fish species that spend part of their life cycle there.

Ecologists tell us that mangroves provide double protection against storms and tsunamis. The first layer of red mangroves with their flexible branches and tangled roots hanging in the coastal waters absorb the first shock waves. The second layer of tall black mangroves then acts like a wall, withstanding much of the sea's fury.

But shrimp farming has continued its destructive spree, eating away more than half of the world's mangroves. Since the 1960s, for instance, aquaculture and industrial development in Thailand have resulted in a loss of over 65,000 hectares of mangroves. In Indonesia, Java has lost 70% of its mangroves, Sulawesi 49%, and Sumatra 36%. At the time the tsunami struck in all its fury, logging companies were busy axing mangroves in the Aceh province of Indonesia to export to Malaysia and Singapore.

In India, mangrove cover has been reduced by over two-thirds in the past three decades. In Andhra Pradesh, more than 50,000 people have been forcibly removed to make way for shrimp farms; throughout the country, millions have been displaced.

Whatever remained of the mangroves in India was cut down by the hotel industry, aided and abetted by the Ministry of Environment and Forests and the Ministry of Industries. Five-star hotels, golf courses, industries, and mansions sprung up all along the coast, warnings from environmentalists notwithstanding. These two ministries worked overtime to dilute the

struction plans are being prepared by a newly created agency, TAFREN, which a recent statement by a coalition of over 170 civil-society organizations describes as "composed entirely of big business leaders with vested interests in the tourist and construction industries, who are completely unable to represent the interests of the affected communities."

Proposals announced by TAFREN and by various government officials call for the building of multi-lane highways and the wholesale displacement of entire villages from the coast. Coastal lands are to be sliced up into designated buffer zones and tourism zones. The government is preventing those fishing families who wish to do so from rebuilding their homes on the coast, ostensibly because of the risk of future natural disasters; at the same time, it's encouraging the opening of both new and rebuilt beachfront tourist hotels.

The plans are essentially roadmaps for multinational hotel chains, telecom companies, and the like to cater to the tourism industry. Small-scale fishing operations by individual proprietors will become more difficult to sustain as access to the beach becomes increasingly privatized and fishing conglomerates move in. The environmental deregulation proposed in the PRSP will open the door to even more un-

---

Coastal Regulation Zone rules, allowing the hotels to take over even the 500-meter buffer zone that was supposed to be maintained along the beach.

The recent tourism boom throughout the Asia-Pacific region coincided with the destructive fallout from industrial shrimp farms. In the past two decades, the entire coastline along the Bay of Bengal, the Arabian Sea, and the Strait of Malacca in the Indian Ocean, as well as all along the South Pacific Ocean, has witnessed massive investment in hotels and tourism facilities. By 2010, the region is projected to surpass the Americas to become the world's number two tourist destination, with 229 million arrivals.

If only the mangroves were intact, the damage from the tsunami would have been greatly minimized. That's what happened in Bangladesh in 1960, when a tsunami wave hit the coast in an area where mangroves were intact. Not a single person died. These mangroves were subsequently cut down and replaced with shrimp farms. In 1991, thousands of people were killed when a tsunami of the same magnitude hit the same region.

In Tamil Nadu, in south India, Pichavaram and Muthupet, with dense mangroves, suffered low human casualties and less economic damage from the recent tsunami than other areas. Likewise, Myanmar and the Maldives suffered much less from the killing spree of the tsunami because the tourism industry had so far not spread its tentacles to the virgin mangroves and coral reefs surrounding their coastlines. The large coral reef surrounding the Maldives islands absorbed much of the tidal fury, limiting the human loss to a little over 100 dead. Like mangrove swamps, coral reefs absorb the sea's fury by breaking the waves.

Let's weigh the costs and benefits of destroying the mangroves. Having grown tenfold in the last 15 years, shrimp farming is now a $9 billion industry. It is estimated that shrimp consumption in North America, Japan, and Western Europe has increased by 300% within the last 10 years. But one massive wave of destruction caused by this tsunami in 11 Asian countries has exacted a cost immeasurably greater than the economic gain that the shrimp industry claims to have created.

World governments have so far pledged $4 billion in aid, and private relief agencies are spending additional billions. The World Bank gave $175 million right away, and then-World Bank president James Wolfensohn said, "We can go up to even $1 billion to $1.5 billion depending on the needs...." But if only successive presidents of the World Bank had refrained from aggressively promoting ecologically unsound but market friendly economic policies, a lot of human lives and dollars could have been saved.   —Devinder Sharma

trammeled exploitation of natural resources. None of the reconstruction planning is being channeled through decision-making processes that are accountable or participatory. Ultimately, it looks like reconstruction will be determined by the deadly combination of a rapacious private sector and government graft: human tragedy becomes a commercial opportunity, tsunami aid a business venture.

Not unpredictably, even the subsidies planned for the tourism industry in the wake of the tsunami are going to the hotel owners and big tour operators, not to the porters and cleaning women who were casual employees in hotels. Many of the local residents who were proprietors or workers in smaller tourism-related businesses, now unemployed, are not classified as tsunami-affected, so they are denied even the meager compensation they should be entitled to. The situation is much worse for the vast informal sector of sex workers, souvenir sellers, and others whose livelihood depended on the tourism industry. If the tsunami highlighted the acute vulnerability that accompanies financial dependence on the industry, the tsunami reconstruction plans look set to exacerbate this vulnerability even further.

A needs assessment study conducted by the World Bank in collaboration with the Asian Development Bank and Japan's official aid agency pegged the loss borne by the tourism industry at $300 million, versus only $90 million for the fishing industry. The ideological assumptions embedded in an assessment methodology that rates a hotel bed bringing in $200 a night as a greater loss than a fisherman bringing in $50 a month have far-reaching consequences. With reconstruction measures predicated on this kind of accounting, we are on a trajectory that empowers the tourism industry to be an even more dominant player than it was in the past, and, concomitantly, one that disempowers and further marginalizes the coastal poor.

Travel and Displacement

Much has been made of the unsightly fishing shanties that will not be rebuilt. Instead, fishing communities are going to be transformed into even more unsightly urban squalor, their residents crowded into "modern" apartment complexes like the sardines they may fish. However, this will be further inland. As they sit on the beach watching the ocean loll onto Lanka's shore, tourists will enjoy the coast in a sanitized, "consumer friendly" environment. Ironically, they may even be sitting in *cadjan* cabanas, a nostalgic nod to the *cadjan* homes of fishing communities of the past—a neatly consumable experience of the exotic without the interference of a more messy everyday.

But perhaps this *is* the new everyday that is proposed: the teeming hordes in designated settlements, a playground for tourists elsewhere. It's a product of the mercantile imagination—the imagination of tourist industry fat cats who will be raking in the tsunami windfall. With the building of planned superhighways, tourists will be able to zoom from airport to beach, shopping mall to spa, while the people who lived in these regions will become less mobile as they are shut out from entire stretches of coastal land. If tourism is about carefully planned displacement from the ordinary for a privileged few, the crossing of boundaries for recreation and adventure, here it is tied to the forced displacement of fishing communities and the instituting of new boundaries that exclude and dispossess.

REPOPULATING NEW ORLEANS

How did San Francisco do what a top economist says New Orleans cannot?

MASON GAFFNEY
March/April 2006

Our latest Nobelist in economics, Thomas Schelling, offered the following advice in the wake of Hurricane Katrina: "There is no market solution to New Orleans. It is essentially a problem of coordinating expectations... ." By that he meant simply that each person's incentive to move home and rebuild depends on his or her confidence that others will do likewise. "But achieving this coordination in the circumstances of New Orleans seems impossible."

So economics has come to this. Only yesterday, the approved posture was not to recommend programs, but merely to advise timidly on how different ones might work, covering one's back with caveats. Now our top dog has gone the next step, and advises us that nothing can work, not even the market. A discipline with roots in Utilitarianism has morphed into Futilitarianism.

Actually, there is a time-tested way to solve the problem that defeats the most advanced economics theory. American urban settlers and investors have a long history of building and rebuilding cities by "coordinating expectations." In 1891 the traveling Lord James Bryce wrote of Americans, "Men seem to live in the future rather than in the present: ... they see the country not merely as it is, but as it will be." They achieved critical urban mass by faith in each other, a mutual faith more economic than theological.

"The chief tax is in every State," Bryce noted in 1891, "a property tax... ." The property tax at that time fell in many places mainly on land values, because that is most of what there was to tax. This tax was the mechanism for "coordinating expectations." Each landowner felt the pressure to use his land, knowing his neighbors felt the same pressure at the same time. (There were also pioneering religious and ethnic groups that fostered mutual faith, as the Greek Orthodox community is doing now in its small part of New Orleans. In the game theory Schelling & co. study, we are all greedy monads, so such things do not happen in the models—and who cares about the extra-modular [i.e., real] world outside the laptop?)

It's not that Schelling never heard of the stimulative effect of taxing land values. In 1969 I had the privilege of presenting it to a seminar at the Brookings Institution. I suggested raising the land tax, and lowering sales taxes and taxes on buildings. Most attendees listened with at least moderate sympathy, notably excepting Schelling, who objected that any change in tax policy would break the social contract, destabilize expectations, shatter investor confidence, and risk bringing the world down in ruins.

In 1966 I had spoken on the same point to a New Orleans civic group, sponsors of a Brookings urbanism program. They were charming hosts, eager for ideas about how to clear "undesirable" neighborhoods but obsessed with preserving *Le Vieux Carré*, which they saw as unique, wholesome, a money machine, and too fragile to survive competition that would replace it with the commonplace. Like Schelling, they chose stasis, with the results that we see today. Actually, there can be no stasis:

buildings depreciate every year, and need constant upkeep, operation, adaptation to markets, and often replacement.

A going city or region, leveled by catastrophe, has an easier time returning to critical mass than does a new city or region flying blind. London renewed itself after the Great Fire of 1666; Schenectady after Frontenac razed it in 1690; Lisbon after the 1755 quake; Dutch cities after flooding themselves out to balk successive Spanish, French, and German invaders; Moscow after 1812; and Washington, D.C., after 1813. In 1848 John Stuart Mill highlighted "the great rapidity with which countries recover from a state of devastation; the disappearance, in a short time, of all traces of the mischiefs done by earthquakes, floods, hurricanes, and the ravages of war." Since then there have been a series of such rebirths: Atlanta after Sherman; Chicago after 1871; swaths of Wisconsin after the epic 1871 fire named for little Peshtigo; Johnstown, Pa., after the killer 1889 flood; San Francisco after the quake and fire of 1906; Flanders after World War I; Tokyo after 1926; the Mississippi Valley after the great flood of 1927; Nanking after Japan's devastating occupation. After World War II came Germany's *Wirtschaftswunder*, and the rebuilding of Coventry, Rotterdam, Tokyo again, Hiroshima, Nagasaki, and Russia after Hitler. There was Anchorage after its quake; Kobe after its; and on and on.

Permanent hazards may remain, as in New Orleans. Yet, Chicago was rebuilt on the foundation of its "stinking swamp," where the city's architects and engineers pioneered the modern skyscraper on deep caissons. Tokyo was rebuilt at the confluence of four tectonic plates, and after 1945 with no navy or army of its own. San Francisco was rebuilt on the San Andreas Fault, and went high-rise on its crazy hills while Los Angeles was still capping building heights and opting for sprawl. Much of the Netherlands thrives below sea level.

After disaster, location remains, and location makes cities. Greater New Orleans was recently the largest port in the world in tonnage shipped. People, enterprise, and investment also make cities. Herein lies the greater hazard, for many American cities wither away not with a bang but with a whimper, like Buffalo, Cincinnati, Detroit, Camden, or St. Louis.

New Orleans today has a kind of dynamism that those cities lack. Demand for its real estate is holding up, and rising in the unflooded areas like Gentilly Ridge. Even in the flooded and abandoned areas there is strong demand from absentee bottom-fishers looking for a free ride up the price elevator as the efforts of others bring back the neighborhoods. Yet this kind of dynamism is worse than stasis. These absentees choke out other buyers aiming to commit themselves—to rebuild and reside and make neighborhoods. As "Each man kills the thing he loves," do-nothing investors collectively drive away the very people who could make their dreams come true. Many of them have no plans, but are waiting for other people's plans. Coordinating expectations like those adds up to nothing. Tragically, the tax system in New Orleans—as nearly everywhere else—penalizes builders and doers, and spares free riders.

Consider born-again San Francisco, 1907 to 1930, as a case study in success. What can it teach New Orleans? It had no state or federal aid to speak of. The state of California had oil, but didn't even tax it, as Louisiana (rightly) does. It did have private insurance, but so does New Orleans today. It had no power to tax sales or incomes. It had no lock on Sierra water to sell dearly to its neighbors, as now; no finished Panama Canal, as now; no regional monopoly comparable to New Orleans' hold on the vast Mississippi Valley. Unlike Los Angeles (whose smog lay in the future) it had cold fog, cold-water beaches, no local fuel nor easy mountain passes to the east. Its rail and shipping connections were inferior to the major rail, port, and shipbuilding complex in rival Oakland, and even to inland Stockton's. It was hilly; much of its flatter space was landfill, in jeopardy both to liquefaction of soil in another quake and to precarious land titles. Its great bridges were unbuilt, so it was more island than peninsula. It was known for eccentricity, drunken sailors, tong wars, labor strife, racism, vice, vigilantism, and civic scandals. In its hinterland, mining was fading and irrigation barely beginning. Lumbering was far north around Eureka; wine around Napa; deciduous fruit around San Jose. Berkeley had the state university, Sacramento the capital, Palo Alto Stanford, Oakland and Alameda the major U.S. Navy supply center.

How did a city with so few assets raise funds to repair its broken infrastructure and rise from its ashes? It had only the local property tax, and much of this tax base was burned to the ground. The answer is that it taxed the ground itself, raising

A Primer on Henry George's "Single Tax"

At the turn of the last century, Henry George and the "Single Tax" movement he inspired were household names. George's 1879 book *Progress and Poverty* captured the imagination of millions in the United States and elsewhere, who found in his ideas a blueprint for an economic system that would retain capitalism's productive dynamism *and* distribute its fruits more fairly.

To summarize George's political-economy: George began from the premise that the land, along with all other natural resources, is the common inheritance of all. No persons or firms should *own* land; they should only be able to rent it. Furthermore, that rent should be paid to the public, as the rightful collective owner of all land.

Individuals and firms should own entirely whatever results from their efforts to make the land productive, however, whether by farming it or building a factory on it. They should also own entirely whatever profit they can create through the investment of accumulated capital. (In other words, George was not a socialist.)

The single-tax program was George's plan for implementing this view. The "single tax" was to be a property tax, on land but not on improvements, at a rate high enough to provide adequate revenue to the government. These tax payments would represent the "rent" those who use the land owe to the public. At the same time, taxes on labor income and on capital earnings would be eliminated.

George argued that the single-tax program would boost the economy. A sound economic system encourages both work and capital investment, so governments should avoid taxing labor income or returns on capital. At the same time, a productive system discourages rentier behavior—holding onto resources like land, living off of rents or waiting for speculation to raise land prices. With a high property tax, he believed, land will tend to end up in the hands of those who can make it most productive.

Echoes of George's ideas can be found in many strains of progressive economic thought today. For example, activists have proposed creating a so-called Sky Trust that would collect fees from firms that emit carbon dioxide. These firms are using up our common inheritance of a low-CO_2 atmosphere, Sky Trust proponents argue, so they owe the public a "rent" that would serve as both an incentive to clean up their emissions and a source of funds for environmental protection efforts or "dividend" payments to the public.

—Amy Gluckman

money while also kindling a new kind of fire under landowners to get on with it or get out of the way.

Historians have obsessed over the quake and fire but blanked out the recovery. We do know, though, that in 1907 San Francisco elected a reform mayor, Edward Robeson Taylor, with a uniquely relevant background: he had helped Henry George, more than anyone else, write *Progress and Poverty* in 1879. George, of course, is the one who wrote and campaigned for the cause of raising most revenues from a tax on the value of land, exempting labor and sales and buildings. (See "A Primer on Henry George's Single Tax.") In 1907, single-tax was in the air, and it was natural to go along with Cleveland (Mayors Tom Johnson and Newton Baker), Detroit (Mayor and later Governor Hazen Pingree), Toledo (Mayors Samuel "Golden Rule" Jones and Brand Whitlock), Milwaukee (the "sewer socialists" and Mayor Dan Hoan), Chicago (Mayor Edward F. Dunne, ex-Governor J.P. Altgeld, muckrakers Ida Tarbell and Henry D. Lloyd, editor Louis F. Post, Nobelist-to-be Jane Addams, Councilman Clarence Darrow, et al.), Vancouver (six-time Mayor Louis Denison "Single-tax" Taylor), Houston (Assessor J.J. Pastoriza), many smaller cities, and doubtless other big cities yet to be researched, that chose to tax buildings less and land more. It was the golden age of American cities when they grew like fury, and also with the grace of the popular "City Beautiful" motif.

San Francisco bounced back so fast its population grew by 22% from 1900 to 1910, in the very wake of its destruction; it grew another 22% from 1910 to 1920 and another 25% from 1920 to 1930, becoming the tenth largest American city. It did this without expanding its land base, as rival Los Angeles did, and without stinting its parks. On its steep gradients it housed, and linked with publicly-owned mass transit, a denser population than any city except the Manhattan borough of New York. It is these people and their good works that made San Francisco so famously livable, the cynosure of so many eyes, and gave it the massed economic power later to bridge the Bay and the Golden Gate, grab water from the High Sierra, finance the fabulous growth of intensive irrigated farming in the Central Valley, and become the financial, cultural, and tourism center of the Pacific coast.

Mayor Nagin of New Orleans tells the world that Katrina wiped out most of his tax base, so he is impotent. By contrast, in 1907 Mayor Taylor's Committee on Assessment, Revenue, and Taxation reported sanguinely that revenues were still adequate. How could that be? Because before the quake and fire razed the city, land value already comprised 75% of its real estate tax base. San Francisco also taxed "personal" (movable) property, but it was much less than real estate, and secured by a lien on land. The coterminous county and school district used the same tax base. They also made extensive use of special assessments on lands benefited by specific public works. In other words, San Francisco had adopted most of Henry George's single tax program *de facto*, whether or not they said so publicly.

It was a jolt to replace the lost part of the tax base by taxing land value more, but small enough to be doable. This firm tax base also sustained the city's credit, allowing it to finance the great burst of civic works that was to follow. Taylor supported the next mayor but one, James Rolph (1911-1930), who oversaw a long period of civic unity and public works. "Sunny Jim" Rolph expanded city enterprise into water supply, planning, municipally owned mass transit, the Panama-Pacific International Exposition, and the matchless Civic Center. Good fiscal policy did not turn all the knaves into saints: Rolph eventually fell into bad company with venal bankers and imperialist engineers. But San Francisco rose and thrived.

New Orleans, sited below the Mississippi River and its levees, has its own special problem. Milton Friedman and his like-thinkers proclaim that markets have solutions for everything that governments botch. Building levees, however, demands cooperation guided by some overall authority, which is what governments are for. A levee protects the land behind it only by shunting water onto other lands, which then require their own levees to shunt the water back, and downstream, and even, as it turned out, upstream. Competition among levee-builders becomes a vicious spiral. Over a century it has led step-by-step to levees four stories high.

Analytically, the problem is analogous to that of rivals pumping water or oil from a common pool, or fishermen competing by taking fish from each other. In those other contexts, private-property fanatics (i.e. most modern economists) see a "tragedy of the commons" and prescribe privatization. Levees, however, are there to protect lands already private, and call for different thinking.

Since the Mississippi Valley covers half the country, the central authority has to be federal. In the great flood of 1927, Calvin Coolidge let Herbert Hoover make himself czar of the river system. Hoover, who fostered cartels in industry, declared that prosperity can be organized by "cooperative group effort and planning"—i.e., by coordinating expectations consciously, from the top down. It was too late, however, to keep the power elite of New Orleans, who ran Louisiana, from dynamiting the levee protecting St. Bernard and Plaquemines Parishes, saving the city by flooding the rednecks. These responded by electing Huey Long governor in 1928, breaking New Orleans' hegemony for good.

Meantime, Hoover and a few rich power-brokers organized the Tri-State Flood Control Commission to coordinate efforts among at least Louisiana, Mississippi, and Arkansas. Hoover's approach achieved coordination by making local governments pathetic supplicants (like Mayor Nagin and Governor Blanco) at the public trough, brokered by the highly politicized U.S. Army Corps of Engineers. Over time this arrangement has come to entail less coordination and more pork.

Hoover's czardom came too late to allocate lands for a bypass or overspill, such as the broad one west of Sacramento that protects the lower Sacramento Valley. Too many oxen would have been gored. And last year the overbuilt levee system, legacy of 150 years of the slow vicious spiral of misdirected competition to beggar-thy-neighbor, finally betrayed the city.

What to do now? A strong dose of Georgist tax policy will revive the private sector of any city, and the surrounding rural areas too. As to flood control, we need an integrated system that will sacrifice some lands to benefit others, and a tax system that will compensate the losers from the gains of the winners. Given such integration, engineers since James B. Eads in 1870 have worked out plans for the whole river system. It would take a catastrophe to shock Americans into such a new mode of thinking—but the catastrophe just happened, so now let us think.

IN VIEQUES, PUERTO RICO, *LA LUCHA CONTINUA*

LIV GOLD
November/December 2006

Last spring, I came across an article in *Caribbean Edge* magazine on Vieques, a small island seven miles off the coast of Puerto Rico. According to the article, Vieques' "lush green rainforest, pristine beaches, and crystal clear waters" are "the perfect place to relax and experience the quiet charms of a truly unspoiled Caribbean island."

They must have mistaken a different island for Vieques, I thought. "Pristine" and "unspoiled" could not possibly describe the Vieques I knew of—a U.S. aerial weapons testing ground for over 50 years whose residents had a 30% higher cancer rate than Puerto Ricans do, a 381% higher rate of hypertension, and a 95% higher rate of cirrhosis of the liver. And phrases like "perfect place to relax" and "quiet charms" hardly seem apt to describe a place that has been the site of demonstrations and arrests, and whose future continues to be contested terrain.

Of course I could have been wrong—and there was only one way to be sure. In June, I packed my bags and headed to Vieques.

Sixty Years of Bombing

The U.S. Navy's occupation of Vieques began on December 10, 1941, three days after Japanese bombs struck Pearl Harbor, when Congress authorized $30 million to build military installations in Puerto Rico, including a dual-use target range/amphibious exercise base in Vieques. Between 1941 and 1947, the Navy expropriated two-thirds of the island and displaced 10,000 Viequenses. It compensated possessors of legally titled land—a small number of mostly white, mostly wealthy plantation owners. Almost overnight Vieques was rebuilt to serve as one side in a defensive triangle, made up of Puerto Rico, Florida, and Panama, that would protect the Panama Canal and hold European fascism at bay.

But by the time construction was completed, the base was already obsolete. The Panama Canal was calm and the Caribbean Sea, initially expected to be a theater of war, had hosted only one minor battle. At the end of World War II the largest base on the Puerto Rican mainland was placed on maintenance status. Some tracts of land were leased back to the Puerto Rican government, but in Vieques the Navy remained planted. It kept Viequenses in the center of the island and poured more capital into munitions storage facilities in the west and weapons testing grounds in the east, all the while insisting that its maneuvers on Vieques were vital to national security. The service members who trained there fought the wars on fascism, on communism, on drugs, and later on terror. During the Navy's 60-year residency, 18,000 tons of bombs fell on the island; napalm and Agent Orange rained from the sky.

Nonetheless, in an official "Vieques White Paper," the Navy asserted that it has been a good steward of the land and water entrusted to its care at Vieques. It has protected and nurtured the wildlife, forests, plants, and resources. ... Its use of a very small part of the island for a live impact area has not harmed the health of its neighbors on Vieques or the environment in which they live. ... To date, the Navy has seen no credible evidence that its activities pose a risk to human health.

That was in 1999, six months after two 500-pound bombs were accidentally dropped on a civilian Viequense named David Sanes. Four years later, a solidarity movement worldwide in reach was conducting large-scale demonstrations and civil disobedience actions to force the Navy off of the island. Over 1,500 people were imprisoned, including some of Puerto Rico's most esteemed religious and political leaders. The mayor of Vieques himself served four months in a federal penitentiary. Finally, in 2003, the Navy deactivated the base. The press stopped reporting on "the struggle in Vieques." In the *New York Times*, Vieques slid seamlessly from social justice talking point to hot tourist destination.

This Is Not Wilderness

When the Navy closed its base, it transferred land administration to the U.S. Fish and Wildlife Service, which applied the term "wilderness area" to 900 acres of the eastern portion of the island. The 1964 Wilderness Act defines "wilderness" as

> [a place] where the earth and its community are untrammeled by man ... retaining its primeval character and influence ... and that generally appears to have been affected primarily by forces of nature, with the imprint of man's work substantially unnoticeable.

It seemed to me that the imprint of man's work would be rather pronounced on an ex-Navy bombing range; that a site with more craters than parts of the moon could only loosely be termed "wilderness." This is more than just semantics. Engaging in an Orwellian name game allows the Navy to evade its decontamination responsibilities. Suppose the land was classified as residential or commercial rather than as "wilderness." Or better yet, imagine that it must one day accommodate an elementary school. Environmental standards and corresponding clean-up processes enjoy a reciprocal relationship with future land use plans. So whether the land must be made suitable for sea turtles or school children makes a big difference. By designating much of the land as wildlife refuge and wilderness area, the U.S. government has reduced the Navy's financial and environmental responsibility to the lowest possible level.

For evidence of the Navy's financial evasion, consider Kahoʻolawe, Hawaii. Like Vieques, Kahoʻolawe was used for conventional and non-conventional military operations for over 50 years. Unlike Vieques, however, Kahoʻolawe was uninhabited. Yet Kahoʻolawe received $400 million for decontamination, while Vieques, with a population above 7,000, received less than half that.

This Is Not Clean-Up

The environmental repercussions of such parsimony are everywhere. The Navy and its contractors say they are "removing" unexploded ordnance and munitions scrap debris. But safe, complete removal requires the use of controlled detonation chambers to explode live ordinance. "Operational limitations" preclude such methods, says the Navy. As a result, 20 tons of explosives have been blown up in place recently, including 1,046 munitions of up to one-ton size, 495 of which were classified as "high explosives."

While I was in Vieques I attended a meeting of the Restoration Advisory Board, which lasted more than four hours and brought together members of the Viequense community with representatives from the Navy, EPA, U.S. Fish and Wildlife Service, and the Vieques municipal government. But most Viequenses do not trust the federal government; they feel angry and alienated and betrayed. "This is still a matter of life or death," shouted Bob Rabin, a long time resident of Vieques. "*Bombs* are being detonated."

Naval contractor CH2M Hill has begun testing for background levels of inorganics (metals) in soil samples from areas on Vieques identified as "not impacted by past Navy activities." These data will be compared with soil tests from sites where Navy activity is a concern. During discussions about background sampling, a resident named Mike Diaz expressed concern that areas "not impacted by past Navy activities" may simply not exist on his small island. "If you can envision a volcano distributing material over the islands," he asked, "why can't you envision the same distribution by bombs?"

Rabin's assertion that lives are at stake is not overstated. Study after study shows that toxic substances from Navy activity have entered the food chain, contaminating surface vegetation like squash, peppers, and pigeon peas, as well as fish. A research group from the University of Puerto Rico School of Public Health examined the dust in residents' homes and found it laced with cadmium, arsenic and lead. Yet until the Navy's own team of contracted experts executes *its* contamination study, the Navy denies any responsibility.

This Is Not Control

The struggle in Vieques was many things, but it was never solely an expression of anti-militarism. It was more about control, or more specifically, about putting control of their land and economy back into the hands of Viequenses.

Consequently, the Navy's 2003 departure was bittersweet because since then, land administration has gone from the U.S. Department of Defense's Naval Facilities Atlantic Command to the U.S. Department of Interior's Fish and Wildlife Service, and ongoing clean-up efforts, though aided by private contractors, are overseen and regulated by the EPA. In each case, the governing body—the body determining the fate of the island—belongs to the U.S. government, not to the people of Vieques.

The economic sub-plot is similar. During the Navy's occupation of the island, Viequenses lost access to their ports, both marine and air, which effectively halted foreign investment and stalled domestic production in industries like sugar, fishing and agriculture. While unemployment soared among Viequenses, the U.S. government took in close to $100 million annually by renting the eastern Live Impact Area to allied militaries. Now that the bombing has stopped, Vieques has a chance to restore its faltering economy. But in the absence of regulatory controls and a sustainable land use plan, Viequenses risk losing control yet again.

Already gentrification has displaced a large segment of the Viequense population. As one local realtor explained, "When the Navy left, land on Vieques was cheap and plentiful, at least from the perspective of foreign investors." Those investors had business experience and capital to front; in just a few years they cultivated a tourism industry that put the island in demand.

As more people come to Vieques, the cost of living rises and the real estate market becomes inflated. "Nobody forces Viequenses to leave," insisted the realtor. "They get offered a hundred thousand dollars for their concrete house and soon they're gone."

Nilda Medina, a Viequense woman, has watched foreign capital displace her friends. "It's like a ghost community has taken over," she said. Absentee owners with bank accounts in Boston are coming into possession of beach-front properties, hotels, and shops. Only they can swallow the sort of land speculation that makes previously untitled properties rapidly triple and quadruple in value. And all of these purchases by foreign investors, renters, and second-home buyers are happening while 600 homeless or underhoused Puerto Rican families bide their time on a waiting list for Section 8 housing assistance.

"After decades of resistance," Nilda told me, "American capital might accomplish what American bombs never could—the erosion and eventual eviction of Viequense population and culture."

Vieques needs a land use plan that will moderate the power of both the real estate and tourism industries and the federal government, a plan that can restore agency to the Viequense people. It needs a plan that will mandate the quick and complete decontamination of the island and pave the way for future economic growth—growth that is not just sustainable, but also endogenous. Given its history, this is a tough task for Vieques. The task is complicated further by the fact that Vieques has not just one, but three official land use plans: one applies to the municipality, one applies to all of Puerto Rico, and one was specially designed for Vieques by a group of Puerto Rican academics. Testing the legal fortitude of each plan has already proven challenging. It may be some time before a stable land use plan is adopted.

The Struggle Continues

For over half a decade, the struggle in Vieques was described in mythic terms, as a battle between David and Goliath, the Viequenses and the Navy. Now that the Navy is gone, the challenges facing Vieques are less clear-cut; instead of bombs and mortars, residents confront poorly regulated markets where absentee ownership and staggering foreign investment threaten wholesale displacement of the native people and culture.

Bob Rabin is one of the founding members of the Committee for the Rescue and Development of Vieques (CRDV), formed in 1995 to articulate a vision of a Navy-free Vieques. He and his colleagues advocate the four Ds: demilitarization, decontamination, devolution, and (community-based, sustainable) development. "Demilitarization" refers specifically to the closure of remaining radar facilities and telecommunications centers that still occupy 200 acres on the island. "Decontamination" broadly demands that the Navy leave Vieques as clean as it was found in 1940, including the complete cleanup of heavy metals, napalm, Agent Orange, depleted uranium, and other land, marine, and aerial contaminants. "Devolution" speaks to the return of all land to Vieques, as opposed to the Fish and Wildlife Service. "Development" urges sustainable economic development by the Viequenses for the Viequenses, which respects the cultural and natural resources of the island.

"You might laugh at this," said Rabin, "but in some ways it used to be easier. The themes and issues were more straightforward. And there was consensus—we all believed there was something fundamentally correct about what we were doing." Today the issues are complicated; each proposal, each plan, and each initiative is controversial.

The same can be said for the solidarity movement that once rallied around the island. The Navy's presence was a unifying force; now the support network is frayed. Many people assume that with the base deactivated, the struggle is over. And those still attuned find it hard to stay informed and difficult to get involved. However, at the core of the struggle are familiar themes—respect for Vieques' land and waters, dignity for its people—and strategies—civil disobedience, town meetings, and referendums.

In the United States, I hope that our solidarity can shift with the circumstances to fight the U.S. military's "war on the earth" and support Vieques' efforts to achieve self-determination. In Vieques, *la lucha continua.*

U.S. MILITARY SPENDING AND THE COST OF THE WARS

BY CHRIS STURR
July/August 2006

For the past several years, the annual inflation-adjusted budget of the Department of Defense has been higher than the Cold War average of $342.4 billion per year (see Figure 1).

The peaks in the early 1950s, the late 1960s, and the mid-1980s reflect spending on the Korean War, the Vietnam War, and the Reagan military buildup respectively. With the United States at war in Iraq and Afghanistan, it might not seem surprising that Defense Department spending is again at a peak. But that's not the explanation: the DoD's regular budget, shown in Figure 1, does not include direct spending on those wars. Add in the special appropriations Congress has made to cover the costs of war-fighting since 9/11, and the current military buildup is even more dramatic (see Figure 2).

U.S. military spending, including spending on the wars, is far and away the highest in the world, dwarfing the next nine top spenders *combined* (see Table 1).

One of the only countries to spend a comparable amount per capita on its military is Israel, whose population is comparable to that of Massachusetts. U.S.

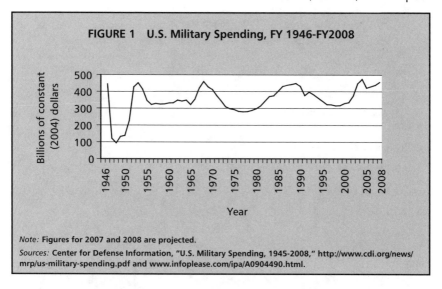

FIGURE 1   U.S. Military Spending, FY 1946-FY2008

Note: Figures for 2007 and 2008 are projected.

Sources: Center for Defense Information, "U.S. Military Spending, 1945-2008," http://www.cdi.org/news/mrp/us-military-spending.pdf and www.infoplease.com/ipa/A0904490.html.

military spending per capita is $1750; Israel's is $1380. Russia spends $432 per capita; China spends $47.

The money the Defense Department has spent on the Iraq war does not exhaust the costs of the war to the government. In a study released last February, Harvard policy analyst Linda Bilmes and Columbia economist Joseph Stiglitz estimated that if we include spending by the Veterans Administration, demobilization costs, and interest on debt incurred because of the Iraq war, the cost of the war to the U.S. government rises to between $750 billion and $1.2 trillion. If we add in economic

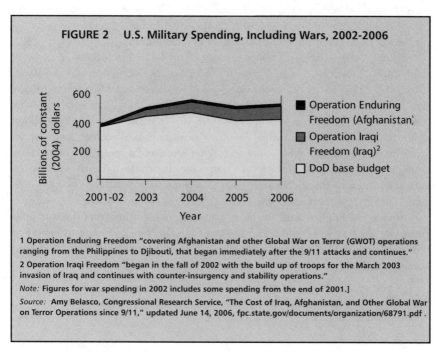

FIGURE 2   U.S. Military Spending, Including Wars, 2002-2006

■ Operation Enduring Freedom (Afghanistan)

■ Operation Iraqi Freedom (Iraq)[2]

☐ DoD base budget

1 Operation Enduring Freedom "covering Afghanistan and other Global War on Terror (GWOT) operations ranging from the Philippines to Djibouti, that began immediately after the 9/11 attacks and continues."

2 Operation Iraqi Freedom "began in the fall of 2002 with the build up of troops for the March 2003 invasion of Iraq and continues with counter-insurgency and stability operations."

Note: Figures for war spending in 2002 includes some spending from the end of 2001.]

Source: Amy Belasco, Congressional Research Service, "The Cost of Iraq, Afghanistan, and Other Global War on Terror Operations since 9/11," updated June 14, 2006, fpc.state.gov/documents/organization/68791.pdf .

TABLE 1
Top Ten Military Spenders, 2005

Rank and Country	2005 Military Budget ($Billions)
1. United States (including funding for Iraq and Afghanistan)	522.0
2. China (2004 expenditures)	62.5
3. Russia (2004 expenditures)	61.9
4. United Kingdom	51.1
5. Japan	44.7
6. France	41.6
7. Germany	30.2
8. India	22.0
9. Saudi Arabia	21.3
10. South Korea	20.7

Source: Center for Arms Control and Non-Proliferation, "U.S Military Spending vs. the World," February 6, 2006, www.armscontrolcenter.org/archives/002244.php (see also www.sipri.org/contents/milap/milex/mex_trends.html).

costs that are not borne by the government—e.g. the lost economic contributions of reservists while they are deployed, or after they are dead or injured—the price tag for the war balloons by another $187 billion to $305 billion.

Bilmes and Stiglitz also attempt to estimate the larger macroeconomic costs of the Iraq war. One source of such costs is the higher price of oil—now over $50 per barrel, vs. $25 per barrel before the war—plausibly due to instability in the Middle East resulting from the war. They argue that even assuming, conservatively, that only 10-20% of the increase is due to the war, this translates into a $25-50 billion dollar added expense. Addressing a number of other possible consequences of the war—increased security threats, higher interest rates, and opportunity costs of devoting so many resources to the war in Iraq—they conclude that even with conservative estimates, its macroeconomic costs "are potentially very large; possibly even a multiple of the direct costs," that is, possibly *several* trillion dollars.

Bilmes and Stiglitz conclude by enumerating many other ways the vast sums going into the Iraq war could have been spent so as to "buy" greater well-being and more security than the war has achieved. They make a plea for governments to undertake cost-benefit analysis of a planned war before starting it:

> The most important things in life—like life itself—are priceless. But that doesn't mean that topics like defense ... should not be subject to cool, hard analysis of the kind for which economics has long earned a reputation.

The kind of analysis mainstream economics has a reputation for can certainly provide a balance sheet for a war. But as the figures above reveal, the U.S. government is accelerating military spending even apart from its actual wars. What mainstream economic analysis, with its categorical blindness to deployments of power in the political economy, cannot do is to explain why.

Sources: Center for Defense Information, "U.S. Military Spending, 1946-2008," http://www. cdi.org/news/mrp/us-military-spending.pdf and www.infoplease.com/ipa/A0904490.html; Amy Belasco, Congressional Research Service, "The Cost of Iraq, Afghanistan, and Other Global War on Terror Operations since 9/11," updated June 14, 2006, fpc.state.gov/documents/ organization/68791.pdf; House Appropriations Committee Democrats, Iraq Funding Timeline, www.house.gov/appropriations_democrats/pdf/iraq-funding-timeline-6-15-2005.pdf; Center for Arms Control and Non-Proliferation, "U.S Military Spending vs. the World," February 6th, 2006, www.armscontrolcenter.org/archives/002244.php (see also www.sipri.org/contents/milap/ milex/mex_trends.html); Linda Bilmes and Joseph Stiglitz, "The Economic Costs of the Iraq War," www2.gsb.columbia.edu/faculty/jstiglitz/cost_of_war_in_iraq.pdf; Christopher Hellman, Center for Arms Control and Nonproliferation, "The Runaway Military Budget: An Analysis," Friends Committee on National Legislation *Washington Newsletter*, March 2006, www.fcnl.org/now/ pdf/2006/mar06.pdf.

Chapter 10

PROGRAMS FOR SOCIAL AND ECONOMIC CHANGE

LABOR'S CAPITAL
Putting pension wealth to work for workers.

ADRIA SCHARF
September/October 2005

Pension fund assets are the largest single source of investment capital in the country. Of the roughly $17 trillion in private equity in the U.S. economy, $6 to 7 trillion is held in employee pensions. About $1.3 trillion is in union pension plans (jointly trusteed labor-management plans or collectively bargained company-sponsored plans) and $2.1 trillion is in public employee pension plans. Several trillion more are in defined contribution plans and company-sponsored defined benefit plans with no union representation. These vast sums were generated by—and belong to—workers; they're really workers' deferred wages.

Workers' retirement dollars course through Wall Street, but most of the capital owned *by* working people is invested with no regard *for* working people or their communities. Pension dollars finance sweatshops overseas, hold shares of public companies that conduct mass layoffs, and underwrite myriad anti-union low-road corporate practices. In one emblematic example, the Florida public pension system bought out the Edison Corporation, the for-profit school operator, in November 2003, with the deferred wages of Florida government employees—including public school teachers. (With just three appointed trustees, one of whom is Governor Jeb Bush, Florida is one of the few states with no worker representation on the board of its state-employee retirement fund.)

The custodians of workers' pensions—plan trustees and investment managers—argue that they are bound by their "fiduciary responsibility" to consider only narrow financial factors when making investment decisions. They maintain they have a singular obligation to maximize financial returns and minimize financial risk for beneficiaries—with no regard for broader concerns. But from the perspective of the teachers whose dollars funded an enterprise that aims to privatize their jobs, investing in Edison, however promising the expected return (and given Edison's track record, it wasn't very promising!), makes no sense.

A legal concept enshrined in the 1974 Employee Retirement Income Security Act (ERISA) and other statutes, "fiduciary responsibility" does constrain the decision-making of those charged with taking care of other people's money. It obligates fiduciaries (e.g., trustees and fund managers) to invest retirement assets for the exclusive benefit of the pension beneficiaries. According to ERISA, fiduciaries must act with the care, skill, prudence, and diligence that a "prudent man" would use. Exactly what that means, though, is contested.

The law does *not* say that plan trustees must maximize short-term return. It does, in fact, give fiduciaries some leeway to direct pension assets to worker- and community-friendly projects. In 1994, the U.S. Department of Labor issued rule clarifications that expressly permit fiduciaries to make "economically targeted investments" (ETIs), or investments that take into account collateral benefits like good jobs, housing, improved social service facilities, alternative energy, strengthened infrastructure, and economic development. Trustees and fund managers are free to consider a double bottom line, prioritizing investments that have a social payoff so long as their expected risk-adjusted financial returns are equal to other, similar, investments. Despite a backlash against ETIs from Newt Gingrich conservatives in the 1990s, Clinton's Labor Department rules still hold.

Nevertheless, the dominant mentality among the asset management professionals who make a living off what United Steelworkers president Leo Gerard calls "the deferred-wage food table" staunchly resists considering any factors apart from financial risk and return.

This is beginning to change in some corners of the pension fund world, principally (no surprise) where workers and beneficiaries have some control over their pension capital. In jointly managed union defined-benefit (known as "Taft-Hartley") plans and public-employee pension plans, the ETI movement is gaining ground. "Taft-Hartley pension trustees have grown more comfortable with economically targeted investments as a result of a variety of influences, one being the Labor Department itself," says Robert Pleasure of the Center for Working Capital, an independent capital stewardship-educational institute started by the AFL-CIO. Concurrently, more public pension fund trustees have begun adopting ETIs that promote housing and economic development within state borders. Most union and public pension trustees now understand that, as long as they follow a careful process and protect returns, ETIs do not breach their fiduciary duty, and may in certain cases actually be sounder investments than over-inflated Wall Street stocks.

Saving Jobs: Heartland Labor Capital Network

During the run-up of Wall Street share prices in the 1990s, investment funds virtually redlined basic industries, preferring to direct dollars into hot public technology stocks and emerging foreign markets, which despite the rhetoric of fiduciary responsibility were often speculative, unsound, investments. Even most collectively bargained funds put their assets exclusively in Wall Street stocks, in part because some pension trustees feared that if they didn't, they could be held liable. (During an earlier period, the Labor Department aggressively pursued union pension trustees for breaches of fiduciary duty. In rare cases where trustees were found liable, their personal finances and possessions were at risk.) But in the past five years, more union pension funds and labor-friendly fund managers have begun directing assets into investments that bolster the "heartland" economy: worker-friendly private equity, and, wherever possible, unionized industries and companies that offer "card-check" and "neutrality." ("Card-check" requires automatic union recognition if a majority of employees present signed authorization cards; "neutrality" means employers agree to remain neutral during organizing campaigns.)

The Heartland Labor Capital Network is at the center of this movement. The network's Tom Croft says he and his allies want to "make sure there's an economy still around in the future to which working people will be able to contribute." Croft estimates that about $3 to $4 billion in new dollars have been directed to worker-friendly private equity since 1999—including venture capital, buyout funds, and "special situations" funds that invest in financially distressed companies, saving jobs and preventing closures. Several work closely with unions to direct capital into labor-friendly investments.

One such fund, New York-based KPS Special Situations, has saved over 10,000 unionized manufacturing jobs through its two funds, KPS Special Situations I and II, according to a company representative. In 2003, St. Louis-based Wire Rope Corporation, the nation's leading producer of high carbon wire and wire rope products, was in bankruptcy with nearly 1,000 unionized steelworker jobs in jeopardy. KPS bought the company and restructured it in collaboration with the United Steelworkers International. Approximately 20% of KPS's committed capital is from Taft-Hartley pension dollars; as a result, the Wire Rope transaction included some union pension assets.

The Heartland Labor Capital Network and its union partners want to expand this sort of strategic deployment of capital by building a national capital pool of "Heartland Funds" financed by union pension assets and other sources. These funds have already begun to make direct investments in smaller worker-friendly manufacturing and related enterprises; labor representatives participate alongside investment experts on their advisory boards.

"It's simple. Workers' assets should be invested in enterprises and construction projects that will help to build their cities, rebuild their schools, and rebuild America's infrastructure," says Croft.

"Capital Stewardship": The AFL-CIO

For the AFL-CIO, ETIs are nothing new. Its Housing Investment Trust (HIT), formed in 1964, is the largest labor-sponsored investment vehicle in the country that produces collateral benefits for workers and their neighborhoods. Hundreds of union pension funds invest in the $2 billion trust, which leverages public financing to build housing, including low-income and affordable units, using union labor. HIT, together with its sister fund the Building Investment Trust (BIT), recently announced a new investment program that is expected to generate up to $1 billion in investment in apartment development and rehabilitation by 2005 in targeted cities including New York, Chicago, and Philadelphia. The initiative will finance thousands of units of housing and millions of hours of union construction work. HIT and BIT require owners of many of the projects they help finance to agree to card-check recognition and neutrality for their employees.

HIT and BIT are two examples of union-owned investment vehicles. There are many others—including the LongView ULTRA Construction Loan Fund, which finances projects that use 100% union labor; the Boilermakers' Co-Generation and Infrastructure Fund; and the United Food and Commercial Workers' Shopping Center Mortgage Loan Program—and their ranks are growing.

Since 1997, the AFL-CIO and its member unions have redoubled their efforts to increase labor's control over its capital through a variety of means. The AFL-CIO's Capital Stewardship Program promotes corporate governance reform, investment manager accountability, pro-worker investment strategies, international pension fund cooperation, and trustee education. It also evaluates worker-friendly pension funds on how well they actually advance workers' rights, among other criteria. The Center for Working Capital provides education and training to hundreds of union and public pension fund trustees each year, organizes conferences, and sponsors research on capital stewardship issues including ETIs.

Public Pension Plans Join In

At least 29 states have ETI policies directing a portion of their funds, usually less than 5%, to economic development within state borders. The combined public pension assets in ETI programs amount to about $55 billion, according to a recent report commissioned by the Vermont state treasurer. The vast majority of these ETIs are in residential housing and other real estate.

The California Public Employees' Retirement System (CalPERS) is an ETI pioneer among state pension funds. The single largest pension fund in the country, it has $153.8 billion in assets and provides retirement benefits to over 1.4 million members. In the mid-1990s, when financing for housing construction dried up in California, CalPERS invested hundreds of millions of dollars to finance about 4% of the state's single-family housing market. Its ETI policy is expansive. While it requires economically targeted investments earn maximum returns for their level of risk and fall within geographic and asset-diversification guidelines, CalPERS also considers the investments' benefits to its members and to state residents, their job creation potential, and the economic and social needs of different groups in the state's population. CalPERS directs about 2% of its assets—about $20 billion as of May 2001—to investments that provide collateral social benefits. It also requires construction and maintenance contractors to provide decent wages and benefits.

Other state pension funds have followed CalPERS' lead. In 2003, the Massachusetts treasury expanded its ETI program, which is funded by the state's $32 billion pension. Treasurer Timothy Cahill expects to do "two dozen or more" ETI investments in 2004, up from the single investment made in 2003, according to the *Boston Business Journal*. "It doesn't hurt our bottom line, and it helps locally," Cahill explained. The immediate priority will be job creation. Washington, Wisconsin, and New York also have strong ETI programs.

In their current form and at their current scale, economically targeted investments in the United States are not a panacea. Pension law does impose constraints.

Many consultants and lawyers admonish trustees to limit ETIs to a small portion of an overall pension investment portfolio. And union trustees must pursue ETIs carefully, following a checklist of "prudence" procedures, to protect themselves from liability. The most significant constraint is simply that these investments must generate risk-adjusted returns equal to alternative investments—this means that many deserving not-for-profit efforts and experiments in economic democracy are automatically ruled out. Still, there's more wiggle room in the law than has been broadly recognized. And when deployed strategically to bolster the labor movement, support employee buyouts, generate good jobs, or build affordable housing, economically targeted investments are a form of worker direction over capital whose potential has only begun to be realized. And (until the day that capital is abolished altogether) that represents an important foothold.

As early as the mid-1970s, business expert Peter Drucker warned in *Unseen Revolution* of a coming era of "pension-fund socialism" in which the ownership of massive amounts of capital by pension funds would bring about profound changes to the social and economic power structure. Today, workers' pensions prop up the U.S. economy. They're a point of leverage like no other. Union and public pension funds are the most promising means for working people to shape the deployment of capital on a large scale, while directing assets to investments with collateral benefits. If workers and the trustees of their pension wealth recognize the power they hold, they could alter the contours of capitalism.

THE LAND TRUST SOLUTION
Land trusts ease control of U.S. farmland away from developers.

MICHELLE SHEEHAN
March/April 2005

It was back in the early 1970s that Steven and Gloria Decater of Covelo, Calif., first started farming an unused plot of land belonging to a neighbor. Over many years, they turned the fallow plot into fertile farmland that yielded a bounty of organic vegetables. They named it "Live Power Community Farm" and launched California's first successful community supported agriculture (CSA) program there in 1988. But the Decaters' hold on the land was vulnerable. Without ownership rights, they risked losing the farm to encroaching development. The couple wanted to buy the property but could not afford the land into which they had poured their lives.

The Decaters found a solution to their land-tenure challenge that gave them ownership rights *and* ensured the land would remain an active organic farm. Their solution creates an important precedent—and a possible path for other small tenant farmers.

With the help of Equity Trust Inc., a Massachusetts-based organization that promotes property ownership reform, the Decaters gained ownership rights to the land in 1995—without having to pay the full value themselves. The couple purchased just its "agricultural use value," while Equity Trust, acting as a conservation land trust (a nonprofit institution that controls land for the benefit of current and future generations), purchased "easements," or deed restrictions, that were equal in value to the land's development rights. Together, the two payments amounted to the original asking price.

Agricultural easements are a good way for small farmers to gain ownership control over land when they're not looking to develop or sell it anyway, because they limit the property's market price to its working agricultural value, making it more affordable—while conserving it.

In transferring development rights to the conservation land trust, the Decaters forever forfeited their rights to subdivide or develop the land for anything other than farming; the terms cannot be changed unless both parties agree through a court process. The transaction unpacked the bundle of property rights associated with land ownership, dividing ownership between two entities and placing deliberate restrictions on how the land could be used in the future.

Ramped Up Land-Use Rules

This approach made sense for the Decaters, because they were interested in more than just owning the farm for themselves. "We wanted to have some sort of relationship where it wasn't merely privatized ownership," Gloria explains, "but a socially and economically responsible form of land tenure." They also wanted to make certain that the land would continue to be cultivated by resident farmers with sustainable methods well into the future.

Their vision for the farm was secured by designing easement provisions that went beyond any existing precedent. For example, most easements on farmland dfine agriculture rather loosely. As Equity Trust's Ellie Kastanopoulos notes, "any-

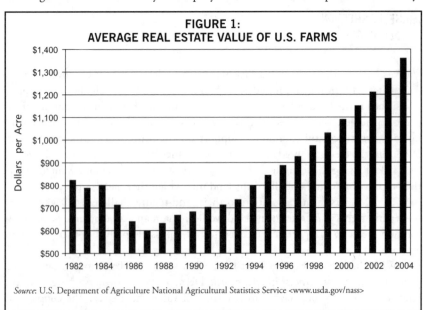

FIGURE 1:
AVERAGE REAL ESTATE VALUE OF U.S. FARMS

Source: U.S. Department of Agriculture National Agricultural Statistics Service <www.usda.gov/nass>

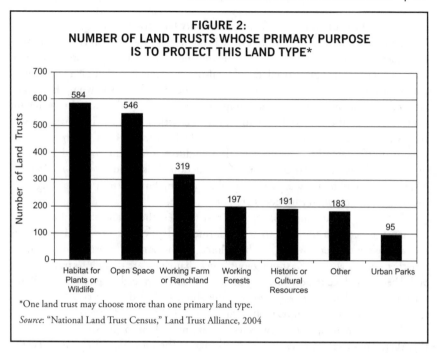

FIGURE 2:
NUMBER OF LAND TRUSTS WHOSE PRIMARY PURPOSE
IS TO PROTECT THIS LAND TYPE*

One land trust may choose more than one primary land type.

Source: "National Land Trust Census," Land Trust Alliance, 2004

one willing to put a few cows on their property and call it a farm" could exploit many agricultural easements. The Decaters and Equity Trust built in a "ramped up" agriculture requirement: Live Power Community Farm must be farmed continually by resident farmers and remain organic or "biodynamic" (a farming philosophy that treats the land as a balanced and sustainable unit and uses the rhythms of nature to maintain the health of the farm).

The Decaters' other major concern was the affordability of their land for future farmers. They see a lot of young farmers for whom "one of the biggest stumbling blocks is getting access to land," Gloria says. While traditional conservation easements ban developers, they do not curb the upward pressure on the price of the land from individual home or estate buyers. Steve worried that when he and Gloria were ready to pass on the land, market forces could "spike the cost of the land so high that any farmer would be bid clear out of the picture." To prevent this, the Decaters and Equity Trust crafted limitations on the resale price of the land into the easement.

Today, Live Power is an active 40-acre horse-powered community supported agriculture (CSA) farm, thriving amidst encroaching development and the huge corporate farms that dominate California agriculture. Not only do the Decaters own their land, but their unique conservation easement ensures that it will permanently remain an affordable, active, and ecologically sustainable farm. The Decaters are true stewards of the land, and the land trust's easement provisions reflect their commitment.

New Ways of Looking at Land Ownership

In addition to conservation land trusts, Equity Trust and others have implemented a second land trust model. So-called "community land trusts" usually focus on low-income housing in urban areas, but have in some cases included agricultural interests. They operate by purchasing tracts of land and then leasing them on a long-term basis to tenants who agree to a detailed land-use agreement. Although a farmer who enters into such a relationship would not own the land, he or she would have agricultural control and would own any improvements made to the land. In the tenant contract, the land trust would retain a purchase option for those improvements so that when the farmer was ready to move on, the land trust could ensure the lands remained affordable for new farmers. The land-use agreement could also include provisions to ensure the land remains in production. This option works well in areas where land is exorbitantly expensive, prohibiting the farmer from purchasing even restricted land, or when easements are not available.

In both land trust models, Equity Trust stresses, there is flexibility in how the relationship between the land trust and farmer is defined. Key to the definition is the land use agreement, which can be tailored for the particular situation according to either party's wishes. Kastanopolous notes that these are complex arrangements and "there is no black and white way of doing things." Indeed, one of Equity Trust's missions is to "change the way people think about and hold property." Their goal is to provide models that can be replicated and adapted to varied situations

These partnerships and new ways of looking at land ownership acknowledge that there are diverse interests in a piece of land. The farmers, the community, the environment, and future users are all considered. Steven Decater is excited by the prospect of agricultural land trusts catching on. "We'll have permanent farms," he says, "and they're going to be needed." He's right about that. Farm real estate values have risen by 70% in the last 20 years (see Figure 1). Across the country, massive mechanized and chemically sustained corporate-controlled farms are rapidly replacing small-time farmers.

The most vulnerable small farmers are ones who sink tremendous energy and resources into improving their soil but are unable to afford the market value of the land they work. Their lack of ownership control puts their land, and their investment, in jeopardy. This is a particularly common experience for operators of CSA

What Are Conservation Land Trusts?

Conservation land trusts are nonprofit organizations designed to protect ecologically fragile environments, open space, or small farms. According to the 2003 National Land Trust Census, there are 1,537 local and national conservation land trusts in operation nationwide, protecting approximately 9 million acres of land, an area four times the size of Yellowstone National Park. This is twice the acreage protected by conservation land trusts just five years ago. New conservation land trusts are formed at the rate of two per week, according to the Land Trust Alliance. They exist in every state; California leads with 173 land trusts, followed by Massachusetts (154) and Connecticut (125). While land trusts protect land in a variety of ways, two of the most common approaches are acquiring land and acquiring conservation easements, legal agreements that permanently restrict the use of land, shielding it from development to ensure its conservation.

For more information on land trusts, see: Land Trust Alliance <www.lta.org>, Equity Trust, Inc. <www.equitytrust.org>, and Vermont Land Trust <www.vlt.org>.

farms, in which producers sell "shares" directly to consumers who receive regular harvest portions during the growing season. According to an informal survey conducted by Equity Trust in the late 1990s, 70% of CSA farms operated on rented land.

Land trusts allow small tenant farms to access land, resist rising property values, and conserve small agricultural tracts. They provide an alternative to unchecked development and farm consolidation, while helping to preserve communities, shield the environment from development, and protect the livelihoods of small farmers. But they are underutilized—in part because the strategy poses certain challenges. It requires:

- resources to purchase the agricultural value of the land,
- willingness by current landowners to sell or donate the land to a land trust,
- technical expertise, and
- in the conservation land trust model, the presence of a conservation land trust with enough resources to pay for easements—which has become more difficult with skyrocketing property values.

Yet thanks to the hard work of the Decaters, Equity Trust, and other organizations including the Vermont Land Trust (VLT) and the Institute of Community Economics (ICE), this innovative approach to land ownership has taken hold in several parts of the country (see "What Are Conservation Land Trusts?"). The VLT oversees many similar transactions every year; it has worked with more than 1,000 landowners and conserved more than 400 farms. Although the group has not quite figured out how to meet the high demand for affordable land as demand pressure drives land prices up across the state, it is nevertheless successfully managing to preserve large areas of farmland in Vermont—and writing affordability restrictions into their easements wherever possible.

Steve Getz, a dairy farmer assisted by the VLT through an easement purchase, says, "We would not have been able to afford the land without the VLT." He and his wife Karen say they respect how the land trust model challenges the "it's my land and I'll do whatever I please with it" mantra that reflects the dominant conception of private land ownership in this country. They now own a successful pasture-based dairy farm in Bridport that will be forever preserved.

SHARING THE WEALTH OF THE COMMONS

PETER BARNES
November/December 2004

We're all familiar with private wealth, even if we don't have much. Economists and the media celebrate it every day. But there's another trove of wealth we barely notice: our common wealth.

Each of us is the beneficiary of a vast inheritance. This common wealth includes our air and water, habitats and ecosystems, languages and cultures, science and technologies, political and monetary systems, and quite a bit more. To say we share this inheritance doesn't mean we can call a broker and sell our shares tomorrow. It does mean we're responsible for the commons and entitled to any income it generates. Both the responsibility and the entitlement are ours by birth. They're part of the obligation each generation owes to the next, and each living human owes to other beings.

At present, however, our economic system scarcely recognizes the commons. This omission causes two major tragedies: ceaseless destruction of nature and widening inequality among humans. Nature gets destroyed because no one's unequivocally responsible for protecting it. Inequality widens because private wealth concentrates while common wealth shrinks.

The great challenges for the 21st century are, first of all, to make the commons visible; second, to give it proper reverence; and third, to translate that reverence into property rights and legal institutions that are on a par with those supporting private property. If we do this, we can avert the twin tragedies currently built into our market-driven system.

Defining the Commons

What exactly is the commons? Here is a workable definition: The commons includes all the assets we inherit together and are morally obligated to pass on, undiminished, to future generations.

This definition is a practical one. It designates a set of assets that have three specific characteristics: they're (1) inherited, (2) shared, and (3) worthy of long-term preservation. Usually it's obvious whether an asset has these characteristics or not.

At the same time, the definition is broad. It encompasses assets that are natural as well as social, intangible as well as tangible, small as well as large. It also introduces a moral factor that is absent from other economic definitions: it requires us to consider whether an asset is worthy of long-term preservation. At present, capitalism has no interest in this question. If an asset is likely to yield a competitive return to capital, it's kept alive; if not, it's destroyed or allowed to run down. Assets in the commons, by contrast, are meant to be preserved regardless of their return.

This definition sorts all economic assets into two baskets, the market and the commons. In the market basket are those assets we want to own privately and manage for profit. In the commons basket are the assets we want to hold in common and manage for long-term preservation. These baskets then are, or ought to be, the yin and yang of economic activity; each should enhance and contain the other. The role of the state should be to maintain a healthy balance between them.

The Value of the Commons

For most of human existence, the commons supplied everyone's food, water, fuel, and medicines. People hunted, fished, gathered fruits and herbs, collected firewood and building materials, and grazed their animals in common lands and waters. In other words, the commons was the source of basic sustenance. This is still true today in many parts of the world, and even in San Francisco, where I live, cash-poor people fish in the bay not for sport, but for food.

Though sustenance in the industrialized world now flows mostly through markets, the commons remains hugely valuable. It's the source of all natural resources and nature's many replenishing services. Water, air, DNA, seeds, topsoil, minerals, the protective ozone layer, the atmosphere's climate regulation, and much more, are gifts of nature to us all.

Just as crucially, the commons is our ultimate waste sink. It recycles water, oxygen, carbon, and everything else we excrete, exhale, or throw away. It's the place we store, or try to store, the residues of our industrial system.

The commons also holds humanity's vast accumulation of knowledge, art, and thought. As Isaac Newton said, "If I have seen further it is by standing on the shoulders of giants." So, too, the legal, political, and economic institutions we inherit— even the market itself—were built by the efforts of millions. Without these gifts we'd be hugely poorer than we are today.

To be sure, thinking of these natural and social inheritances primarily as economic assets is a limited way of viewing them. I deeply believe they are much more than that. But if treating portions of the commons as economic assets can help us conserve them, it's surely worth doing so.

How much might the commons be worth in monetary terms? It's relatively easy to put a dollar value on private assets. Accountants and appraisers do it every day, aided by the fact that private assets are regularly traded for money.

This isn't the case with most shared assets. How much is clean air, an intact wetlands, or Darwin's theory of evolution worth in dollar terms? Clearly, many shared inheritances are simply priceless. Others are potentially quantifiable, but there's no current market for them. Fortunately, economists have developed methods to quantify the value of things that aren't traded, so it's possible to estimate the value of the "priceable" part of the commons within an order of magnitude. The surprising conclusion that emerges from numerous studies is that the wealth we share is worth more than the wealth we own privately.

This fact bears repeating. Even though much of the commons can't be valued in monetary terms, the parts that can be valued are worth more than all private assets combined.

It's worth noting that these estimates understate the gap between common and private assets because a significant portion of the value attributed to private wealth is in fact an appropriation of common wealth. If this mislabeled portion was subtracted from private wealth and added to common wealth, the gap between the two would widen further.

Two examples will make this point clear. Suppose you buy a house for $200,000 and, without improving it, sell it a few years later for $300,000. You pay off the mortgage and walk away with a pile of cash. But what caused the house to rise in value? It wasn't anything you did. Rather, it was the fact that your neighborhood became more popular, likely a result of the efforts of community members, improvements in public services, and similar factors.

Or consider another fount of private wealth, the social invention and public expansion of the stock market. Suppose you start a business that goes "public" through an offering of stock. Within a few years, you're able to sell your stock for a spectacular capital gain.

Much of this gain is a social creation, the result of centuries of monetary-system evolution, laws and regulations, and whole industries devoted to accounting, sharing information, and trading stocks. What's more, there's a direct correlation between the scale and quality of the stock market as an institution and the size of the private gain. You'll fetch a higher price if you sell into a market of millions than into a market of two. Similarly, you'll gain more if transaction costs are low and trust in public information is high. Thus, stock that's traded on a regulated exchange sells for a higher multiple of earnings than unlisted stock. This socially created premium can account for 30% of the stock's value. If you're the lucky seller, you'll reap that extra cash—in no way thanks to anything you did as an individual.

Real estate gains and the stock market's social premium are just two instances of common assets contributing to private gain. Still, most rich people would like us to think it's their extraordinary talent, hard work, and risk-taking that create their well-deserved wealth. That's like saying a flower's beauty is due solely to its own efforts, owing nothing to nutrients in the soil, energy from the sun, water from the aquifer, or the activity of bees.

The Great Commons Giveaway

That we inherit a trove of common wealth is the good news. The bad news, alas, is that our inheritance is being grossly mismanaged. As a recent report by the advocacy group Friends of the Commons concludes, "Maintenance of the commons is terrible, theft is rampant, and rents often aren't collected. To put it bluntly, our common wealth—and our children's—is being squandered. We are all poorer as a result."

Examples of commons mismanagement include the handout of broadcast spectrum to media conglomerates, the giveaway of pollution rights to polluters, the extension of copyrights to entertainment companies, the patenting of seeds and genes, the privatization of water, and the relentless destruction of habitat, wildlife, and ecosystems.

This mismanagement, though currently extreme, is not new. For over 200 years, the market has been devouring the commons in two ways. With one hand, the market takes valuable stuff from the commons and privatizes it. This is called "enclosure." With the other hand, the market dumps bad stuff into the commons and says, "It's your problem." This is called "externalizing." Much that is called economic growth today is actually a form of cannibalization in which the market diminishes the commons that ultimately sustains it.

Enclosure—the taking of good stuff from the commons—at first meant privatization of land by the gentry. Today it means privatization of many common assets by corporations. Either way, it means that what once belonged to everyone now belongs to a few.

Enclosure is usually justified in the name of efficiency. And sometimes, though not always, it does result in efficiency gains. But what also results from enclosure is the impoverishment of those who lose access to the commons, and the enrichment of those who take title to it. In other words, enclosure widens the gap between those with income-producing property and those without.

Externalizing—the dumping of bad stuff into the commons—is an automatic behavior pattern of profit-maximizing corporations: if they can avoid any out-of-pocket costs, they will. If workers, taxpayers, anyone downwind, future generations, or nature have to absorb added costs, so be it.

For decades, economists have agreed we'd be better served if businesses "internalized" their externalities—that is, paid in real time the costs they now shift to the commons. The reason this doesn't happen is that there's no one to set prices and collect them. Unlike private wealth, the commons lacks property rights and institutions to represent it in the marketplace.

The seeds of such institutions, however, are starting to emerge. Consider one of the environmental protection tools the U.S. currently uses, pollution trading. So-called cap-and-trade programs put a cap on total pollution, then grant portions of the total, via permits, to each polluting firm. Companies may buy other firms' permits if they want to pollute more than their allotment allows, or sell unused permits if they manage to pollute less. Such programs are generally supported by business because they allow polluters to find the cheapest ways to reduce pollution.

Public discussion of cap-and-trade programs has focused exclusively on their trading features. What's been overlooked is how they give away common wealth to polluters.

To date, all cap-and-trade programs have begun by giving pollution rights to existing polluters for free. This treats polluters as if they own our sky and rivers. It means that future polluters will have to pay old polluters for the scarce—hence valuable—right to dump wastes into nature. Imagine that: because a corporation polluted in the past, it gets free income forever! And, because ultimately we'll all pay for limited pollution via higher prices, this amounts to an enormous transfer of wealth—trillions of dollars—to shareholders of historically polluting corporations.

In theory, though, there is no reason that the initial pollution rights should not reside with the public. Clean air and the atmosphere's capacity to absorb pollutants are "wealth" that belongs to everyone. Hence, when polluters use up these parts of the commons, they should pay the public—not the other way around.

Taking the Commons Back

How can we correct the system omission that permits, and indeed promotes, destruction of nature and ever-widening inequality among humans? The answer lies in building a new sector of the economy whose clear legal mission is to preserve shared inheritances for everyone. Just as the market is populated by profit-maximizing corporations, so this new sector would be populated by asset-preserving trusts.

Here a brief description of trusts may be helpful. The trust is a private institution that's even older than the corporation. The essence of a trust is a fiduciary relationship. A trust holds and manages property for another person or for many other people. A simple example is a trust set up by a grandparent to pay for a grandchild's education. Other trusts include pension funds, charitable foundations, and university endowments. There are also hundreds of trusts in America, like the Nature

Conservancy and the Trust for Public Land, that own land or conservation easements in perpetuity.

If we were to design an institution to protect pieces of the commons, we couldn't do much better than a trust. The goal of commons management, after all, is to preserve assets and deliver benefits to broad classes of beneficiaries. That's what trusts do, and it's not rocket science.

Over centuries, several principles of trust management have evolved. These include:

- Trustees have a fiduciary responsibility to beneficiaries. If a trustee fails in this obligation, he or she can be removed and penalized.
- Trustees must preserve the original asset. It's okay to spend income, but don't invade the principal.
- Trustees must assure transparency. Information about money flows should be readily available to beneficiaries.

Trusts in the new commons sector would be endowed with rights comparable to those of corporations. Their trustees would take binding oaths of office and, like judges, serve long terms. Though protecting common assets would be their primary job, they would also distribute income from those assets to beneficiaries. These beneficiaries would include all citizens within a jurisdiction, large classes of citizens (children, the elderly), and/or agencies serving common purposes such as public transit or ecological restoration. When distributing income to individuals, the allocation formula would be one person, one share. The right to receive commons income would be a nontransferable birthright, not a property right that could be traded.

Fortuitously, a working model of such a trust already exists: the Alaska Permanent Fund. When oil drilling on the North Slope began in the 1970s, Gov. Jay Hammond, a Republican, proposed that 25% of the state's royalties be placed in a mutual fund to be invested on behalf of Alaska's citizens. Voters approved in a referendum. Since then, the Alaska Permanent Fund has grown to over $28 billion, and Alaskans have received roughly $22,000 apiece in dividends. In 2003 the per capita dividend was $1,107; a family of four received $4,428.

What Alaska did with its oil can be replicated for other gifts of nature. For example, we could create a nationwide Sky Trust to stabilize the climate for future generations. The trust would restrict emissions of heat-trapping gases and sell a declining number of emission permits to polluters. The income would be returned to U.S. residents in equal yearly dividends, thus reversing the wealth transfer built into current cap-and-trade programs. Instead of everyone paying historic polluters, polluters would pay all of us.

Just as a Sky Trust could represent our equity in the natural commons, a Public Stock Trust could embody our equity in the social commons. Such a trust would capture some of the socially created stock-market premium that currently flows only to shareholders and their investment bankers. As noted earlier, this premium is sizeable—roughly 30% of the value of publicly traded stock. A simple way to share it would be to create a giant mutual fund—call it the American Permanent Fund—

that would hold, say, 10% of the shares of publicly traded companies. This mutual fund, in turn, would be owned by all Americans on a one share per person basis (perhaps linked to their Social Security accounts).

To build up the fund without precipitating a fall in share prices, companies would contribute shares at the rate of, say, 1% per year. The contributions would be the price companies pay for the benefits they derive from a commons asset, the large, trusted market for stock—a small price, indeed, for the hefty benefits. Over time, the mutual fund would assure that when the economy grows, everyone benefits. The top 5% would still own more than the bottom 90%, but at least every American would have some property income, and a slightly larger slice of our economic pie.

Sharing the Wealth

The perpetuation of inequality is built into the current design of capitalism. Because of the skewed distribution of private wealth, a small self-perpetuating minority receives a disproportionate share of America's nonlabor income.

Tom Paine had something to say about this. In his essay "Agrarian Justice," written in 1790, he argued that, because enclosure of the commons had separated so many people from their primary source of sustenance, it was necessary to create a functional equivalent of the commons in the form of a National Fund. Here is how he put it:

> There are two kinds of property. Firstly, natural property, or that which comes to us from the Creator of the universe—such as the earth, air, water. Secondly, artificial or acquired property—the invention of men. In the latter, equality is impossible; for to distribute it equally, it would be necessary that all should have contributed in the same proportion, which can never be the case .... Equality of natural property is different. Every individual in the world is born with legitimate claims on this property, or its equivalent.

Enclosure of the commons, he went on, was necessary to improve the efficiency of cultivation. But

> The landed monopoly that began with [enclosure] has produced the greatest evil. It has dispossessed more than half the inhabitants of every nation of their natural inheritance, without providing for them, as ought to have been done, an indemnification for that loss, and has thereby created a species of poverty and wretchedness that did not exist before.

The appropriate compensation for loss of the commons, Paine said, was a national fund financed by rents paid by land owners. Out of this fund, every person reaching age 21 would get 15 pounds a year, and every person over 50 would receive an additional 10 pounds. (Think of Social Security, financed by commons rents instead of payroll taxes.)

A Progressive Offensive

Paine's vision, allowing for inflation and new forms of enclosure, could not be more timely today. Surely from our vast common inheritance—not just the land, but the atmosphere, the broadcast spectrum, our mineral resources, our threatened habitats and water supplies—enough rent can be collected to pay every American over age 21 a modest annual dividend, and every person reaching 21 a small start-up inheritance.

Such a proposal may seem utopian. In today's political climate, perhaps it is. But consider this. About 20 years ago, right-wing think tanks laid out a bold agenda. They called for lowering taxes on private wealth, privatizing much of government, and deregulating industry. Amazingly, this radical agenda has largely been achieved.

It's time for progressives to mount an equally bold offensive. The old shibboleths—let's gin up the economy, create jobs, and expand government programs—no longer excite. We need to talk about fixing the economy, not just growing it; about income for everyone, not just jobs; about nurturing ecosystems, cultures, and communities, not just our individual selves. More broadly, we need to celebrate the commons as an essential counterpoise to the market.

Unfortunately, many progressives have viewed the state as the only possible counterpoise to the market. The trouble is, the state has been captured by corporations. This capture isn't accidental or temporary; it's structural and long-term.

This doesn't mean progressives can't occasionally recapture the state. We've done so before and will do so again. It does mean that progressive control of the state is the exception, not the norm; in due course, corporate capture will resume. It follows that if we want lasting fixes to capitalism's tragic flaws, we must use our brief moments of political ascendancy to build institutions that endure.

Programs that rely on taxes, appropriations, or regulations are inherently transitory; they get weakened or repealed when political power shifts. By contrast, institutions that are self-perpetuating and have broad constituencies are likely to last. (It also helps if they mail out checks periodically.) This was the genius of Social Security, which has survived—indeed grown—through numerous Republican administrations.

If progressives are smart, we'll use our next New Deal to create common property trusts that include all Americans as beneficiaries. These trusts will then be to the 21st century what social insurance was to the 20th: sturdy pillars of shared responsibility and entitlement. Through them, the commons will be a source of sustenance for all, as it was before enclosure. Life-long income will be linked to generations-long ecological health. Isn't that a future most Americans would welcome?

VENEZUELA'S COOPERATIVE REVOLUTION

BETSY BOWMAN AND BOB STONE
July/August 2006

Zaida Rosas, a woman in her fifties with 15 grandchildren, works in the newly constructed textile co-op Venezuela Avanza in Caracas. The co-op's 209 workers are mostly formerly jobless neighborhood women. Their homes on the surrounding steep hillsides in west Caracas were almost all self-built.

Zaida works seven hours a day, five days a week, and is paid $117 a month, the uniform income all employees voted for themselves. This is much less than the minimum salary, officially set at $188 a month. This was "so we can pay back our [government start-up] loan," she explained. Venezuela Avanza cooperativistas have a monthly general assembly to decide policy. As in most producer co-ops, they are not paid a salary, but an advance on profits. Workers paying themselves less than the minimum wage in order to make payments to the state was, Zaida acknowledged, a bad situation. "We hope our working conditions will improve with time," she said.

To prepare the co-op's workers to collectively run a business, the new Ministry of Popular Economy (MINEP) had given them small scholarships to train in cooperativism, production, and accounting. "My family is a lot happier—I've learned to write and have my 3rd grade certificate," she said.

Zaida is now also part of a larger local web of cooperatives: her factory is one of two producer co-ops, both built by a local bricklayers' cooperative, that, along with a clinic, a supermarket co-op, a school, and a community center, make up a so-called "nucleus of endogenous development." These nucleos are at the core of the country's plan for fostering egalitarian economic development.

U.S. media coverage of Venezuela tends to center around the country's oil and the—not unrelated—war of words between President Hugo Chávez and the White House. Chávez, for example, likes to refer to George W. Bush as "Mr. Danger," a reference to a brutish foreigner in a classic Venezuelan novel. Somewhat more clumsily, Defense Secretary Donald Rumsfeld recently compared Chávez to Hitler. While this makes for entertaining copy, reporters have missed a major story in Venezuela—the unprecedented growth of cooperatives that has reshaped the economic lives of hundreds of thousands of Venezuelans like Zaida Rosas. On a recent visit to Caracas, we spoke with co-op members and others invested in this novel experiment to open Venezuela's economy from the bottom up.

Explosion of Cooperatives

Our first encounter with Venezuela's co-op movement was with Luis Guacarán, a taxi co-op member who drove us to the outskirts of Caracas. Settled into the rainy trip, we asked Luis what changes wrought by the Chávez government had meant for him personally. Luis replied that he now felt that as a citizen he had a right to share in the nation's oil wealth, which had always gone to an "oligarchy." The people needed health, education, and meaningful work; that was reason enough for Chávez to divert oil revenues in order to provide these things. Two of Luis's five sons are in the military, a daughter is studying petroleum engineering, another has a beauty shop. All were in vocational or professional studies.

Almost everyone we met during our visit was involved in a cooperative. The 1999 constitution requires the state to "promote and protect" co-ops. However, it was only after the passage of the Special Law on Cooperative Associations in 2001 that the totals began to skyrocket. When Chávez took office in 1998 there were 762 legally registered cooperatives with about 20,000 members. In 2001 there were almost 1,000 cooperatives. The number grew to 2,000 in 2002 and to 8,000 by 2003. In mid-2006, the National Superintendence of Cooperatives (SUNACOOP) reported that it had registered over 108,000 co-ops representing over 1.5 million members. Since mid-2003, MINEP has provided free business and self-management training, helped workers turn troubled conventional enterprises into cooperatives, and extended credit for start-ups and buy-outs. The resulting movement has increasingly come to define the "Bolivarian Revolution," the name Chávez has given to his efforts to reshape Venezuela's economic and political structures.

Now MINEP is trying to keep up with the explosion it set off. While pre-Chávez co-ops were mostly credit unions, the "Bolivarian" ones are much more diverse: half are in the service sector, a third in production, with the rest divided among savings, housing, consumer, and other areas. Cooperativists work in four major sectors: 31% in commerce, restaurants, and hotels; 29% in transport, storage and communications; 18% in agriculture, hunting, and fishing; and 8.3% in industrial manufacture. Cooperativism is on the march in Venezuela on a scale and at a speed never before seen anywhere.

Most cooperatives are small. Since January 2005, however, when the government announced a policy of expropriation of closed industrial plants, MINEP has stood ready to help workers take control of some large factories facing bankruptcy. If the unused plant is deemed of "public utility," the initiation of expropriation proceedings often leads to negotiation with the owners over compensation. In one instance, owners of a shuttered Heinz tomato processing plant in Monagas state offered to sell it to the government for $600,000. After factoring in back wages, taxes, and an outstanding mortgage, the two sides reached an amicable agreement to sell the plant to the workers for $260,000, with preferential loans provided by the government. In a more typically confrontational example, displaced workers first occupied a sugar refinery in Cumanacoa and restarted it on their own. The federal government then expropriated the property and turned it over to cooperatives of the plant's workers. The owners' property rights were respected inasmuch as the government loaned the workers the money for the purchase, though the price was well below what the owners had claimed. Such expropriated factories are then often run by elected representatives of workers alongside of government appointees.

There are strings attached. "We haven't expropriated Cumanacoa and Sideroca for the workers just to help them become rich people the day after tomorrow," said Chávez. "This has not been done just for them—it is to help make everyone wealthy." Take the case of Cacao Sucre, another sugar mill closed for eight years by its private owners, leaving 120 workers unemployed in a neighborhood of grinding poverty. The state's governor put out a call for the workers to form a co-op. After receiving training in self-management, the mill co-op integrated with the 3,665-

strong cane growers' co-op. In July 2005, this large cooperative became the first "Social Production Enterprise." The new designation means that the co-op is required to set aside a portion of its profits to fund health, education, and housing for the local population, and to open its food hall to the community as well.

With only 700 plants on the government's list of closed or bankrupt candidates for expropriation, cooperativization of existing large-scale facilities is limited, and so far a bit slow. Unions are identifying more underproducing enterprises. But there is a long way to go.

Cooperatives are at the center of Venezuela's new economic model. They have the potential to fulfill a number of the aims of the Bolivarian revolution, including combating unemployment, promoting durable economic development, competing peacefully with conventional capitalist firms, and advancing Chávez's still-being-defined socialism.

Not Your Grandfather's WPA

Capitalism generates unemployment. Neoliberalism aggravated this tendency in Venezuela, producing a large, stable group of overlooked people who were excluded from meaningful work and consumption. If not forgotten altogether, they were blamed for their plight and made to feel superfluous. But the Bolivarian revolution is about demanding recognition. In March of 2004 Chávez called Venezuelans to a new "mission," when MINEP inaugurated the "Misión Vuelvan Caras" program—Mission About-Face. Acting "from within themselves and by their own powers" to form cooperatives, the people were to "combat unemployment and exclusion" by actually "chang[ing] the relations of production."

In Venezuela, "vuelvan caras" evokes an insurgent general's command to his troops upon being surrounded by Spaniards in the war of independence. In effect: stop playing the role of the pursued; turn and attack the enemy frontally. The new enemy is unemployment, and the goal of full employment is to be achieved by groups—especially of the unemployed—throwing in their lot with each other and setting to work together. Vuelvan Caras teaches management, accounting, and co-op values to hundreds of thousands of scholarship students. Graduates are free to seek regular jobs or form micro-enterprises, for which credit is offered; however, co-ops get priority for technical assistance, credits, and contracts. But the original spark—the collective entrepreneurship needed for cooperativization—is to come from the people. Over 70% of the graduates of the class of 2005 formed 7,592 new co-ops.

Vuelvan Caras seems to be paying off. Unemployment reached a high of 18% in 2003 but fell to 14.5% in 2004, and 11.5% in 2005. MINEP is planning a "Vuelvan Caras II," aiming to draw in 700,000 more of the jobless. But with a population of 26 million, Venezuela's battle against structural causes of unemployment has only begun.

Economic Development from Within

Cooperatives also advance the Chávez administration's broader goal of "endogenous development." Foreign direct investment continues in Venezuela, but the government aims to avoid relying on inflows from abroad, which open a country to capitalism's usual blackmail. Endogenous development means "to be capable of producing the seed that we sow, the food that we eat, the clothes that we wear, the goods and services that we need, breaking the economic, cultural and technological dependence that has halted our development, starting with ourselves." To these ends, co-ops are ideal tools. Co-ops anchor development in Venezuela: under the control of local worker-owners, they don't pose a threat of capital flight as capitalist firms do.

The need for endogenous development came home to Venezuelans during the 2002 oil strike carried out by Chávez's political opponents. Major distributors of the country's mostly imported food also supported the strike, halting food deliveries and exposing a gaping vulnerability. In response, the government started its own parallel supermarket chain. In just three years, Mercal had 14,000 points of sale, almost all in poor neighborhoods, selling staples at discounts of 20% to 50%. It is now the nation's largest supermarket chain and its second largest enterprise overall. The Mercal stores attract shoppers of all political stripes thanks to their low prices and high-quality merchandise. To promote "food sovereignty," Mercal has increased its proportion of domestic suppliers to over 40%, giving priority to co-ops when possible. Venezuela still imports 64% of the food it consumes, but that's down from 72% in 1998. By cutting import dependence, transport costs, and middlemen while tapping local suppliers, Mercal aims to wean itself from its $24 million-a-month subsidy.

Displacing Capitalism and Building Socialism

Another reason the architects of the so-called "Bolivarian revolution" are vigorously pushing the co-op model is their belief that co-ops can meet needs better than conventional capitalist firms. Freed of the burdens of supporting costly managers and profit-hungry absentee investors, co-ops have a financial buoyancy that drives labor-saving technological innovation to save labor time. "Cooperatives are the businesses of the future," says former Planning and Development Minister Felipe Pérez-Martí. Not only are they non-exploitative, they outproduce capitalist firms, since, Pérez-Martí holds, worker-owners must seek their firm's efficiency and success. Such a claim raises eyebrows in the United States, but a growing body of research suggests that co-ops can indeed be more productive and profitable than conventional firms.

To test whether co-ops can beat capitalist firms on their own terms, a viable co-op or solidarity sector must be set up parallel to the securely dominant capitalist one. Today Venezuela is preparing this "experiment." More than 5% of the labor force now works in cooperatives, according to MINEP. While this is a much larger percentage of cooperativistas than in most countries, it is still small relative to the size of a co-op sector that would have a shot at out-competing Venezuela's capitalist sector. Chávez's supporters hope that once such a sector is launched, cooperativization will expand in a "virtuous circle" as conventional workforces, observing co-ops, demand similar control of their work. Elias Jaua, the initial Minister of Popular Economy, says, "The private sector can understand the process and incorporate itself into the new dynamic of society, or it will be simply displaced by the new productive forces which have a better quality production, a vision based much more on solidarity than consumption." One could claim that MINEP's credits, trainings, and contracts prejudice the outcome in favor of co-ops. But Vuelvan Caras graduates are free to take jobs in the capitalist sector. And MINEP's policy of favoring employee-owned firms is not that different from U.S. laws, subsidies, and tax benefits that favor investor-owned ones.

Finally, by placing the means of production in workers' hands, the co-op movement directly builds socialism. Cooperativization, especially of idle factories occupied by their workforces, promotes "what has always been our goal: that the workers run production and that the governments are also run by the workers," according to Labor Minister Maria Cristina Iglesias. Co-ops, then, are not just means to what Chávez calls "socialism for the 21st century": they actually constitute partial realizations of it.

Managing the Experiment's Risks

Cooperativization is key to achieving the aims of the Bolivarian revolution. But the revolution's leaders acknowledge that a long struggle lies ahead. Traditional capitalist enterprises still dominate Venezuela's economy. And even if all of the country's current cooperativization programs succeed, will that struggle—and it will be a struggle—result in socialism? Michael Albert of Z Magazine grants that co-ops may be more productive, and he strongly supports Venezuela's experiment. But in the absence of plans for de-marketization, he has doubts that it will reach socialism. For the effect on cooperatives themselves of "trying to out-compete old firms in market-defined contests may [be to] entrench in them a managerial bureaucracy and a competitive rather than a social orientation," leading to a market socialist system "that

---

Democracy: Economic and Political

Alongside the co-op movement, Venezuelans are engaged in building a new form of local political democracy through so-called Communal Councils. Modeled on Brazil's innovative participatory budgeting process, these councils grew out of the Land Committees Chávez created to grant land titles to the many squatters in Caracas's barrios. If a community of 100 to 200 families organizes itself and submits a local development plan, the government grants land titles. Result: individuals get homes, and the community gets a grassroots assembly.

The councils have budgets and make decisions on a range of local matters. They delegate spokespersons to the barrio and the municipality. Today, a few thousand Communal Councils exist, but within five years the government plans to bring all Venezuelans into local counsels. In conjunction with cooperativization in the economy, the Community Council movement may portend the creation of a new decentralized, democratic polity..

still has a ruling managerial or coordinator class." Albert's concern is well founded: the history of co-ops from the Amana colonies of Iowa to the Mondragón Cooperative Corporation in the Basque country shows that even when they start out with a community-service mandate, individual co-ops, or even networks of co-ops, tend to defensively re-internalize capitalist self-seeking and become indistinguishable from their competitors when made to compete alone against an array of capitalist firms in a capitalist economy.

Disarmingly, members of Chávez's administration acknowledge these risks. Juan Carlos Loyo, deputy minister of the popular economy, noting that community service has been part of the cooperative creed since its beginning, asks for patience: "We know that we are coming from a capitalist lifestyle that is profoundly individualistic and self-centered." Marcela Maspero, a national coordinator of the new, Chavista UNT labor federation, acknowledges "the risk of converting our comrades into neo-liberal capitalists." In Venezuela's unique case, however, construction of a viable co-op sector is the goal of a government with considerable financial resources, and its aim of thereby building socialism is also a popular national project. In Venezuela, success is therefore a plausible hope. A loose analogy would hold with May 1968 if both the de Gaulle government and the French Communist Party had been in favor of student-worker demands for "auto-gestion" or self-management.

There are problems, of course. Groups may register as "phantom co-ops" to get start-up grants, then simply walk away with the money. And since co-ops are favored in awarding government contracts, there is a significant amount of fraud. "There are cooperatives that are registered as such on paper," Jaua, the former head of MINEP, reports, "but which have a boss who is paid more, salaried workers, and unequal distribution of work and income." SUNACOOP admits that its enforcement is spotty. Many of the new cooperatives have also suffered as a result of inadequate self-management training. Government authorities are attempting to address these problems by increasing visits to local co-ops, augmenting training and support services, and decentralizing oversight to local councils.

Despite the obstacles, the new co-ops, with government support, are building a decentralized national movement with its own momentum and institutions. This May, the National Executive Cooperative Council (CENCOOP) was launched. The council is made up of five co-op members from each of Venezuela's 25 states, elected by their State Cooperative Councils, which are in turn elected by Municipal Councils composed of local cooperativists. CENCOOP will represent Venezuela at the International Cooperative Alliance—the global body embracing 700 million individual members in hundreds of thousands of cooperatives in 95 countries.

The pre-Bolivarian co-op movement at first felt left out, and criticized hasty cooperativization. But its advice was sought at each stage of the planning for CENCOOP, and it finally joined the council, sharing its valuable experience with the new movement. The new state and municipal co-op councils are part of a plan to decentralize MINEP's functions. Having helped organize CENCOOP, MINEP Superintendent Carlos Molina says his office will adopt a hands-off approach to assure the cooperative movement's increasing autonomy. Today, however, many of the new co-ops remain dependent on MINEP's support.

A Movement's Opponents

Whatever success cooperativization achieves carries its own risks, both internal and external. So far, the Chávez government has compensated capitalists for expropriations and has targeted for co-op conversion only firms that are in some sense in trouble. But at a certain point, workers in healthy firms, seeing their cooperativist neighbors enjoying newfound power in the workplace and a more equal distribution of income, may want to cooperativize their firms too. And having for years had profit extracted as a major portion of the value their labor has created—in many cases enough to cover their firm's market value many times over—won't they have grounds to demand transfer without compensation? In short, to further expand and strengthen revolutionary solidarity before new counter-revolutionary efforts take root, won't the revolution have to start a real redistribution of productive wealth— to cooperativize firms directly at the expense of Venezuela's capitalists? Sooner or later, Venezuela's cooperative experiment will have to address this question.

After joining in the World Social Forum in Caracas in last January, we caught some glimpses of the "Bolivarian revolution" moving at full speed, and we've followed it since then. We are convinced that for those around the world who believe "another world is possible," the stakes of this experiment are enormous. Predictably, then, it faces genuine external threats. The short-lived coup in April of 2002 and the destructive strike by oil-industry managers that December were the works of a displaced and angry elite encouraged by the United States at every step. And the campaign continues: State Department-linked groups have been pumping $5 million a year into opposition groups that backed the coup. Yet the democratizing of workplaces proceeds relentlessly, bringing ever more Venezuelans into the revolutionary process. This inclusion is itself a defense since it expands, unites, and strengthens the resistance with which Venezuelans would greet any new effort to halt or divert their revolution.

Sources: Many valuable articles have been collected at www.Venezuelanalysis.com, including: C. Harnecker, "The New Cooperative Movement in Venezuela's Bolivarian Process" (from Monthly Review Zine) 5/05; S. Wagner, "Vuelvan Caras: Venezuela's Mission for Building Socialism of the 21st Century," 7/05; "Poverty and Unemployment Down Significantly in 2005," 10/05; F. Perez-Marti, "The Venezuelan Model of Development: The Path of Solidarity," 6/04; "Venezuela: Expropriations, cooperatives and co-management," Green Left Weekly, 10/05; M. Albert, "Venezuela's Path," Z-Net, 11/05; O. Sunkel, Development from Within: Toward a Neostructuralist Approach for Latin America (L. Rienner Publ., 1993); H. Thomas, "Performance of the Mondragón Co-operatives in Spain," in Participatory and Self-Managed Firms, eds. D. C. Jones and J. Svejnar (Lexington Books, 1982); D. Levine and L. D'A. Tyson, "Participation, Productivity and the Firm's Environment," in Paying for Productivity: A Look at the Evidence, ed. A. Blinder (Brookings Inst., 1990); D. Schweickart, After Capitalism (Rowman & Littlefield, 2002); M. Lebowitz, "Constructing Co-management in Venezuela: Contradictions along the Path," Monthly Review Zine 10/05; Z. Centeno, "Cooperativas: una vision para impulsar el Desarrollo Endogeno," at www.mci.gob.ve.

WORKER-OWNERS AND UNIONS:
Why can't we just get along?

DAN BELL
September/October 2006

You have probably heard the story of the scorpion that convinces a frog to carry it across a river. Halfway across, the scorpion stings the frog, which means both will drown. The frog does not understand; the scorpion explains, "I couldn't help myself. It's my nature."

In the abstract, worker-owned enterprises and labor unions would appear to have much in common. Both share the goal of improving pay and working conditions. Both aim to give workers a say in the workplace. And both belong on any progressive's short list of strategies for building a more just economic system.

But when unions and worker-owned businesses actually interact, they sometimes act more like the fabled arachnid.

The Ohio Employee Ownership Center at Kent State, where I work, provides preliminary technical assistance on worker buyouts. I once met with a group of employees exploring a worker buyout of a failing paper mill in southwest Ohio. When I asked them why they thought they would do any better, they gave me an example. Pointing to a large machine, they explained that it broke down regularly, resulting in lost production. Any repairs they could make were only temporary, until permanent replacement parts could be installed. They went on to explain that the mill had been bought and sold three times over the past two years. Two owners ago the parts had been purchased, but they were still sitting in a storeroom. When these employees became the owners, they were going to install the parts.

But would the workers really cooperate with management as employee owners, and would management really cooperate with them and empower them to make decisions and act independently? Or, as with the scorpion, were the decades of confrontational labor-management relations so engrained in the nature of both groups that they would sink their own company? In that instance we'll never know, because the buyout effort did not go forward.

Competing Models?

Worker-owned businesses can take a variety of forms, from full-fledged worker cooperatives to companies whose structure and management practices are indistinguishable from ordinary capitalist firms except for the fact that their employees own some or all of the company's shares (see sidebar, "The Many Forms of Worker Ownership"). Because most of the manufacturing companies where worker buyouts have been used to avert plant closures were unionized, unions have had to grapple with reshaping their role in this new context.

While unions and worker-owners share many aims, there are also profound differences. True cooperatives address working conditions through direct democracy at the company level. Members have the right to participate in making decisions on matters such as compensation and business planning. Co-op members do not like being restricted in their decision-making by factors external to the cooperative—even factors like industry-wide collective bargaining agreements. When co-ops interact with other co-ops, they typically form secondary cooperatives controlled by the member co-ops, which run them to serve their common needs. One might say that co-ops tend toward decentralization.

In contrast, unions depend on numbers to build their strength. They need to maintain a degree of discipline among their locals, insisting on relative uniformity around key issues. Unions' most effective strategy for bringing about changes in the workplace is the collective refusal to work. If the central leadership cannot count on each local to follow its direction, the threat of a strike loses credibility. Thus, unions depend on centralization in order to create enough power to offset that of the owners.

Why Worker-Owners Need Unions

Moreover, union representation might seem to be superfluous for worker-owners, who after all are supposed to have decision-making authority by virtue of being owners. Most ESOPs are not structured so as to give workers significant decision-making authority. But even in the most democratic ESOP, a union can have an important role to play. One way to look at the role of unions is to observe the balance of power that exists between the three branches of government in the United States. The legislative branch makes the laws, as the board of directors in a company sets policy by which management must manage. The executive branch implements or executes the laws on a daily basis, as management runs the day-to-day operations. Even in those ESOPs where the worker-owners have the right to participate in electing the board of directors, that right does not protect any individual employee from the power that management enjoys to hire and fire, for example. Just as the judicial branch protects individual citizens from the misuse of power by an executive, the union protects individual workers from the arbitrary use of power by management.

Collective bargaining is another role that unions play. A union can help worker-owners to assess their situation in the context of industry-wide working conditions and compensation practices. And via the union, information flows both ways. In a cooperative or an ESOP practicing so-called open book management, the employees have full access to the company's financial information. With such transparency, the union negotiating team does not have to guess about what the company can afford; it has the information required to calculate what is available for compensation. Using this as a frame of reference, the union is also in a better position to bargain for strong agreements throughout the industry.

Access to group rates on benefits like health insurance or multi-employer pensions can be another advantage that unions bring, especially in the case of cooperatives, which tend to be much smaller than ESOP companies.

Unions also bring a ready-made communication structure, which can be helpful in building an ownership culture among workers who are accustomed to having little say in the business.

Some of the positive synergies between union representation and worker ownership were at play in a Toledo textile firm. In 1991, GenCorp was planning to close down an unprofitable division, but instead agreed to sell it to the 200-plus employees as Textileather. The Amalgamated Clothing and Textile Workers Union (ACTWU) supported the buyout and joined with management in building successful employee participation. Training in participatory practices was implemented from the beginning, and an effective jointly led employee involvement structure resulted in a 28% increase in productivity, a 40% drop in scrap, and greatly reduced machine downtime in the first year. The company was immediately profitable. Ultimately, though, Textileather's worker-owners decided that their primary goal was job security, not ownership. In 1996, when the acquisition debt was paid off, man-

---

The Many Forms of Worker Ownership

The term "worker ownership" can describe a variety of business structures. At one end of the spectrum, the worker-owned cooperative model rejects the very notion that capital should control the business and enjoy an unlimited return. To the contrary, as political economist David Ellerman describes it, in the cooperative model labor hires capital, governance is based on membership in the firm, and the return to capital is limited. As a result, investors are not easily attracted. Workers themselves typically have little capital to invest. So co-ops are rarely found in capital-intensive industries; most of the 400 for-profit co-ops in the United States are in labor-intensive service industries, which do not require expensive tools.

Another model involves direct worker ownership of voting stock. Unlike the cooperative, this model accepts the capitalist system but rejects the capitalist. Here, the workers accept the assumption that control and profits should be allocated according to the number of shares one owns, but reject absentee ownership of shares by those who do not work at the firm. Only a handful of worker-owned companies are structured this way because workers typically lack capital to invest and are averse to risking the little they may have.

By far the most common structure of worker ownership is the Employee Stock Ownership Plan, or ESOP, which has been used in over 11,000 U.S. companies since first being written into legislation in 1974. About 9,225 ESOPs are active today, according to the National Center for Employee Ownership. ESOP participants often share ownership of the company with large investors. Moreover, in most companies with ESOPs the worker-owners not only accept that capital, not labor, has the right to govern the business, but also allow someone else to vote their shares of that capital.

The ESOP itself is a trust that receives tax-deductible retirement contributions from the company. Two characteristics set ESOPs apart from other retirement plans, such as 401(k)s. First, ESOPs are not only allowed, but required, to invest a majority of their assets in the employer company's own stock. Second, an ESOP can borrow money to acquire stock, releasing shares to individual participants as future contributions are made. While employees may not possess credit, cash, or collateral, the ESOP provides a vehicle for the sponsoring employer to fill this gap with the credit, cash, and collateral of the company itself. In other words, ESOPs provide workers with a tax-advantaged structure for financing the acquisition of their company.

The legal owner of the capital is the ESOP trust, overseen by a trustee appointed by the board of directors. In managing the ESOP's assets, under current law the trustee is allowed to consider only the workers' interest in increasing the value of their retirement holdings—not their interests as employees with concerns such as job security.

While worker buyouts to avoid shutdowns account for only about 3% of all ESOPs, a majority of these are companies with union representation prior to the buyout. Without the leadership, structure, and protection afforded by a union, employees generally cannot build common cause quickly enough to present themselves as viable buyers, before machinery has been moved out and customers turned away.

agement and workers agreed to sell the company. The buyer not only paid 160% of the valuation price, but also agreed to increase wages, bring in additional work creating more jobs, and give the employees the first right of refusal if it decided to sell the plant in the future.

At another worker-owned firm, an initially strong union-ESOP relationship failed to prevent a breakdown of the worker-ownership structure. Republic Engineered Steels' 4,500 employees, spread among eight plants in four states and primarily organized by the United Steelworkers (USWA), chose to buy their division from steel giant LTV in 1989 to avoid a shutdown. The new contract defined a structure for employee participation: Work groups would meet regularly to identify opportunities for change. They could implement actions that affected only their area; other proposals would be kicked up to the department level, the plant level, and in some cases to a corporation-wide joint labor-management committee. To get this structure to work, 100 managers and their corresponding 100 union representatives trained jointly for a week to become co-facilitators. Union and management also formed a joint committee to direct the ownership training program.

With a solid foundation of worker-owner participation, the company successfully cut $80 million out of its annual $800 million expenses in only 18 months— not by cutting compensation, but by implementing employees' ideas for improving operations.

Two events changed the picture. First, to provide equity for the buyout, employees had agreed to roll over $20 million from their LTV retirement plan in exchange for preferred stock that paid annual dividends at 16%. In order to retire this expensive debt, management convinced the employees to let the company go public. But management miscalculated the price the shares would obtain, disappointing the workers and shaking their confidence in company leadership. Furthermore, in an attempt to enhance the company's reputation with its new outside shareholders and raise its share price, management became less sensitive to the priorities of its worker-owners.

Then, in the late 1990s the price of steel took a deep plunge. Instead of responding to the crisis by taking advantage of the participatory structures that had so methodically been created, management fell back on its traditional MO, implementing changes with no worker input. When management made plans to open a new plant where it could get the most concessions from the local government—a decision that would have put many of its Massillon, Ohio, worker-owners on the street—the union became so frustrated that it sought out an investor to buy the company, giving up ownership in order to dislodge an entrenched management.

Unions have other ways of getting management's attention, short of selling the company. Some choose the traditional union weapon: the strike. In 1998, the worker-owners at the 100% employee-owned Republic Storage Systems, represented by the Steelworkers, chose to go on strike, ostensibly over a few pennies. In fact, this was their way of expressing a vote of no confidence in the CEO. Soon after, the CEO did resign, and the employees found a new leader they were prepared to follow. In fact, in 2003, when the entire plant was severely damaged by a flood, employees came in on their own time to clean up the plant.

Communication and Tranparency

Union members are conditioned to be suspicious of management. Worker buyouts are far more likely to be successful if workers and management build trust; the experience of a number of companies shows that the best way for managers to build that trust is to operate with transparency and open up workers' access to information.

The union bargaining committee at Dimco-Gray, a 100% employee-owned company with about 110 worker-owners, was refusing to budge on management's proposed profit sharing formula. Management wanted to reserve an amount equivalent to 5% of the company's assets before paying out 50% of the remainder as profit-shares to the employees. The bargaining committee members decided the trigger for profit sharing should be no more than 3% of assets.

The impasse was broken after an Ohio Employee Ownership Center trainer met with the committee. After reviewing the basics of the profit and loss statement and the balance sheet, employees asked, "Where does the company's share go?" The trainer explained that it went to build up the company's equity, in the same way that the principal portion of monthly mortgage payments increases a homeowner's equity. The union team realized that the issue was not how much do we get and how much do they get. As a 100% employee owned company, the employees get it all. The question is, rather, how much do we take out for current consumption, and how much do we re-invest for a stronger retirement. Agreement on the contract was reached the very next day.

At Republic Engineered Steels, a group of 50 employee-owners, half blue collar and half white collar, attended an offsite peer-training workshop. Believing the program to be a sham, some of the union members had signed up to be trainers so they could expose it. I recall overhearing some union participants discussing how the company had brought them there to be brainwashed. But when they realized they were getting real information, they became much more supportive of the changes and became the company's best trainers. Their reversal in attitude got the attention of others, who had known them to be outspoken skeptics.

Reasonable Doubt

Although workers and companies can clearly benefit from maintaining union representation following a worker buyout, unions have historically been skeptical about worker ownership. For one thing, they have had to contend with a string of companies that have engaged in deceptive practices in connection with creating ESOPs or selling plants to workers.

For instance, the International Brotherhood of Teamsters has good reason to be suspicious of employee ownership. In the 1980s, when deregulation was exposing trucking companies to lower-cost competition, the Teamsters refused to negotiate any changes to the master contract. At the same time, the union did not object if individual locals chose to exchange specific items in the contract for an equivalent amount of company stock held in an ESOP.

With this hands-off position, neither opposing nor encouraging employee ownership, the union left its locals at the mercy of the companies. Some trucking company owners were able to get away with matching their workers' concessions with stock in assetless "front" companies that leased their trucks from the owner's separate asset-holding company. When the front companies failed, the workers had neither revenue nor assets to give their stock any value.

One of the Ohio Employee Ownership Center's first employee buyout efforts was with Atlantic Foundry in Akron, Ohio. The owners had announced a shutdown because the foundry was unable to turn a profit. A quick analysis showed that the revenues did cover the direct costs, generating a gross profit, and that with sufficient sales volume, the buyout would be able to cover its indirect and debt service costs.

Despite this good news, the Steelworkers showed little initial support for the buyout effort and eventually took a clear position opposing it. Why was the union not willing to help these workers save their jobs?

The reason the foundry was losing money was its pension obligations to past workers; the plant simply did not generate sufficient income to cover this additional non-operating expense. Deeper analysis revealed that the owners had withdrawn a significant amount of non-operating assets and placed them in a separate company, whose balance sheet did not show the obligations to the retirees. The owners had offered to sell the company "for a song" as long as the workers took the retiree obligation with them. The union believed that the new company would fail if saddled with this obligation, and that the retirees would then have a more difficult time going after the original owners.

In the case of a deceptive sale, as with Atlantic Foundry, the union did exactly the right thing. Had the Steelworkers not drawn attention to the deceptive offer, the workers would have taken on more debt—the obligation to the retirees—than the operation could service. This would have left them bankrupt and unemployed—and left the retirees with a more difficult legal battle in any attempt to salvage their pensions. In essence, the active employees and the seller were negotiating a sale based on the risk capital of an absent voice: the retirees. The union brought that voice to the table. With this transparency, a more feasible transaction might have been possible. For example, negotiators could have placed a fair value on the retiree obligation; a trust could have been funded with a note from the new worker-owned company, equal to the fair market value of the operating business, and with cash from the seller to cover the balance. Of course, this was exactly the outcome that the unethical sellers were attempting to avoid. Not surprisingly, the foundry still sits idle today, two decades later.

Unions also have legitimate concerns about worker buyouts leading to decertification of the union. For the most part, if a company does not have a union before becoming worker-owned, it probably will not form a union afterward. Employees reason, "If we didn't need a union when we were owned by someone else, why would we need one now that we own the place?" Similarly, companies that have a union before the buyout often continue with the union under worker ownership. However, in some instances sellers have forced workers to disband their union as a condition of the buyout deal. In the case of Plymouth Locomotive, the owners refused to sell to a union workforce. The UAW agreed to decertification in order to let the buyout move forward. In the case of the Brainard Rivet Division of Textron, the employees did not decertify; the union local simply ceased to exist when the plant was closed.

When Fastener Industries, a successful 100% employee-owned company, offered the Brainard workers the opportunity to reopen as a subsidiary, the workers agreed not to re-establish the union.

On the other hand, organizing drives sometimes do succeed at employee-owned companies where workers view the union as a mechanism for reshaping the ESOP along more democratic lines. At Voto Sales and Manufacturing in Steubenville, Ohio, for example, the management controlled the initial board of directors following the buyout, allowing them to put a hand-picked trustee in charge of the ESOP. In other words, while owning only a minority of the company stock, management had positioned itself as the controlling shareholder group. The workers brought in a union as a way to establish a balance of power. After establishing a Steelworkers local, the employees were able to get the ESOP modified to pass through voting rights directly to the participants, in effect, bringing management under the control of the owners again.

Finally, unions have a duty to workers across an industry as well as to those in a particular workplace. Recently a worker co-op member contacted me looking for guidance on resolving a difficult conflict between his co-op and the union that organizes a few of its employees. Most of the workers at this site had supported the worker buyout and joined the co-op. A few of the workers, who are represented by a union, chose not to become members. In order to generate the surplus necessary to pay off the acquisition debt, the members agreed to reduce their wages and benefits. However, the union insisted that the terms of the collective bargaining agreement not be altered. The co-op members believed that to stick to the contract would be unfair to the members who were not in the union, because they were making sacrifices to help the co-op survive. And if all of the members were compensated as the union members expected to be, the business would fail. Since one of the principles of a co-op is autonomy from outside organizations, it seemed inappropriate for the union to be insisting on sticking to the contract, when even the members affected were willing to adapt.

But the co-op members had to recognize that the union was not dealing with their company in a vacuum. A union has to bargain with the entire industry and try to get the best possible deal for all of its members. Any time a local agrees to a lower-cost contract with one employer, that undercuts the union's bargaining position with all other employers. Each employer will expect to get the same contract as the competition, so the result is that wages fall. Industry-wide worker solidarity is just as important to union members as autonomy is to co-op members.

As it turns out, in this instance both the need to respect an industry-wide collective bargaining agreement and the co-op members' right to compensate everyone fairly and according to cooperative values can probably be satisfied. For the co-op members, their compensation is not wages per se, but rather an advance on their profit share. If the union-member employees are to receive higher pay in accord with their contract, that can be offset by giving them a smaller share of the surplus as owners. The nonunion co-op members, who get a smaller "advance" now, will receive a larger profit-share down the road.

The Road Ahead

Can worker-owners and unions get along? Notwithstanding the profound differences between worker ownership and union representation as strategies for improving working conditions and giving workers a voice, and in spite of unions' sometimes valid skepticism, the simple answer is: They must! Globalization has exposed both the labor movement and worker-owned cooperatives to intense competition within a framework of laws and policies that relentlessly favor corporations over workers. To respond effectively, workers need a varied toolkit; they cannot afford to abandon solidarity merely because different groups pursue different strategies.

The collaboration between the Hotel Employees and Restaurant Employees union (HERE) and Cooperative Home Care Associates, a large, Bronx, N.Y.-based co-op, provides a good case study. When HERE sought to organize CHCA's employees, the workers, who already had significantly better pay and working conditions than most home health aides, initially showed little interest. CHCA's management, on the other hand, saw an opportunity: a successful industry-wide organizing campaign would raise the payroll of the competition closer to the co-op's costs.

CMCA's managers believed a union organizing drive would benefit their co-op. Likewise, creating co-ops may benefit a union's organizing work, according to Lisabeth Ryder, an American Federation of State, County, and Municipal Employees (AFSCME) administrator. Ryder believes that when public-sector jobs are contracted out to large corporations, unions such as AFSCME, instead of repeating traditional organizing drives that face growing obstacles and often fail, could help the privatized workers to turn their units into worker-owned cooperatives that could then bid against the corporation for the government contract.

Today, the worker-ownership and labor movements are engaged in an expanding dialogue. This June, several union leaders participated in a symposium in Halifax, Nova Scotia, on cooperatives and their workers. In September, the Canadian Worker Co-op Federation hosted over a dozen regional labor leaders at a two-day workshop in Saskatoon to explore the development of a joint strategy for worker-driven interventions to avert plant closures. Retired Steelworkers President Lynn Williams set the tone for the meeting with a brief review of his union's development of a proactive position on employee buyouts. Participants ended the meeting by forming the Prairie Labour-Worker Cooperative Council; with the Ohio Employee Ownership Center as a model, the council aims to create a regional program and infrastructure to support worker buyouts and foster collaboration between the worker-ownership and labor movements.

The U.S. Federation of Worker Cooperatives hopes that its effort to engage labor leadership at its biannual conference this October in New York will prove just as successful as that of its Canadian counterpart.

As unions and co-ops engage in further discussion and collaboration, they may discover unexpected synergies between the two strategies. Ideally, such collaborations will turn out to strengthen and invigorate both the union staff and members and the worker-owners who are willing to cross over and work together toward a common goal of empowering workers.

CONTRIBUTORS

Randy Albelda, a *Dollars & Sense* Associate, teaches economics at the University of Massachusetts-Boston.

Dean Baker is the co-director for the Center for Economic and Policy Research.

Peter Barnes is a successful entrepreneur and co-founder of Working Assets.

Paul Bigman has been a labor activist for more than 30 years, including over 20 years as a full-time union organizer. He is currently the Western Regional Field Organizer for Jobs with Justice.

Dan Bell is currently the international program coordinator at the Ohio Employee Ownership Center at Kent State University.

Betsy Bowman is on the editorial collective of *Grassroots Economic Organizing*. She is among the cofounders of the bilingual Center for Global Justice in San Miguel de Allende, Mexico, where she serves as a research associate,

Paul Cummings is a software engineer with a long-standing interest in environmental and social issues.

James M. Cypher is profesor-investigador, Programa de Doctorado en Estudios del Desarrollo, Universidad Autónoma de Zacatecas, Mexico, and a *Dollars & Sense* associate.

Michael Engel is an emeritus professor of political science at Westfield State College in Massachusetts. He is the author of *The Struggle for Control of Public Education: Market Ideology vs. Democratic Values* (2000).

Ellen Frank is senior economist at the Poverty Institute at Rhode Island College and a member of the *Dollars & Sense* collective.

Mason Gaffney is professor of economics at the University of California, Riverside.

Ross Gelbspan is a former reporter for the *Boston Globe*.

Teresa Ghilarducci, associate professor of economics at University of Notre Dame, served twice on the PBGC Advisory Board under President Clinton.

Amy Gluckman is co-editor of *Dollars & Sense.*

Liv Gold is a member of the *Dollars & Sense* collective.

William Greider has been a political journalist for more than 35 years. He is currently the National Affairs Correspondent for the Nation magazine.

Monique Harden is co-director of Advocates for Environmental Health Rights, a nonprofit, public interest law firm in New Orleans.

Katy Himmelstein is a former *Dollars & Sense* intern.

Howard Karger is professor of social policy at the University of Houston. He is the author of *Shortchanged: Life and Debt in the Fringe Economy* (2005).

Dena Libner is a former *Dollars & Sense* intern.

Nina Martin is a researcher at the Center for Urban Economic Development.

James McBride is a member of the *Dollars & Sense* collective.

Siobhán McGrath is a Policy Research Associate with the Economic Justice Project at the Brennan Center for Justice.

John Miller is a member of the *Dollars & Sense* collective, and teaches economics at Wheaton College.

Vasuki Nesiah is a senior associate at the International Center for Transitional Justice and co-editor of lines magazine.

Doug Orr teaches economics at Eastern Washington University.

Thomas I. Palley is an economist, who has held positions at the AFL-CIO, Open Society Institute, and the U.S.-China Economic and Security Review Commission.

Adam D. Sacks is executive director of the Center for Democracy and the Constitution.

Adria Scharf is director of the Richmond Peace Education Center in Richmond, Va., and a former co-editor of *Dollars & Sense.*

Devinder Sharma is a food and trade policy analyst, and chairs the New Delhi-based Forum for Biotechnology and Food Security.

Michelle Sheehan is a member of the *Dollars & Sense* collective.

William E. Spriggs is a senior fellow at the Economic Policy Institute, and was formerly the executive director of the National Urban League Institute for Opportunity and Equality.

Barbara Sternal is a former intern at *Dollars & Sense*.

Bob Stone is on the editorial collective of *Grassroots Economic Organizing*. He is among the cofounders of the bilingual Center for Global Justice in San Miguel de Allende, Mexico, where he serves as a research associate,

Chris Sturr is co-editor of *Dollars & Sense*.

Sam Uretsky is a retired hospital pharmacist who frequently writes about health care policy and finanacing.

Ramaa Vasudevan teaches economics at Barnard College and is a member of the *Dollars & Sense* collective.

Jessica Weisberg is a former intern at *Dollars & Sense*.

Jeannette Wicks-Lim is an economist and research fellow at the Political Economy Research Institute at the University of Massachusetts-Amherst.

Timothy A. Wise, a former editor at *Dollars & Sense*, is deputy director of Tufts University's Global Development and Environment Institute.

James Woolman is a health policy analyst and a member of the *Dollars & Sense* collective.

Jenna Wright is a former *Dollars & Sense* intern.